The Food
Lobbyists

The Food Lobbyists

Behind the Scenes of Food and Agri-Politics

Harold D. Guither
University of Illinois

LexingtonBooks
D.C. Heath and Company
Lexington, Massachusetts
Toronto

Library of Congress Cataloging in Publication Data

Guither, Harold D
   The food lobbyists.

   Includes index.
   1. Agriculture and state—United States. 2. Lobbying—United States.
I. Title.
HD1765 1980.G84   338.1'873   79-6734
ISBN 0-669-03539-4

Published simultaneously in Canada.

Printed in the United States of America.

International Standard Book Number: 0-669-03539-4

Library of Congress Catalog Card Number: 79-6734

Contents

v

List of Figures
and Tables

Foreword

This book fills a long-standing need for a reliable directory and analysis of the organized forces that seek to influence the course of agribusiness legislation in Washington. To my knowledge nothing like it has been published before and certainly not in the nineteen years during which I have been intimately involved in the legislative process. It is comprehensive, concise, well-organized, and dispassionate.

It is a splendid example of public service rendered by professionals who work within the United States' great system of land-grant universities. The author, Dr. Harold D. Guither, is a prominent member of the Department of Agricultural Economics at the University of Illinois College of Agriculture. I have a better appreciation of his talents than most, because he spent part of a sabbatical working effectively with me in the development of the Famine Prevention Program (Title XII of the Foreign Assistance Act), through which agricultural teaching institutions in the United States are given a new long-term responsibility to upgrade local systems for educating farmers in developing countries.

Dr. Guither headed the outstanding and widely praised study, "Who Will Control U.S. Agriculture?" published several years ago. This book is a worthy sequel.

I will keep a copy of this book near my desk, and I am sure hundreds of other people will do the same. It provides a ready index of the teams and players with which we must deal in this legislative game. I use the word *must* advisedly, because I am convinced that lobbyists are a valuable—indeed an essential—part of good government. They serve special interests, of course. But in the process of serving these interests often they confront legislators with important facts and arguments that otherwise might be overlooked. I never complain about too much lobbying, only about too little lobbying of good quality.

In my experience lobbyists are rarely the shadowy, sinister figures popular with editorial cartoonists. For the most part they are decent, thoughtful, well-informed people who present their information in a reasonable way. Some are superb, others mediocre. A few are offensive. Several are so reliable and resourceful that I find myself calling them more often than they call me.

Lobbyists sometimes provide financial support to the campaigns of legislators whose views they like, but I have found that they carefully separate these donations from their legislative efforts. Only once in nineteen years did a lobbying group that contributed to my political campaign fund try to use that donation as a lever on me. It did not work, of course, and I had no further relationship with the group.

Successful lobbyists recognize that their most important asset is integrity. Their job is a continuing one. They must keep the door open for future opportunities and needs. If they are misleading or abusive—even to a slight degree—they risk destroying beyond repair an important relationship.

The publication of this book is timely because many of the groups seeking to influence agricultural legislation are already making preparations for a major legislative endeavor in 1981—the extension of general farm programs.

By the time hearings begin in the spring of 1981, this book will be well thumbed. And I venture to predict it will have a salutary influence on the role of lobbyists on Capitol Hill.

Paul Findley
Congress of the United States,
House of Representatives

Preface and Acknowledgments

Despite the many changes in how we live and work, food is still a basic necessity. However, the role of government involvement in agriculture and food production has changed significantly during the last forty years.

This book was written to identify and briefly describe the many organizations and groups that have had vital interests and concerns about federal government decisions in some phase of agriculture, food production, and distribution in the late 1970s. Such a task requires certain decisions about which groups should be included and which omitted. Although every effort has been made to include all producers, business and industry, citizens, and professional groups with major regional and national interests in food and agricultural issues, some unintended omissions are likely, for which we express regrets.

To keep the book within manageable bounds, most groups and organizations whose major concerns involve wilderness and natural resources, public lands and mineral rights, forest production and use, energy production, and transportation were excluded.

The appendixes are intended to serve as a reference directory for readers interested in more details about specific organizations. Almost every organization mentioned in the text is included in the appendixes. With more than 400 identified organizations, changes in staff, addresses, and phone numbers can be expected, although they were as up to date as possible when this book went to press.

Sincere appreciation is due to the staff of several hundred organizations that submitted reports, newsletters, and publications describing their policies and activities and responded to questions. Without the willingness of many staff members of the Senate and House agriculture committees and the staff of individual members of those committees to be interviewed, chapter 8 would not have been written. Many employees at the Federal Election Commission; Departments of Justice, Agriculture, and Labor; and Community Services Administration provided valuable data and information.

The term *agri-politics* is used with permission of Prairie Farmer Publishing Company, Oak Brook, Illinois.

Here at the University of Illinois this book could never have been written without the vision and support of Dan Alpert, director of the Center for Advanced Study; Dan Padberg, head of the Department of Agricultural Economics; and J.B. Claar, director of the Cooperative Extension Service.

Funds for travel were provided by the Center for Advanced Study and the Illinois Agricultural Experiment Station.

A special note of appreciation is extended to Sam Aldrich, Bob Spitze, Harold Halcrow, Gary Orfield, Lloyd Witter, Dave Gardner, Willard Visek, Robert Metcalf, John Erdman, John Garst, Dave Anderson, Glenn Schmidt, John Romans, J.B. Wyckoff, Robert Wichser, Marijo Gorney, and many others who participated in "brown-bag seminars" on food policy, reviewed drafts of manuscripts, and provided information that has contributed to the development of this book. Rich Boyd, Jan Fauble, Joy Elliott, and Sharon Ormiston provided valuable research assistance. At the Center for Advanced Study, Peggy Harris, Angela Di Maria, and Caroline Fertig provided valuable typing, clerical, and administrative assistance. In the Department of Agricultural Economics, Mary Howell deserves a very special note of appreciation as she patiently typed and retyped the drafts of each chapter and the appendixes to make the finished manuscript possible. And last, but not least, my wife Lois provided the patience and pleasant home environment to make the completion of this effort possible.

The Food
Lobbyists

1

Setting the Stage, Naming the Cast: Government in Food and Agriculture

Food, its production and distribution, will be the overriding social, political, economic, environmental and moral issue of the next decade.
—Congressman Fred Richmond

Today we have a lot of 'new actors' in the political process.—Wallace Barr[a]

People in the United States will spend $250 to $300 billion a year for food in the first years of the 1980s.[1] About 90 percent of it will be produced in the United States.

U.S. agriculture, besides providing a basic life necessity, is an integral part of the country's economy. Even though farmers represent less than 4 percent of the total population, much of the U.S. workforce either processes and markets farm commodities or produces equipment and supplies for the farmer. When agricultural production and the output of direct agri-support industries are included, about 25 percent of the total gross national product is involved. So, directly or indirectly the agricultural food system employs more people than any other industry.[2]

The Evolution of Government Involvement

The federal government spends an estimated $40 billion annually on various programs to ensure good nutrition.[3] Most of these are carried out by the Departments of Agriculture and Health, Education, and Welfare (HEW).

The role of the federal government in food and agricultural production is not new or unexpected. From 1785 to 1862, the major government role was to establish the rules for sale and distribution of land in the public domain. By 1860, the federal government had acquired all the land to the Pacific Coast, which now forms the forty-eight contiguous states in North America. During this period, various groups and special interests pleaded with Congress to change these laws to promote easier access to the vast public lands by more and more people and to promote development and settlement. The outcome of this effort was the Homestead Act of 1862 which granted land free to anyone who would settle on it for five years.

---

[a]Wallace Barr, "Implications for Policy Education," in *Increasing Understanding of Public Problems and Policies, 1978* (Oak Brook, Ill.: Farm Foundation, 1978), p. 42.

1

From 1860 to 1933, the role of government in agriculture and food still included land distribution and development, but an enlarged role in scientific research and education was added. In 1862, Congress established the U.S. Department of Agriculture (USDA) and passed the Morrill Act, which established land-grant colleges of agriculture and mechanical arts (engineering) in each state. The Hatch Act in 1887 provided federal grants to states for research, and the Smith Lever Act in 1914 established the federal-state cooperative arrangement for an extension service. During its first seventy years, the USDA only slowly expanded its original roles of scientific inquiry and education.[4]

The first Pure Food and Drug Act was passed in 1906.[5] Laws to regulate and maintain competition in marketing of agricultural products and encourage farmer cooperatives were passed in the 1920s. But the major shift toward more government involvement with food and agriculture began in 1933. The Depression of the 1930s was particularly severe in agriculture. Farm organization leaders called on the federal government for help that could not be met by the traditional teaching, research, and extension programs of the USDA.

The Agricultural Adjustment Act of 1933 and succeeding legislation provide the foundation for price and income support programs for producers.[6] The Farm Credit Act of 1933 set a new direction for government-assisted credit to farmers.[7] The Soil Conservation Service was established in the USDA in 1935,[8] and it provides the foundation for conservation and environmental programs. The Rural Electrification Administration Act of 1936 opened another important direction of government involvement affecting farmers and rural communities.[9] Marketing orders and agreements for milk, fruits, and vegetables were established under the Agricultural Marketing Agreement Act of 1937.[10]

With high unemployment and surpluses of certain agricultural commodities, the first food stamp program began in 1939 as a surplus disposal effort. This program was discontinued in 1943 during World War II.

Key Food and Agricultural Legislation

Although government involvement in food and agriculture dates back more than 200 years, a few key laws since World War II have established the foundation for most of the controversy, confrontation, and lobbying efforts on food and agriculture issues of the 1970s and 1980s.

The Agricultural Act of 1948 set the stage for postwar price support and income assistance for farmers. It has been revised and renewed every four or five years since that time.[11] The Agricultural Trade and Development Assistance of 1954, known as Public Law 480, opened the way for expanding subsidized exports of U.S. agricultural products through use of local currencies, low-interest loans, and donations.[12] Current issues center on how much should be spent on these programs, who should get it, and how it will be distributed.

In 1958, Congress enacted the Food Additives Amendment to the Federal Food, Drug, and Cosmetics Act. Section 409(c)(3)(A) of this amendment, referred to as the "Delaney clause," provides that "No additive shall be deemed to be safe if it is found to induce cancer when ingested by man or animal or if it is found, after tests which are appropriate for the evaluation of the safety of food additives, to induce cancer in man or animal. . . ." Since there is no room for scientific judgment as to the risks involved, this clause has created major debate among scientists, consumers, public interest groups, producers, and government officials.

The Food Stamp Act of 1964 established a new national policy to use food stamps to distribute food to low-income persons.[13] Amendments in 1971 which stated that each low-income household should have the opportunity for "a nutritionally adequate diet" added a significant new dimension to food assistance programs.[14]

The Federal Insecticide, Fungicide, and Rodenticide Act of 1947 set up a registration of all pesticides, including those used in agricultural and food production.[15]

The Environmental Protection Agency was established in 1970. Offices of several agencies were incorporated into it, including the Pesticide Registration Division of the USDA.[16]

The Federal Environmental Pesticide Control Act (FEPCA), adopted in 1972, amended the 1947 act.[17] It permitted the regulation of the use of pesticides and their classification, and it established qualifications for certification. It extended control over pesticides marketed within a state as well as those in interstate commerce. The act recognized the environment as a quality to be protected.

The Food and Agricultural Act of 1977 is part of the continuing evolution of national food and agricultural policy.[18] However, additional features make this act the most comprehensive statement of a national food and agricultural policy ever passed in a single bill. The major features set the course for commodity price support programs through 1981, established a farmer-held grain reserve, amended food assistance and food stamp programs, and established new directions for research and education in agriculture, food, and nutrition.[19]

A New Agenda with a Larger Power Cluster

As the federal government has expanded its role in food and agriculture, the cast of characters participating in writing the laws and implementing them also has grown. These new groups and organizations have added new items to the food and agricultural policy agenda.

The old agenda in agricultural policy making was concerned primarily with land use and distribution, commodities, and the influencing of supplies and prices in the farmers' interest. This agenda was developed and controlled by what Paarlberg has labeled the "agricultural establishment"—the farm organizations, the agricultural committees of Congress, the USDA, and the land-grant universities. While these groups do not agree on all issues, they have long agreed on one thing—that they should be the farm policy decisionmakers.[20]

However, new actors have entered to play a part in the expanded government involvement in food and agriculture. As Paarlberg observes, "The Agricultural establishment had the ball for a hundred years, but sometime during the last ten years there was a turnover. It was not rapid, or clean cut, or dramatic, as in a football game. But the initiative has changed hands nonetheless."[21]

The new agenda includes all government-sponsored food assistance programs, conservation, land use, environmental quality, food prices, advertising and nutrition, hunger around the world, small farms, and rights and protection for farm workers.

Some participants in the agricultural establishment have voiced alarm and concern about this shift in control of the policy-making agenda. Luther Tweeten, an Oklahoma State University agricultural economist, observed, "While some consumer interests voice reasoned and entirely justifiable concerns worthy of immediate alleviation by public policy or other means, other 'consumer' advocates seem woefully uninformed. That this group so completely alien to farmers' thinking and tradition would determine farm policy is a turn of events unthinkable a few years ago."[22]

From a political scientist's perspective, the power cluster that traditionally has made the nation's food and agricultural policy expanded during the 1970s. Daniel Ogden, a political scientist, sees public policy making as segmented and decentralized through various "power clusters." He characterizes such policy making through the use of a system of power clusters, organized around broad subject areas including agriculture and food, natural resources, health, education, defense, transportation, justice and law enforcement, and others which operate in relative isolation from one another.

Within each power cluster the federal government's executive agencies, congressional standing committees and appropriations subcommittees, organized interest groups, professionals, certain special individuals, and an attentive public interact to identify problems, arrive at acceptable solutions, and provide the resources to carry out the decisions.[23]

However, the newly expanded power cluster in food and agriculture policy making is diverse, includes many groups and interests, and represents almost all segments of the population. One new group describes it this way:

> Concern and activism around farm, land and food related issues is growing. Soaring food prices and the 1978 farmers' strike reaffirm the fundamental inadequacies of American agricultural policy.
>
> The potential for building broad based coalitions around food and land related issues is enormous . . . the people working on these issues come from the widest of backgrounds, perspectives and occupations. Family farmers and progressive farm organizations are in the forefront, as are consumer, environmental and religious groups, and increasingly neighborhood and community based organizations.[24]

Identifying the Actors—Old and New

The actors in the food and agriculture political process enter in many different scenes and play leading roles and bit parts. They write laws; issue regulations; testify before congressional hearings; contact government officials; write letters; conduct educational programs; pique public awareness through the media; try to influence decisions through direct contact with officials; conduct research and issue reports; write newsletters, publications, and books; bring lawsuits into the courts; collect and disperse funds through political action committees; and represent the special and specific interests of their clients in many different ways.

Congress

The Senate Committee on Agriculture, Nutrition and Forestry and the House Committee on Agriculture take the center of the stage in holding hearings, conducting investigations, and writing laws. The Agriculture Appropriations subcommittees also play a significant role. The makeup of these committees and their operations are discussed in chapter 2.

The Executive Branch

The President holds a key role in recommending agricultural and food policies, in proposing a budget, and in signing laws passed by Congress. The USDA carries a major role, but does not perform all functions, in implementing the actions of Congress. The USDA spent $20.6 billion during the 1979 fiscal year and has been budgeted an estimated $23.6 billion during the 1980 fiscal year ending September 30, 1980.[25] Although the USDA budget comprises only 4 percent of the total, the number of persons affected by the decisions of USDA agencies is much greater than this budget percentage would suggest.

Other Cabinet departments also play a role in food and agriculture issues. The Department of State has an interest in international trade and negotiations which affect agricultural products and foreign aid conducted through the Agency for International Development. The Commerce Department conducts the Census of Agriculture and is concerned with trade balances. The Treasury Department is concerned with monetary policy, the effect of agricultural trade on the foreign-exchange value of the dollar, and tax policies that affect revenues and taxes paid by farmers and consumers.

The Labor Department is responsible for implementing the Occupational Safety and Health Act which includes coverage of farm workers. The Older Americans Act allots benefits to older persons in rural communities, including meals on wheels. The Department of Health and Human Services (formerly part of HEW) includes the Food and Drug Administration, which is responsible for food safety and purity. Through the Community Services Administration, the government also provides grants for community action agencies and other groups to implement USDA food assistance programs and improve rural community living conditions. The Department of Transportation is concerned with regulation of railroads, trucking, and roads—all vital parts of moving food and agricultural products from producer to consumer. The Department of Energy is concerned with energy supplies to all parts of the economy, including agriculture.

The Department of Justice is responsible for enforcing the antitrust laws. The growth and merging of corporations and cooperatives which produce and process agricultural products have stimulated their interest in food and agriculture.

The Environmental Protection Agency, an independent agency, is responsible for administering the Federal Insecticide, Fungicide, and Rodenticide Act (FIFRA), which affects the registration and use of several thousand chemicals and compounds used in agricultural and food production. The Federal Trade Commission has jurisdiction over the advertising of food products.

The Judiciary

The Constitution also provided for a system of federal courts to interpret the laws and serve as part of the system of checks and balances. In recent years, the federal courts have played a significant role in interpreting, implementing, and enforcing the Food Stamp Act of 1964 and other federal food assistance programs. Specific examples are cited in chapter 5.

Special and Public Interests

Although the Constitution provides for a Congress to represent the U.S. people and decide what laws are to be passed, the growth of the federal government and the concentration of power in the executive branch have brought the entrance of a new set of actors into the political scene. They are known as special interests, Washington representatives, lobbyists, public interest groups, consultants, or a combination of these. They may represent trade associations, membership organizations, unions, individual companies or firms, churches or religious groups, professional associations, state or local governments, foreign governments or firms, or the "public" interest.

Exactly how many individuals or groups are involved is not certain because the numbers change as groups and individuals come and go. One estimate places the total number at 6,000. They have been described as the cutting edge of the special interests, or, less boldly, "an interface between the American public and its government."[26] These individuals and organizations have one common purpose—they represent their client's interest to the federal government. They are lobbyists in the sense that they are pleading or defending their views or those of their clients to Congress or other agencies of government. A common definition of a lobbyist is a person who tries to get legislators to introduce or vote for measures favorable to a special interest that he or she represents.[27]

However, with many decisions being made in the executive branch, lobbying involves representation not only in Congress but also in many government agencies and bureaus. The public image of lobbying is often one of a threat to good government. However, in recent years the emergence of citizens' or public interest lobbies may have helped to change this image. Organized efforts to influence legislation may still be looked on unfavorably, particularly among those who oppose the point of view being expressed. On the other hand, the lobbyist has been described as filling an indispensible function in the legislative process, as knowledgeable experts on their subjects, capable of explaining complex issues in a clear, understandable fashion. Often they can provide information not available elsewhere.[28]

In 1946 Congress passed the Federal Regulation of Lobbying Act. Although it is generally regarded as ineffective, its purpose is described as being "to keep members of Congress and the public informed of the lobbyists' special areas of interest and the financing of legislative activities to promote such special interest."[29] The law has two basic requirements—registration and reporting. A person must report if he directly or indirectly solicits, collects, or receives money or any other thing of value to be used principally to aid in the passage or defeat of any legislation, or to influence Congress directly or indirectly in the passage or defeat of any legislation.

A court decision involving the law and the Justice Department stipulated that employees of state and local government lobbying groups were exempt from the act. A 1954 Supreme Court case (*U.S.* v. *Harriss*) resulted in an opinion by Chief Justice Earl Warren that the law applied to lobbying only in the commonly accepted sense of direct communication with members of Congress on pending or proposed federal legislation. Those whose actions and work have only an incidental purpose of influencing legislation would also be excluded from the registration requirement. Consequently it is generally accepted among close observers of the lobbying law that those who register include only part of those carrying on lobbying activities with some branch or agency of the federal government. Part of this may be due to the lack of an enforcement mechanism, because congressional officials who administer the law see their role as custodians and not as law enforcers. No effort is made to determine how many registrants remain active. The Justice Department, which has an obligation to enforce all laws, either avoids the responsibility or says the violations are technical.[30] Efforts to strengthen the lobbying laws have been made several times, but by 1979 they had not yet succeeded.

Who Are the Food Lobbyists?

In this book, a *food lobbyist* includes any organization, group, association, firm, or individual who seeks in some way to influence the decisions made by Congress or other federal officials related to food and agriculture. Some of these persons will have public policy concerns outside of food and agriculture, but this will not exclude them from also being identified as food lobbyists.

Food and agricultural interests include production of food and fiber crops; livestock, poultry, dairy, and other animals grown for food purposes; use of private agricultural land or property; manufacture and sale of farm equipment, pesticides, feeds, fertilizers, petroleum, and other inputs used in agricultural production; and the marketing, processing, and distribution of agricultural and food products in this country and abroad.

In this book, food lobbyists are identified through at least one of these criteria:

Appearance as a witness before House or Senate committees in Washington on matters relating to food and agriculture during 1977, 1978, or 1979[31]

Registration as a lobbyist with the Clerk of the House

Registration as a foreign agent with the Department of Justice for an organization or group related to food and agriculture

Providing written statements which appear in the hearings of House or Senate committees on related food and agricultural matters

Representing groups, organizations, or associations with food and agricultural concerns before agencies or departments in the executive branch

Publicly advocating a specific course of action by some branch of the federal government in the public media or a printed publication

Representing a client in court in which the decision affects the operations or implementation of federal laws relating to food and agriculture

Being connected with an organization or group which collects or disperses money through political action committees and is registered with the Federal Elections Commission

The food lobbyists perform on the dramatic, dynamic, and often confusing Washington stage that produces our nation's food and agricultural policy. They play both lead and supporting parts. They come and go. And many of the "stage crew" behind the scenes may never appear in public; yet they contribute to and influence the process by which decisions are made in a representative form of government such as ours.

The roles played by the food lobbyists can be classified in many ways. To grasp this complex cast of characters, we put them in five broad categories according to whom they represent: (1) producer advocates; (2) agribusiness and industry; (3) consumer, citizen, and specific interest groups including organized labor; (4) public agencies and employees; and (5) professional organizations.[32] The names, addresses, and brief description of many of these groups are found in appendix A.

Producer Advocates

Within this broad category are those who represent the farm and ranch operator and landowner. Although they advocate and work for decisions to help the producer, they are not in complete agreement on every issue that comes up. And some organizations have concerns over a much broader range of issues than others. The five major types of producer advocate groups are the general farm organizations, commodity groups, cooperatives, farm women, and others that fall outside the above. A more complete picture of these groups is drawn in chapter 3.

Agribusiness and Industry Representatives

Many organizations and firms that provide equipment and production supplies or handle or process agricultural and food products engage in some form of lobbying. Associations and firms whose business is primarily with the agricultural and food industry can be quickly identified. Many of the conglomerates who may or may not register as lobbyists and have both agricultural and nonagricultural interests are more difficult to identify. The nature of lobbying varies widely among this group. Some are registered as lobbyists, others testify before congressional committees, and still others make personal contacts with members of Congress and agency officials. Some carry out all these activities. A more complete discussion is found in chapter 4.

Consumer, Citizen, and Special-Interest Groups

The organizations and groups in this category, frequently referred to as "public-interest groups," usually seek a collective good whose achievement will not selectively and materially benefit the membership or activists of the organization. Some are membership organizations, and some are not. The latter are supported by foundations or public grants to try to develop latent interest within society. Within this category are organizations with broad interests in public policy that include food and agriculture; a primary interest in conservation of the land, natural resources, and environment; and major concerns for the poor and their needs for food, both in this country and abroad. A more complete discussion of these groups appears in chapter 5.

Organized Labor

In some ways, the food and agricultural interests of labor unions parallel the interests of citizen, consumer, and public interest groups. But in other ways, their interests differ. Industrial and craft unions are concerned about the welfare of their members. Food stamp eligibility for union members is of special concern. In recent years, farm workers' unions have grown. The concerns among farm workers' unions include food assistance as well as other issues. These are discussed in chapter 5.

Public Agencies and Employees

The distribution of federal funds to states, counties, cities, and public institutions has attracted a stream of representatives to request funds, to recommend how such funds should be distributed, and to suggest which programs should be carried out. Officials with common interests have formed state, regional, and national organizations. Some of these groups are discussed in chapter 6.

Professional Organizations

Certain groups of scientists and educators with training and knowledge in specialized disciplines have contributions to make in food and agricultural policy decisions. With these groups the distinction between the food lobbyist and the auxiliary organization may not be completely clear. In some situations they be advocates; in others they supply information used by the lobbyists. These groups are discussed in chapter 6.

Auxiliary Food and Agricultural Interests

In addition to the food lobbyists identified above, there are others with interests and knowledge about food and agriculture. They perform research, develop educational materials and programs, gather information, and publish data and statistics; but they do not publicly advocate a policy direction for public officials. Their reports may be used in testimony or in discussion by the food lobbyists who do have a specific point of view on a given issue. At times the line between a food lobbyist and an auxiliary interest may be hard to determine. Some of these auxiliary interests are listed in appendix A and discussed in chapter 6.

Can Food Lobbyists Succeed?

With hundreds of actors playing their parts on the federal food and agricultural policy stage, can any of them really succeed? Obviously, when two lobbyists represent two opposite positions, either a final decision will please one or the other, or a compromise will give neither all that he wants. Food lobbyists, like other Washington representatives, use different strategies and tactics. Sometimes they form coalitions—groups of organizations with similar interests—to present a united position on a specific issue. Some lobbyists concentrate most of their food and agricultural concerns on a single issue; others have many concerns. Those who observe food lobbyists believe that some are more effective than others. And they have reasons for these views. An assessment of lobbyist's strategies and tactics for successful representation is made in chapter 8.

How Large Is the Cast?

The number of actors in each of these food lobby groups changes from week to week, month to month, and year to year depending on the economic

Table 1-1
The Food Lobbyists: Witnesses and Statements to Agriculture Committees and Subcommittees, 1977[a]

	National Groups	Regional, State, County, and City Groups	Individuals
Producer Advocates			
General farm organizations	4	16	
Commodity groups	15	26	
Cooperatives	6	12	1
Farm women	2	6	6
Other	5	6	54
	32	66	61
Agribusiness and Industry			
Suppliers of inputs	8	1	61
Commodity handlers, processors	40	8	15
Other	6	2	
	54	11	76
Consumers, Citizens, Special-Interest Groups (General)			
Hunger and welfare	25		3
Conservation and environment	16	60	6
Organized labor	12	11	
Other	5	3	
	66	74	9
Public Agencies and Officials			
Members of Congress	64		
Federal agencies	16		

State and local officials			
National organizations	13	67	
	93	67	2
Professional	6	3	
Totals[b]	243	221	148

[a]Witnesses at, and statements submitted to, the following hearings:

U.S. House Committee on Agriculture hearings, *General Farm Bill*, February 17, 22, 24, 25, 28; March 1, 2, 3, 4, 15, 24, 1977; *Federal Insecticide, Fungicide, and Rodenticide Act*, March 7, 8, 9.

U.S. Senate Committee on Agriculture, Nutrition, and Forestry hearings, *General Farm and Food Legislation*, February 22, 23, 24, 25, 28; March 1, 3, 4, 7, 8, 9, 10, 11, 14, 23, 31; April 7, 1977.

U.S. House Subcommittee on Domestic Marketing, Consumer Relations and Nutrition and House Committee on Agriculture hearings, *Food Stamp Program*, February 28; March 21, 22, 23, 24, 25; April 5, 1977.

U.S. Senate Agricultural Subcommittee on Foreign Agricultural Policy hearings, *Future of Food Aid*, April 4, 5, 1977.

Senate Subcommittee on Nutrition, Committee on Agriculture, Nutrition, and Forestry hearings, *Child Nutrition Legislation*, May 5, 6, 1977.

U.S. Senate Agricultural Subcommittee on Agricultural Research and General Legislation hearings, *Extension of the Federal Insecticide, Fungicide, and Rodenticide Act*, June 8, 9, 1977.

U.S. Senate Agricultural Subcommittee on Agricultural Production, Marketing, and Stabilization of Prices hearings, *Agricultural Transportation Problems*, July 12, 15, 1977.

U.S. Senate Agricultural Subcommittee on Agricultural Credit and Rural Electrification hearings, *Changes in Farmers Home Administration Loan Programs*, October 11, 1977.

U.S. Senate Agricultural Subcommittee on Nutrition hearings, *Food Stamps*, March 25, 1977.

[b]Witnesses who testified at or sent statements to more than one hearing were counted only once.

conditions, time of the year, and nature of the issues before Congress or regulatory agencies. Several approaches to a census would yield different answers. One sample measure of the scope of legislative lobbying is to tabulate and classify witnesses who testified before the House and Senate agriculture committees during 1977. With this as a basis, a total of 612 different persons and groups were identified. The different interests are shown in table 1-1. An additional measurement of the population of food and agricultural lobbyists is a census of the registered lobbyists, foreign agents, political action committees, and other closely related groups that carry out informational activities dealing with legislation and regulations. About 460 major national and regional groups are identified individually in appendix A.

Notes

1. U.S. Department of Agriculture, *National Food Review*, NFR-5, December 1978, p. 22. The 1977 total expenditure for food was $221 billion. If this figure is projected ahead at an increase of 7.5 percent per year, the early 1980s will see expenditures in the range of $250 to $300 billion.

2. U.S. General Accounting Office, *Changing Character and Structure of American Agriculture, An Overview*, Washington, CED-78-178, September 26, 1978, pp. 7-9.

3. U.S. General Accounting Office, "Future of the National Nutrition Intelligence System," CED-79-5, November 7, 1978.

4. For greater detail on the economic and political developments in food and agriculture in the United States, the following readings are suggested: Harold Guither, *Heritage of Plenty, A Guide to the Economic History and Development of U.S. Agriculture* (Danville, Ill.: Interstate Printers and Publishers, 1972); Harold G. Halcrow, *Food Policy in America* (New York: McGraw-Hill, 1977); and A. Desmond O'Rourke, *The Changing Dimension of U.S. Agricultural Policy* (Englewood Cliffs, N.J.: Prentice-Hall, 1978); "American Agriculture, The First 300 Years," in *Farmers in a Changing World*, The Yearbook of Agriculture (Washington: GPO, 1940), pp. 171-296.

5. Public Law 384, 59th Cong., June 30, 1906.

6. Public Law 10, 73d Cong., May 12, 1933.

7. Public Law 77, 73d Cong., June 16, 1933.

8. Public Law 49, 74th Cong., April 27, 1935.

9. Public Law 605, 74th Cong., May 20, 1936.

10. Public Law 137, 75th Cong., June 3, 1937.

11. Public Law 897, 80th Cong., July 3, 1948.

12. Public Law 480, 68 Stat., 83d Cong., July 10, 1954.

13. Public Law 88-525, 78 Stat., 88th Cong., August 31, 1964.

14. Public Law 91-671, Sec. 1, January 11, 1971, 84 Stat. 2048; U.S. Code Title 7, Sec. 2011.

15. Public Law 86, U.S. Code 61 Stat. 163-172, June 25, 1947.

16. U.S. Code, 80 Stat. 393, Reorganization Plan No. 3 of 1970, December 2, 1970.

17. Public Law 92-516, 86 Stat. 975, October 21, 1972.

18. Public Law 95-113, 91 Stat. 913, September 29, 1977, 7 USC, note 1281.

19. For more details of the Food and Agricultural Act of 1977, see Thomas A. Stucker and William T. Boehm, *Guide to Understanding the 1977 Food and Agricultural Legislation*, National Economic Analysis Division, U.S. Department of Agriculture, AER-411, September 1978; and Robert G.F. Spitze, "The Food and Agriculture Act of 1977: Issues and Decisions," *American Journal of Agricultural Economics* 60, 2 (May 1978):225-234.

20. Don Paarlberg, "The Farm Policy Agenda," in *Increasing Understanding of Public Problems and Policies, 1975* (Chicago: Farm Foundation, 1975), p. 95.

21. Ibid., p. 96.

22. Luther Tweeten, "Domestic Food and Farm Policy Issues and Alternatives," in *Increasing Understanding of Public Problems and Policies, 1975*, p. 103.

23. Daniel M. Ogden, Jr., "Recent Changes in the Federal Policymaking Process," in *Increasing Understanding of Public Problems and Policies, 1977* (Oak Brook, Ill.: Farm Foundation, 1977), p. 3.

24. Joe Belden, Gibby Edwards, Cynthia Guyer, and Lee Webb (eds.), *New Directions in Farm, Land and Food Policies* (Washington: Agriculture Project, Conference on Alternative State and Local Policies, 1978), p. 9. Reprinted with permission.

25. Executive Office of the President, Office of Management and Budget, *The Budget for Fiscal Year 1981*, Washington, January 1980.

26. Craig Colgate, Jr. (ed.), *Directory of Washington Representatives of American Associations and Industry, 1978* (Washington: Columbia Books, Inc., 1978), p. 5.

27. *Webster's New World Dictionary of the American Language* (New York: World Publishing Co., 1960).

28. Colgate, *Directory of Washington Representatives*, p. 7.

29. Richard R. Cohen, "Lobbying Report: Ineffective Report Law Likely to Be Toughened, Extended," *National Journal Reports*, April 19, 1975, p. 571.

30. Ibid., pp. 571-572.

31. Many individuals and groups also appeared at field hearings conducted by Senate and House agriculture subcommittees in various parts

of the country. In most cases these witnesses were members of groups also represented at hearings in Washington or were individuals who expressed points of view similar to those of the Washington witnesses.

32. For a revealing analysis of the public-interest lobby groups, see Jeffrey M. Berry, *Lobbying for the People, The Political Behavior of Public Interest Groups* (Princeton, N.J.: Princeton University Press, 1977).

2

Congress and the Agriculture Committees: Foundation for Policy Decisions

It is not the farmers versus the consumers, as some say it now is. The real issue is between the White House which has concern for the entire economy, and the Congress, where the special interests are strongly entrenched.
—Don Paarlberg[a]

Most of the issues dealing with food and agriculture come under the jurisdiction of the Senate Committee on Agriculture, Nutrition, and Forestry and the House Committee on Agriculture. The Senate Committee in the 96th Congress (1979-1980) was made up of ten Democrats and eight Republicans. The House Committee on Agriculture was comprised of twenty-seven Democrats and fifteen Republicans.

To handle the broad range of issues to which they are assigned, the committees in both Senate and House are divided into subcommittees where the first discussions, hearings, and debate take place. The Senate subcommittees are Agricultural Credit and Rural Electrification; Agricultural Production, Marketing, and Stabilization of Prices; Agricultural Research and General Legislation; Environment, Soil Conservation, and Forestry; Foreign Agricultural Policy; Nutrition; and Rural Development. The House subcommittees are Conservation and Credit; Cotton; Dairy and Poultry; Department Investigations, Oversight, and Research; Domestic Marketing, Consumer Relations, and Nutrition; Family Farms, Rural Development, and Special Studies; Forests; Livestock and Grains; Oilseeds and Rice; and Tobacco. Members of the subcommittees and their home states and party affiliations are shown in appendix B.

The appropriations committees in both the House and the Senate have jurisdiction over the appropriation of specific amounts of money for the support of government programs and activities. An agriculture appropriations subcommittee deals with food and agricultural programs. The appropriations committees cannot appropriate more than is authorized by the agriculture committees and approved by Congress, but they can appropriate less, which they often do.

---

[a]Don Paarlberg, *Food and Agricultural Policy* (Washington: American Enterprise Institute for Public Policy Research, 1977), p. 6. Reprinted with permission.

Other committees of the House and Senate also become involved in issues related to food and agriculture. A few examples will illustrate the long list of involvements by other committees. The Subcommittee on Fisheries, Wildlife, Conservation, and the Environment of the House Committee on Merchant Marine and Fisheries has obvious interests. The House Committee on Government Operations held hearings on implementation of the Pesticides Control Act. The Subcommittee on Oversight and Investigations of the Committee on Interstate and Foreign Commerce held hearings on cancer-causing chemicals; the Subcommittee on Health and the Environment held hearings on food safety and nutrition amendments. The House Committee on Foreign Affairs has jurisdiction over nontariff aspects of international trade and the foreign policy aspects of the Food for Peace Program. The Senate Committee on Small Business held hearings on farmland ownership.

By House rules, Democrats and Republicans are to be assigned to committees at a ratio approximating that of the two parties. Democrats also stress geographical representativeness in making committee assignments.[1]

Changes in the makeup of Congress, the rules under which it operates, and the choice of committee chairmen affect the environment under which associations and groups with legislative concerns and interests carry out their activities.

Since 1950, the rapid decline in the number of persons engaged in agriculture and associated occupations, coupled with the constitutional requirements for reapportionment and redistricting after each national census, has changed the geographical constituencies and composition of the House of Representatives. Rural states have lost districts, the number of rural districts has declined, and within rural districts only a small proportion of the workforce is engaged in farming. Farm area congressmen in the 1970s often spoke of an urban Congress lacking understanding of agricultural issues.[2]

The formation of the Democratic Caucus has brought about changes in the method of selecting chairmen of committees and appropriations subcommittees. The removal of W.R. Poage of Texas as chairman of the House Agriculture Committee in 1975 and the selection of Thomas S. Foley of Washington brought a new leadership style and more dispersion of decision making to the subcommittees. Foley was also the first Democrat from outside the South to chair the committee in many years.

The House Agriculture Committee

The forty-two members of the House Agriculture Committee in the 96th Congress came from twenty-nine states. States with major sources of income from agriculture had more than one member: California had four members; Texas, Iowa, and North Carolina had three; and Illinois, Minnesota, and Missouri each had two members on the committee. The locations of the districts represented by members on the House Agriculture Committee are shown in figure 2-1. Thomas Foley of Washington is chairman, and William Wampler of Virginia is the ranking minority member.

The House Agriculture Committee places more emphasis on commodities with separate subcommittees for cotton, dairy and poultry, forests, livestock and grains, oilseeds and rice, and tobacco. The chairmen of these subcommittees represent districts with a strong interest in these commodities.

The Subcommittee on Domestic Marketing, Consumer Relations, and Nutrition has jurisdiction over the domestic food programs including food stamps. Representative Fred Richmond of New York, who represents the most urban and densely populated district of any member of the House Agriculture Committee, serves as chairman. Although two members of the committee represent almost completely urban districts, the more usual constituency of committee members is a mixed rural-urban setting. In many districts the agricultural and rural interests are strong, which explains why their representative is a member of the committee. Among the forty-two members of the committee, eighteen are attorneys, fifteen had served in their state legislatures, eight had farmed or had direct interests in farm operations, nine had managed or operated private businesses, and seven had been teachers or instructors in schools or universities.

The Senate Agriculture Committee

Senator Herman Talmadge, chairman of the committee, has served in the Senate since 1957. The second-ranking Democrat is Senator George McGovern of South Dakota. The ranking minority member is Senator Jesse Helms of North Carolina.

In 1977, the Senate Agriculture Committee was renamed to include nutrition as it absorbed the operations of the Senate Select Committee on Nutrition. The Senate Agriculture Committee has fewer subcommittees than the House. The Subcommittee on Agricultural Production, Marketing, and Stabilization of Prices handles all commodity programs.

The eighteen members of the committee in the 96th Congress came from eighteen states. An examination of the geographic locations of the members shows the strongest representation from the Great Plains and Southern states (figure 2-2). The Corn Belt was represented with members from Indiana, Iowa, and Minnesota; the Great Plains with members from North Dakota, South Dakota, Nebraska, Kansas, and Oklahoma; and the South-

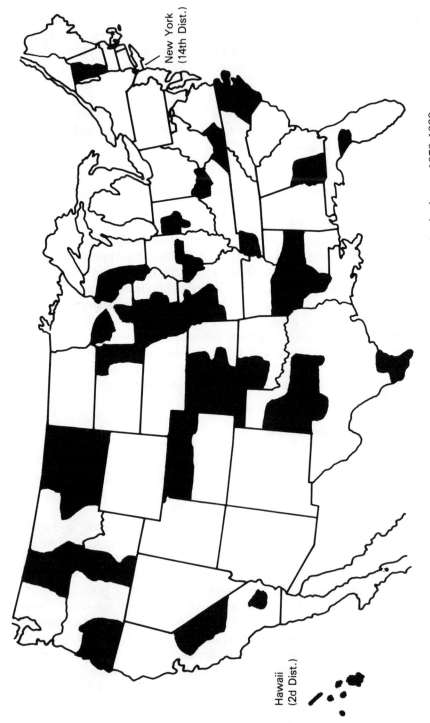

Figure 2-1. Districts Served by Members of the House Committee on Agriculture, 1979-1980.

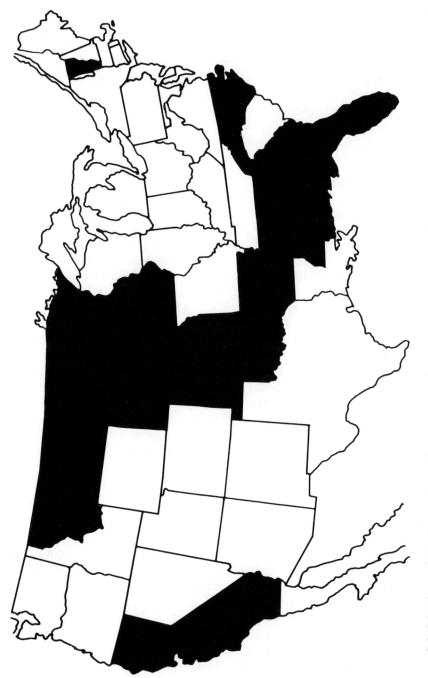

Figure 2-2. Members of the Senate Committee on Agriculture, Nutrition, and Forestry: Geographic Distribution, 1979-1980.

east had members from Arkansas, Mississippi, Alabama, Georgia, North Carolina, and Florida. Except for California, the most urban states in the country were not represented on the Senate Agriculture Committee.

The senators on the committee represent a cross section of professional, business, and political experience. Among the eighteen members, eight are attorneys, one is a veterinarian, three had been governors of their states, at least three had been engaged in farming or had farming interests, five had previously served in the House of Representatives, and eight had previously been elected to state or municipal offices.

Budget Controls

The Budget and Impoundment Act of 1974 created a budget committee with staff in each house and a Congressional Budget Office. The act established a timetable that attempted to structure all legislative efforts and bring total spending under control. Under the act, standing committees must present their budget requests to their budget committees by March 15 and report proposals for new authorizations, appropriations, and tax measures between April 15 and May 15. The first budget resolution for the ensuing fiscal year is to be passed by both houses by May 15.

Bills authorizing programs, appropriating funds, or raising revenue must be passed by the week after Labor Day. A binding budget resolution establishing ceilings for seventeen budget functions is to be passed by September 25. All adjustments and reconciliations must be handled by the committees before the new fiscal year starts on October 1.[3]

Although the budget process has not resulted in balanced federal budgets, it was a step toward more organized planning of total federal expenditures and revenues. It could affect many groups and organizations seeking additional government assistance or attempting to control federal expenditures.

Support Staff

Besides information which members of Congress may receive from outside organizations and associations seeking to influence the direction of legislation, there are certain sources of information and assistance which committees or individual members may use to help in the decision-making process.

The Congressional Research Service, part of the Library of Congress, has a large professional staff of specialists who can provide information to members of Congress upon request. The specialists include persons trained in agriculture, economics, and natural resources who have prepared reports on these subjects.

The Office of Technology Assessment has a staff of scientists and professional persons who prepare reports analyzing and assessing the effects of proposed legislation on new technology, the environment, and the health and well-being of the population.

The General Accounting Office, which originally provided investigations of how appropriated funds were spent, has expanded its role as an investigative and research unit of Congress. Some of its reports deal with issues relating to food and agriculture. Although any member of Congress may request studies by the General Accounting Office, work for committees receives first priority. Such reports are often quoted and provide an input into the policy-making process.

The largest support for members of Congress has come from the staffs of the committees, subcommittees, and the offices of the individual members. Seeking more help to analyze and gain understanding of the many complex issues it faces during the 1970s, Congress greatly enlarged the authorized staff positions for their members and committees.

The staffs have grown so rapidly that an undercurrent of concern running on Capitol Hill is that congressional staff are exercising increasing influence on decisions their bosses were elected to make. An accelerating turnover among members of Congress may well be accentuating the problem. One estimate placed the number of congressional employees at over 20,000. The threat of staff intrusion on decision making has always been regarded as greater in the Senate because senators, being fewer in number, must deal with more legislative subjects and have larger staffs to assist them.[4]

For organizations and groups concerned with legislation, the staff members become key persons to contact, to keep informed, and to become acquainted with. Committee staff members play a key role in holding and inviting witnesses for hearings, preparing committee reports, keeping members of Congress informed about the situations affecting legislative decisions, preparing news releases and press contacts, and setting up appointments for meetings with their bosses. Some lobbyists devote most of their efforts to keeping in contact with congressmen through their staff members.

Staff members, however, serve only as long as the members to whom they are responsible want them to serve. When differences in viewpoints occur, the members and the committees have the final authority. Such a situation occurred in 1977 when the staff of the Senate Select Committee on Nutrition prepared the report on dietary goals for the United States. The first printing of the report recommended less consumption of meat. After protests by the livestock industry and some professional organizations, the committee decided to revise the report and change the wording to recommend eating less animal fat and more lean meat, fish, and poultry. Senator Percy led the revision effort, and Senator McGovern agreed to the change.

But objections by staff member Nick Mottern, who had written the first report, resulted in Senator McGovern's asking him to leave the committee staff.[5]

Coalitions and Tradeoffs

Despite the decline in numbers of farmers in the total population, the decline in number of congressional districts composed primarily of farmers, and the increase in numbers of urban members of Congress, major farm legislation was passed in 1965, 1973, and 1977. A closer examination of the legislation in 1973 and 1977 reveals sections covering concerns of interest to the nonfarm population such as food assistance programs, food stamps, and nutrition. The titles have been changed—"Agriculture and Consumer Protection Act of 1973," "Food and Agriculture Act of 1977"—to reflect and attract support from both farm and consumer groups.

Weldon V. Barton discerned an example of intricate coalition building in the House of Representatives that made the 1973 act appear more than accidental. A coalition within agriculture including wheat, feed grains, and cotton—but with cotton no longer dominant—then achieved a logrolling deal with organized labor's representatives, backing minimum wage and food stamps for strikers in return for labor's backing of farm price supports and subsidies. Barton sees the farm-labor coalition as essential to the retention of an effective farm price support policy for farmers. Charles Hardin sees the durability of such a coalition as "problematic."[6]

James Bonnen also found that coalition building among labor, consumers, and agriculture contributed much to the passage of the 1973 act. He believes that presidential leadership is essential in securing agricultural price support legislation. Bonnen also suggests that making a coalition between agricultural and consumer representatives would require bargaining on a price level that appears neither too low to farmers nor too high to consumers—in effect, the achievement of a workable compromise.[7]

Whether you call it logrolling, coalition, or cooperation, the 1977 act in its final form came about through compromise between those supporting the commodity programs for farmers and the consumer and welfare interests seeking expanded food assistance and nutrition programs.

Future comprehensive food and agricultural legislation will also be influenced by coalitions and tradeoffs among the interested groups. The political climate for such legislation in the 1980s will be conditioned by the extent of food price inflation, domestic production, foreign demand and the U.S. trade balance, and the needs for food assistance at home and abroad. Other groups concerned with social welfare, the economically disadvantaged, human nutrition, the environment, conservation of natural resources, and agricultural land will also participate in the future food and agricultural policy decision-making process.

The next four chapters identify these groups and some of their major interests and concerns.

Notes

1. Laurellen Porter, "Congress and Agricultural Policy," *Policy Studies Journal* 6, 4 (Summer 1978):474. Reprinted with permission.

2. Ibid., pp. 472-473.

3. Ibid., p. 477.

4. "With Shorter Stays for Legislators, Bigger Staffs, Who'll Run Congress?" *Science*, January 19, 1979, p. 245.

5. Nick Mottern, "Dietary Goals," *Food Monitor*, no. 3, March-April 1978, p. 10.

6. Charles M. Hardin, "Agricultural Price Policy: The Political Role of Bureaucracy," *Policy Studies Journal* 5, 4 (Summer 1978):468. Reprinted with permission.

7. Ibid., p. 468.

3

Producer Advocates: To Preserve and Protect the Family Farm

Cultivators of the earth are the most valuable citizens, the most vigorous, the most independent, the most virtuous. They are tied to their country, and wedded to its liberty and interests, by the most lasting bonds.
—Thomas Jefferson[a]

Thomas Jefferson's fundamental beliefs in land ownership and control by the men who cultivated the land are deeply rooted in the beliefs and values of U.S. farm people. The organizations and groups representing farmers and ranchers include the general farm organizations, commodity groups, cooperatives, farmwives, and some other groups brought together by a mutual interest.

General Farm Organizations

General farm organizations include among their members those producers with many interests, usually living in different parts of the country. They carry out a broad range of business activities and services for their members. Their legislative efforts cover a variety of issues dealing with food and agriculture.

Throughout our two-hundred-year history, financial troubles and other hardships have spawned farmers' movements and protests to develop sympathy from the rest of the population and gain assistance from government. Many of these movements and the organizations have disappeared.

The National Grange, National Farmers Union, and American Farm Bureau Federation have survived through war and depression and have provided services to their members for more than sixty years. The National Farmers Organization began in the recession of the mid-1950s, and through emphasis on collective-bargaining contracts with processors and marketing services to its members it has emerged as a fourth major national organization. Each maintains a Washington office and employs registered lobbyists.

Just as not all farmers have the same economic or political philosophy, the major farm organizations do not agree on all legislative issues dealing with food and agriculture.

---

[a]U.S. Department of Agriculture, "Washington, Jefferson, and Agriculture," Mimeograph, 1937.

The National Grange

The National Grange was founded in 1867 as the Patrons of Husbandry, a fraternal and social organization for farmers. It grew rapidly as a voice for farmers against high freight rates being charged by railroads. It also laid the foundation for farmer cooperatives.[1] Besides its continuing interest in farm issues, it carries out many community and family projects through its state and local Grange units.

The Grange supported the Food and Agriculture Act of 1977 and fought for increased target prices for wheat and feed grains when the bill was before the House. Historically it has given strong support for family farms and opportunities for family farmers. However, even though it was sympathetic to the aim of the American Agricultural Movement in 1978 to increase farm income, it was fearful that "their demand for 100 percent of parity mandated by Government will lead to a rapid escalation in land values, placing the family farmer at an extreme financial disadvantage."[2]

Trying to be continuously aware of the changing conditions in agriculture, the National Grange leadership has cautioned about the "quick fix" for farm prices that may have an adverse effect on the agricultural economy in the future. Instead, it calls for a return on investment, labor, and management for farmers equal to other segments of society. At the same time it has publicly supported a grain reserve with 80 percent held by farmers and 20 percent by government, updated disaster payments, price supports based on cost of production but including a 35-year average acquisition cost for land, 90 percent of parity support for milk prices, elimination of tax incentives that favor nonfarm corporate investments in agriculture, adequate funding for agricultural research, and increased agricultural exports under Public Law 480. It has encouraged more flexible regulation of pesticides, more rapid expediting of registration, and developing new pesticides before withdrawal of products already in use.

It favored continuation of food stamps but did not want the program to become a welfare program. It favored keeping the purchase requirement, denying stamps to workers voluntarily away from their jobs, providing better nutritional information to recipients, tightening of eligibility criteria, and transferring the program to the Department of Health, Education, and Welfare.[3]

The Grange maintains its national headquarters in Washington. In 1977 the Grange also participated in the National Farm Coalition, an informal alliance of thirty-six general, commodity, and cooperative farm organizations leaders who testified at hearings on the 1977 Food and Agriculture Act.

Most legislative testimony is handled by the officials in the national headquarters, although local Grange members submitted a statement supporting a mandatory set-aside program and higher loan rates.[4] The national headquarters also sends "hot-line" memos to state nad local units to rally support through their congressional representatives. State officers may testify at field hearings. The oldest national farm organization, the Grange is active in some parts of the country and almost nonexistent in others. There is some feeling that its membership is made up of fewer commercial and young farmers than other farm organizations. Membership has dropped about 100,000 in the last fifteen years.

National Farmers Union

The National Farmers Union (NFU) emerged in 1902 out of the ashes of the declining Farmers Alliance groups which flourished in the 1880s and 1890s. It first spread rapidly across the South. Later growth occurred in the upper Midwest and Great Plains as it absorbed the American Society of Equity and the Nonpartisan League. As it grew, it attracted those farmers who did not respond to the conservative Farm Bureau and the Grange. Today its major membership is in the Great Plains states from Texas to North Dakota, but it is organized in thirty states in the West, Midwest, South, and East.[5]

The NFU is strongly committed to the parity formula, using the base years 1910 to 1914 as the standard by which farm prices should be determined.[6] It believes the family farm and ranch is the keystone to the highly successful U.S. agricultural system, and the welfare of the nation's consumers is increasingly related to preservation of a family farm and ranch system. It strongly opposes farming by publicly owned industrial corporations. It strongly believes that government policies and programs are essential to protect family farmers and ranchers against the hazards of the marketplace where almost everyone else, except the farmer and the rancher, is protected.[7]

In its testimony before Congress it has asked for an objective of 100 percent of parity, for farm policies and programs and for price support through loans of 90 percent of parity. It supported a grain reserve held by farmers and government, but wanted no government release of stocks at less than 110 percent of parity. The use of a monthly parity price index is preferred over an annual cost of production for calculating support prices. It would also like to see more commodities eligible for marketing orders and agreements. It supports strict production control programs if price supports are raised to 90 percent of parity.

The Farmers Union favors expansion of Public Law 480 to include more countries, a world grain reserve held by producing countries, expanding food aid programs, guaranteeing a nutritionally adequate diet for everyone in the United States, and more cooperation in developing international commodity agreements among the major grain-exporting countries.

Farmers Union history is closely associated with cooperatives serving its members. So it is making a major attack on the National Commission to Review Antitrust Laws and Procedures that recommended repeal or reduction in the scope of antitrust exemptions for cooperatives under the Capper Volstead Act, the Clayton Act, and Marketing Agreements Act of 1937. It supports the 160-acre limitation established in the Reclamation Act of 1902.[8]

Headquartered in Denver, the Farmers Union also maintains a Washington office. The Farmers Union schedules state group "fly-ins" to Washington for contacts with home-state members of Congress. At hearings before congressional agriculture committees, state and local officers and members testify. The Farmers Union gave strong support to the American Agricultural Movement (AAM) in its 1978 efforts to achieve 100 percent of parity prices, but remained uncommitted in the AAM's 1979 efforts. In 1977 the NFU did not participate as part of the National Farm Coalition, but two Farmers Union cooperatives—Farmers Union Grain Terminal Association and Farmers Union Central Exchange (CENEX)—did participate.

The Farmers Union has cooperated with consumer and labor groups to further its legislative goals more than other general farm organizations. It is represented on the board of the Consumers Federation of America (see chapter 5). President Tony Dechant, who served as secretary before becoming president in 1968, has announced plans to retire in March 1980.

Some of its officials have served in important administrative posts in government. Robert G. Lewis, national secretary, was administrative assistant to Senator William Proxmire from 1957 to 1959, deputy administrator of the Agricultural Stabilization and Conservation Service, vice-president of the Commodity Credit Corporation from 1961 to 1965, and administrator of the Rural Community Development Service from 1965 to 1967. Legislative director, Reuben Johnson was employed in the Department of Agriculture before he joined the NFU in 1954. When Charles Brannan left his post as Secretary of Agriculture in early 1953, he moved to Denver to become general counsel to the NFU.

The NFU is the national sponsor of the Green Thumb Program, a rural community improvement and service organization that hires and finds jobs for low-income men and women fifty-five-years old and older in rural areas. The program is funded by the Department of Labor under the Older Americans Act. John A. Baker, an assistant Secretary of Agriculture from 1961 to 1968, administered the program for the Farmers Union until he retired in 1979. The national executive board of Farmers Union is also the board of directors of Green Thumb.

Federal funding for the program has expanded in recent years as follows: 1974, $3.6 million; 1975, $17.2 million; 1976, $22.7 million; 1977,

$50.6 million; 1978, $65.7 million; and 1979, $72.2 million. The 1978 program operated in forty-seven states and territories. Although federal regulations permit a maximum of 15 percent of this allocation for administration, the actual administrative costs paid to Farmers Union have been around 12 percent according to Department of Labor officials. This amount is probably less than direct government administration would cost. The Farmers Union, as the national sponsor, helps find participants, selects work sites, and manages the payrolls. One Capitol Hill observer, learning of the scope of the program, commented, "It looks like *green thumb* also means green backs."

American Farm Bureau Federation

The American Farm Bureau Federation is the largest farm organization in the United States with membership that includes farm operators, farmland owners, and others who have an interest in agriculture. Unlike the three other major national farm groups, Farm Bureau began during a period of relative prosperity for farmers. The first local group was sponsored by the chamber of commerce in Broome County, New York, in 1912 to encourage improved farm methods and education among adult farmers. When the Smith-Lever Act was passed in 1914, the law required that the local Extension Service have a local farm group sponsor. In many counties, the sponsoring group was the local farm bureau. In their early years, Farm Bureau and Extension developed together and supported each other. The American Farm Bureau was organized in 1919.[9] As Farm Bureau became active in legislative and lobbying activities, the Department of Agriculture called for separation of the Extension Service and Farm Bureau.

Through county, state, and national conventions, Farm Bureau members develop extensive resolutions dealing with public food and agricultural policy issues, as well as other issues relating government and society. In its 1979 resolutions, Farm Bureau members declared continued support for a market-oriented agriculture as the most efficient means of producing food and fiber and providing farmers with the greatest opportunity for economic well-being. If their plan is effectively implemented, they state that market orientation should avoid the need for and use of price and income support measures, maximize agricultural efficiency, and increase net farm income. They believe that a national farm policy should include unrestricted access to domestic and world markets; help for farmers to obtain needed crop and market information, research, education, and credit; eradicate and control plant and animal pests and diseases; implement programs to encourage conservation of land and water; and prevent exercise of monopoly power.

Developing a position on government price and income support programs has been difficult for Farm Bureau because of regional differences and the national scope of its membership. It testified in favor of extension of the 1973 Agriculture and Consumer Protection Act when the 1977 act was being considered. It called for supports and target prices at lower levels than most other farm groups because they do not want farmers to become dependent on government payments on a continuing basis. It has supported acreage set-aside programs when necessary and has been critical of the 10 percent feed grain set-asides of 1978 and 1979 which it felt were too limited to be effective. Neither does it want government to establish a grain stockpile, so that government could control prices, or high support prices that would create artificial incentives to produce or limit the demand for export.

In line with their strong market orientation, Farm Bureau has called for improved marketing strategies for its members, including authority for collective bargaining through contracts with handlers, workable grades and standards to safeguard product quality, expanded export promotion programs, farmers' rights to organize cooperatives and promote sales of their products.

In the area of food policy, it strongly opposes any efforts to "mislead" the consuming public and cause a decrease in consumption of meat, to dictate what foods should and should not be eaten, to ban nitrites in cured meat products in "the absence of adequate competent research showing undue risk to human health," to limit school lunches to three eggs per child per week, to substitute cash payments for food stamps, to provide food stamps to families of workers on strike. It also opposes federally financed radio and television advertisements to increase the number of food stamp recipients and efforts to transfer school lunch, special milk, or food stamps out of the USDA.

Farm Bureau would like to see less regulation of farming operations; more flexible labeling requirements for pesticides; more administration by state and less by the federal government; exemption of family farms from EPA regulation; and a transfer of administration of the Federal Insecticide, Fungicide, and Rodenticide Act to the USDA.

Farm Bureau has taken more positions in opposition to organized labor, including farm workers' unions, than other farm groups. It has stated that farmers believe in the right of free collective bargaining and the contribution of labor organizations to maintaining a balance of forces in the economy. But it opposes strikes by public employees and excessive monopoly power by which any group can close down an entire industry that brings an area or the entire country under its power. It recognizes the right of farm workers to form or join unions, but it opposes any law that would require workers to join.

Farm Bureau has called for expanded agricultural research to improve agricultural productivity and continued funding of the Extension Service. It has expressed concern that new Extension Service programs for nonfarm people should not come at the expense of programs for farm and ranch families. It favors program decisions being made by local participants and opposes dictation by federal government through earmarking of more funds for specific, federally directed, nonfarm Extension Service programs.[10]

The American Farm Bureau Federation has its national headquarters at Park Ridge, Illinois, on Chicago's northwest side. In its Washington office, it has the largest staff of registered lobbyists of any of the general farm organizations.

State Farm Bureaus sponsor trips to Washington where members call on their congressmen to discuss their concerns. Testimony before congressional committees may be handled by the national president, Washington staff, or state Farm Bureau officers who have special knowledge of the issues being discussed. When special concerns of the membership come up, members may be asked to write or wire their congressmen or specific committee chairmen involved in the legislation.

While legislative activity is an important part of Farm Bureau, many members place as much or more value on the many services provided through affiliated companies and cooperatives. Farm Bureau insurance, farm supplies, and marketing information and services are substantial business enterprises in many states.

The American Farm Bureau Federation conducts a program of political education and action for its members. But it does not have any affiliated political action committee. However, Farm Bureaus in Missouri, Alabama, Ohio, California, and Michigan do have registered political-action committees. These committees receive donations from individual members and contribute to the campaign committees of individual candidates running for office. The candidates may be running for Congress, governor, or state legislature.

National Farmers Organization

The National Farmers Organization (NFO) emerged as a national organization when hog prices dropped to $12 per hundredweight in southwest Iowa and northern Missouri in 1955. One-dollar membership contributions were used to send a delegation to Washington to obtain government assistance. By 1958, the group decided a new approach was needed. Collective bargaining in agriculture became the main thrust, and dedicated farmers in all parts of the country joined together under this principle. Holding actions by farmers to promote contracts with processors were staged during the 1960s. During the 1970s the organization expanded its activities to include a "collection, dispatch, and delivery" system for members along with continued efforts to negotiate contracts with processors.

Although NFO supported the Agricultural Act of 1977, its major effort has been to organize farmers so they can influence prices and incomes. It has based its activities on authority which it believes was given to farmers under the Capper-Volstead Act in 1922.

In its 1977 testimony, it called for higher target prices and loan rates, based on costs of production. It supports production control in order to influence prices, a revised system of crop insurance, and milk supports at 80 percent of parity.[11]

As a new organization, NFO has urged farmers to continue membership in their present farm organization to get whatever benefits are available, but to join NFO to price their products. In pushing for new members and encouraging participation of previously inactive members, it has estimated that 30 percent of the total U.S. production in any commodity would be adequate to allow farmers to determine their own prices.[12]

The national headquarters is at Corning, Iowa. The NFO also maintains a Washington office. Testimony before congressional committees is handled by the national president or the Washington representative.

The organization traditionally has had county units and a national headquarters. In 1978, there were fifty-seven members on the national board from twenty-seven states. State committees and sixteen county operating units have also been organized.

Midcontinent Farmers Association (Missouri Farmers Association)

The Midcontinent Farmers Association (MFA) is a farm legislative organization with membership in Missouri and surrounding states. In a sense, it is the legislative arm of Missouri Farmers Association, which provides many business and cooperative services to Missouri farmers. At times its philosophy and stands on issues have been similar to those of the National Farmers Union. Its leaders have called for target prices at the cost of production, including five-year adjustment for land costs, with loan rates for wheat, rice, feed grains, cotton, and soybeans at 80 percent of the cost of production. They also called for a farm commodity reserve largely under farmer control with release from government-held stocks only under prescribed conditions. It has favored expansion of Public Law 480 Food for Peace and opposed government interference in farm export shipments. It has called for continuing the food stamp program.[13]

Major organization changes occurred in August 1979 when the membership voted out Fred Heinkel, eighty-one, its long-time president, and elected Eric G. Thompson, thirty-six, a five-year MFA employee and director of employee relations. Three vice-presidents were asked to resign. Less legislative activity and lobbying and more emphasis on cooperative and business services are likely to result from the change.

Testimony before congressional committees is given by the officers. It was one of the twenty-one organizations invited to the White House on February 14, 1978, to discuss low farm incomes and financial problems facing farmers.

Commodity Producers Organizations

The commodity producers organized to meet special needs and provide services to those who produce a specific commodity or agricultural product. In some respects, the commodity organization is a trade association for producers who have a common economic interest in the successful production and marketing of that product. Members of the commodity producers organizations may also be members of the general farm organizations.

Commodity groups may be organized as cooperatives to produce or market that commodity; some integrate producers, processors, and handlers into a single association for legislative marketing and public relations efforts.

Unlike the general farm organizations with a broad range of policy resolutions on different topics affecting farming and living conditions in rural areas, the commodity groups are usually concerned with one or a few limited issues affecting their product. Legislative activity may be only a small part of their program of activities. Other services to members may include information through newsletters or other reports, annual conventions, and trade shows, market development to expand demand for their product both at home and abroad, and specific export marketing services to facilitate shipments to overseas locations.

In some way, federal government legislation or regulations affect all producer members of the commodity organizations. However, since legislative activity may be only a small part of the total program, some do not maintain Washington offices or register as lobbyists. The groups identified here have testified before congressional hearings or engaged in other major legislative efforts. Further details about the organization and other lobby groups appear in appendix A.

The American Association of Nurserymen represents firms producing nursery stock, fruit trees, vines, small fruits, trees, and shrubs. It has objected to regulations on pesticides that may permit use of a product on a food crop but prohibits its use on nursery stock. They have sought more flexibility in the labeling requirements for pesticides so that products which can legally be used for sensitive uses around the home or on food crops may also be used for nursery crops.[14]

The American Beekeeping Federation represents beekeepers but also includes equipment suppliers and honey packers. It is concerned by a drop in bee colony numbers from 7 million in 1958 to 4.1 million in 1972. Latest estimates place the population at 4.3 million hives.[15] Since honeybees are the only major pollinators for sixty important fruit, nut, and seed crops, the beekeepers request continuation of indemnity payments which make it possible to build up declining bee colony numbers. Indemnity payments have been authorized by law for beekeepers who have had bees killed by pesticides.

The American Honey Producers is a national organization of beekeepers who formed a new organization in 1969 because they opposed a federal honey market order supported by the American Beekeeping Federation. Its executive secretary is also a registered lobbyist. It has also called for closer monitoring of crops before pesticides are applied to reduce exposure to honeybee colonies. It sees both the Environmental Protection Agency (EPA) and the USDA as bee killers because of their approval of widespread spraying programs that kill bees.

The American Horse Council is a federation of organizations whose members have an interest in horses. It favors more allocation of research funds for animal health and would like to have one person from the horse industry on the animal health research advisory board. If research funds are allocated according to inventory figures, they feel that a new census of horses is needed to show the importance of horses in the nation's animal industry and to be able to properly fund research and vaccination plans.[16]

The American Soybean Association worked to get a permanent mandatory support program established for soybeans in the 1977 Food and Agriculture Act. However, it wanted soybeans treated separately from feed grains. It did not want price supports set too high, suggesting 65 percent of the cost of production, a lower figure than some other farm groups requested for wheat and feed grains. It also would like to see soybeans eligible for crop insurance but not for disaster payments; it opposed target prices and acreage allotments for soybeans; it opposed putting soybeans in the farmer-held grain reserve; it called for protection against export restrictions and embargoes which badly damaged the reputation of the United States as a dependable export supplier in 1973 and 1974; and it favored more funding for research and Extension Service programs.[17]

The American Sugarbeet Growers Association's major concerns deal with national sugar policy. Since production costs for both beet and cane sugar are higher than the price at which sugar could be imported, the survival of the U.S. sugar industry depends on government intervention, which protects U.S. producers. Without this protection, U.S. consumers would be dependent on foreign sources for sugar. Since World War II, our national policy has been to protect and maintain a domestic sugar industry that provides about half of our total needs. This organization favors a system of import fees and quotas to control imports and protect domestic producers. It also supports the concept of an International Sugar Agreement.[18] More discussion of sugar lobbying appears in chapter 4.

The Catfish Farmers of America see aquaculture as a means of supplying more food to a growing population. They want to see aquaculture recognized in the funding of agricultural research programs, specifically in providing for animal health research. They feel that aquaculture should have a representative on the research users advisory board. To properly allocate research funds, they believe that a census of aquaculture is needed so the volume and value of production would be more fully recognized.[19]

The Grain Sorghum Producers Association draws its membership from the major sorghum producing states—the Great Plains area which frequently faces drought and adverse growing conditions. So it has a strong interest in the price support programs. It has called for target prices based on cost of production including land costs based on current cash rent; recommended each producer restrict his output in line with market demand; favored farmer-held over government-held grain reserves; proposed limiting the size of the reserve and not releasing any of it until prices reach 175 percent of the loan rate; strongly opposed any restrictions on grain exports and favored government support of 100 percent of parity should any export restrictions be imposed; and has called for raising the limits on loans to farmers from Farmers Home Administration above $50,000 and $375,000 gross sales.[20]

The Holstein Friesian Association of America generally supports the policy positions of the National Milk Producers Federation. It would like to see market forces operate to set prices for farm products. Although it favors a grain reserve, it would like to see it owned and controlled by farmers. Since it has a direct interest in expanding exports of dairy breeding cattle, it would like to see more competitive international financing arrangements and cooperative efforts between private organizations to expand export sales. It would also like to see more priority placed on research relating to the dairy industry to keep a balance in food and agricultural policy.[21] The association expressed disapproval of the Senate Select Committee on Nutrition Report that suggested less consumption of whole milk and high-fat dairy products.[22]

The National Association of Wheat Growers maintains a strong interest in the economic well-being of its members. Its major policy concerns deal with wheat price supports, disaster assistance, and export market development.

Wheat growers called for target prices at 80 percent of parity, around $4 per bushel, and a loan rate of at least 60 percent of parity, or about $3 per bushel. To encourage participation in the set-aside program, they recommended land diversion payments and disaster benefits if growers had less than two-thirds of the normal yield. They favored waiving interest charges on loans when growers stored their wheat from one to five years under the reserve program. They wanted the release price on government-held wheat raised from 150 to 180 percent of the loan rate or 100 percent of parity, whichever is lower. They favored 25 cents per bushel annual payment for those who store in the grain reserve. They oppose any policy which would encourage wheat for feed use at a lower price than for food uses. They favor expanded programs to increase exports and use of Public Law 480 as a market development tool.[23] The organization has its national headquarters in Washington, and two registered lobbyists are listed on the staff.

The National Cattlemen's Association has sought to limit government involvement in its members' business. It opposes price support on cattle but accepts grain reserves as long as they are held by farmers. It sees government interference with markets, such as the 1971 price freeze, as contributing more to the problems of cattle producers than helping them. It views government as one of the greatest burdens to agriculture because of inflation, excessive interference with technology such as reduction of antibiotic use in animal feeds, legislative and regulatory action to control private and public land use, recommendations for diets which suggest eating less foods with animal fats, and efforts to limit acreage receiving water from federal water projects.[24]

It does see a role for government in guiding research in energy use and setting pollution standards, improving the balance of trade, developing trade agreements on live cattle, tax reform, and correcting abuses of the Food and Drug Administration and Environmental Protection Agency.[25] It supports more funding for agricultural research, but feels that competitive grants often lead to inefficient use of expensive research equipment and do not encourage good continuity of research and research staffs.

The association is the largest commodity membership organization and employs three registered lobbyists on its staff and two others from a private law firm.

The National Corn Growers Association is involved in educational, legislative, and market development programs for its members. Its major legislative interest concerns the price and income support and market expansion programs. In 1977, it called for corn loan rates at no less than 70 percent of parity, around $2.30 per bushel, with loans for three years to give more control of when growers would market their grain. By 1978, it suggested increasing the corn loan to $2.50 per bushel, but did not favor a law requiring 100 percent of parity prices. It would favor payments for diverting land from production, increased conservation payments and wildlife protection, farmer-held grain reserve in which farmers would receive payments after one year in storage, and loans to build storage and purchase drying equipment.

It supports continuation of Public Law 480 export programs, but would limit exports to those countries making honest efforts and progress in family planning, modernizing grain storage and handling, and controlling grain storage insects. It believes Congress should approve any type of export embargo. It also called for reduced fraud and review of alleged abuses in the food stamp program.[26]

The National Peanut Growers Group is most concerned with the peanut price support program. During the 1960s and early 1970s the national acreage allotment program remained at 1.6 million acres each year while average yields more than doubled.[27] The government acquired large stocks and experienced substantial losses in disposing of them by selling for crushing into oil and meal. Secretary of Agriculture Butz wanted to eliminate the program, but growers objected.

The National Peanut Growers Group recognized a need for change. They called for reducing the national acreage allotment by not more than 6 percent in 1977 and in 1978 only by 10 percent as long as the total supply was not less than 115 percent of domestic edible and related needs.

Goldkist, Inc.—a major regional farm cooperative that processes, stores, and markets peanuts and represents about 25 percent of the allotment holders—argued for the strict allotment control program and urged that any change should be gradual so growers could adjust. The 1977 act set a price support of $420 a ton for peanuts grown under the government-assigned acreage quota but only $250 per ton for peanuts grown outside the quota.

In 1978 the growers group asked that the $420 per ton support be increased in view of rising costs to producers. They also called for increased returns for peanuts grown outside their quota to improve grower returns, although Congress had set a lower support price for the "additional" (surplus) peanuts to discourage excess production. By 1979, the 1977 act was providing favorable incomes to peanut growers as exports went up. Their future goal is to maintain a cash market above government price supports by expanding both the domestic and export markets. As the market expands, their goal is to gradually increase acreage by increasing the allotments of growers.[28]

The National Pork Producers Council, headquartered in Des Moines, Iowa, provides educational, business, and market development services for its members. The national organization has refrained from legislative activity not specifically relating to pork production, leaving the general farm organizations and state organizations to discuss general farm policy issues.[29] It is interested in research to increase efficiency of production and to decrease the effects of disease, expanding the export market for pork products, and opposing any efforts that would decrease domestic demand through government regulation or dietary recommendations.

The National Wool Growers Association's major legislative concerns deal with sheep and wool. It would like to see the wool price support program begun in 1954 continued, but at a higher support for both wool and mohair. It is also concerned with restrictions on controls for coyotes and predators on sheep flocks, red tape in importing labor for herding sheep, and the public land policies that discourage grazing of sheep. The organization is concerned with the steady decline in the sheep population of about 50 million in the 1940s to about 12 million in 1977. The chairman of the association board told the Senate Agricultural Committee that coyotes kill 6 to 7 percent of the sheep each year. Many growers have reported higher losses.[30]

The association maintains its national legislative office in Washington and a Western office at Salt Lake City.

Other Commodity Groups

In addition to the commodity groups organized to cover most of the production in the country, there are specialized regional associations which testify before congressional committees in Washington and at field hearings. Some are registered lobbyists; others are not. They do have special food and farm policy concerns.

California has many special commodity interests. Although 200 crops are grown commercially in California, about twenty crop and livestock commodities account for about 82 percent of the state's gross farm income. The California Canners and Growers Association has a registered lobbyist. Many of these crops are not affected by government price support programs, such as grains, cotton, and tobacco. But many are affected by marketing agreements and market orders by which growers work together to stabilize supplies and maintain product quality.

The California Tomato Growers Association with 700 members produces most of the tomatoes canned and processed in California. This group has banded together to achieve a uniform contract with the processors who buy their crop. They would like to see legislation, such as the proposed National Agricultural Bargaining Act of 1978, which would establish standards of fair practices by handlers and producer associations to bargain with respect to production, sale, and marketing of agricultural products.[31]

The Florida winter vegetable growers also have special interest in federal policies that affect their business. Three associations—the Southwest Florida Winter Vegetable Growers Association, the Palm Beach-Broward County Farmers Committee for Legislation Action, and the South Florida Tomato and Vegetable Growers Association—represent almost 99 percent of the winter vegetable production in that state. They express their views at congressional hearings, and each group has a registered lobbyist representing it in Washington. Their major concern is the large volume of vegetables shipped in from Mexico during the winter months, which affects their markets and prices. They adhere to quality standards, wage standards, pesticide and insecticide standards, and OSHA standards; yet they believe that foreign producers are not meeting the same standards, but are permitted to ship their products in to compete with domestic production.[32]

Some commodity producers groups join with handlers and processors of their product to engage in legislative activities. The cotton producers participate in the National Cotton Council. The broiler growers are part of the National Broiler Council. The turkey producers are part of the National Turkey Federation. Rice producers participate in legislative activities through the regional cooperatives that process and package their product.

Regional associations may be part of a national industry groups, but also engage in individual association legislative activity. The Western Cotton Growers Association of California has Kenneth E. Frick, an assistant Secretary of Agriculture during the Nixon administration and a cotton producer, as their lobbyist. The Plains Cotton Growers, Inc., of Lubbock, Texas, also are registered as lobbyists.

Other registered-lobbyist, special commodity producer groups include the Forest Farmers Association of Atlanta, Georgia, and the Hawaiian Sugar Planters Association of Aiea, Hawaii.

Cooperative Organizations

The federal government has aided and stimulated the establishment and growth of cooperatives in the twentieth century. The Capper-Volstead Act of 1922 exempted farm cooperatives from prosecution under the antitrust laws as long as they did not enhance prices unduly. In 1926 a division of cooperative marketing was established in the Department of Agriculture to assist and foster development of cooperatives.[33] The legislation which established the Federal Land Bank system in 1916, the Farm Credit Administration in 1933, and the Rural Electrification Act in 1936 added new government financial support and assistance for development of farmer-owned cooperative business enterprises.

Most legislative activity and lobbying is handled by national associations representing many member cooperatives. Some major regional cooperatives also participate in hearings and have their own registered lobbyists.

The Cooperative League of the USA represents all types of cooperatives but has taken a major role in representing farm cooperatives. In 1978 hearings on the impact of foreign investments in farmland, president Glenn Anderson declared, "What is being threatened here is the most efficient system in the world for producing food at affordable prices. Quarterbacking this system and making it work has been the family farmer. . . . But if outside interests can run up the price of land until it is out of the reach of the next generation, it will effectively foreclose a way of life that has worked in favor of the producer and consumer alike."

The Cooperative League has also opposed removing the child nutrition program from the USDA and lodging it in a new Department of Education.

They believe that food growing, food marketing, and feeding programs are central concerns of the USDA. They feel that to "chip off any part of this basic food mission and assign it in piecemeal fashion to other untried parts of the bureaucracy is not good management."[34]

The National Council of Farmer Cooperatives claims 5,800 co-operatives among its membership and represents a broad array of their interests. One of its major concerns in recent years has been the administration of the Federal Insecticide, Fungicide, and Rodenticide Act (FIFRA) since cooperatives sell about $1 billion of pesticides annually, or about 35 percent of all farmers' purchases. Council representatives cited delay, diversion, and confusion in the five years of Environmental Protection Agency authority over federal pesticide programs and expressed the view that the EPA was both reluctant and unprepared to assume a strong technical and regulatory role. It was critical of the administrator's inability to arbitrate positions of pesticide manufacturers and formulators and to finalize guidelines for registering pesticides. So it urged a study of possibly returning all authorities of FIFRA to the USDA except certain enforcement provisions. It also called for an agricultural impact statement to be required on all future pesticide limitations and bans.[35]

Agricultural transportation is another important concern of the council since cooperatives are engaged in marketing many farm products. It would like to see truck service improved by broadening trucking exemptions for hauling agricultural commodities, maintenance of rail lines to move agricultural products to market, and improvement of bridges and roads through federal assistance. It would like to see more USDA involvement in rail abandonment decisions.[36]

The National Council of Farmer Cooperatives has also supported gradual natural-gas deregulation, supported building of Locks and Dam 26 at Alton, Illinois, on the Mississippi River, favored the Trade Expansion Act of 1978, called for retention of agricultural antitrust laws in their present form, opposed the energy tax package, supported exemption of agricultural cooperative trucking from a change in rules proposed by the Interstate Commerce Commission, opposed a consumer protection agency, supported a gas rationing plan that would give agricultural users full requirements, and supported the Secretary of Agriculture's decision permitting cooperatives to obtain price support loans on wheat and feed grains pooled by their members.

The National Milk Producers Federation has played a strong role in maintaining the dairy price support program. It called for a minimum support of 80 percent of parity with a quarterly review in 1977. The final bill provided for 80 percent minimum support for 1978 and 1979, a minimum of 75 percent for the next two years, and review every six months. As 1980 and 1981 approached, the federation called for keeping the 80 percent minimum support.

It has also urged the government not to sell nonfat dry milk at less than 115 percent of the purchase price and to limit imports to avoid pressure on domestic prices and high government costs for holding surplus stocks. During the review of farm policies early in 1978, it urged that dairy product donations through CARE, Catholic Relief Services, Church World Service, and other agencies be increased. It would also like to see more use of nonfat dry milk in calf milk replacers to substitute for the imported casein now being used.[37]

The National Milk Producers Federation has supported federal nutritional assistance programs designed to supplement the diets of low-income families and children and urged expansion and extension of these programs in a manner that will ensure maximum nutritional value for the recipients. Lynn Stalbaum, their chief lobbyist was a Congressman from Wisconsin from 1965-1967.

When called to the White House with other farm groups early in 1978, the federation representative stressed that dairymen were not striking because they had a system in the federal price support program, milk marketing orders, cooperative structure, and dairy import restrictions—a system that works.[38]

Although the National Milk Producers Federation has been the registered Washington lobbyist and voice for dairy cooperatives, a wave of cooperative mergers in the late 1960s and early 1970s brought the creation of large, interregional "supercooperatives." Most prominent in their legislative and political activity are the Associated Milk Producers, Inc., headquartered in San Antonio; Mid-American Dairymen at Springfield, Missouri; and Dairymen, Inc., at Louisville, Kentucky. They have testified at congressional hearings, formed political action committees, and negotiated higher milk prices than the normal federal pricing formula would provide.

Their testimony has supported the National Milk Producers Federation position for higher price supports at a minimum of 85 to 90 percent of parity and quarterly adjustments of support price levels.[39] More details of their activities with political action committees are discussed in chapter 7. The new economic strength and increased political activity by the three large milk regional cooperatives have brought reactions from consumers groups such as Consumers Federation of America, National Consumers Congress, Congress Watch, and some research and educational groups.[40]

The National Rural Electric Cooperative Association's major concern is the support for energy production by its members. Much of its energy is used in agricultural production in the rural areas which it serves. It sees the availability of reliable and adequate supplies of electric energy as the end to pain and drudgery of manual labor and the key role in bringing vast improvements to the quality of life for farmers, ranchers, and other electric cooperative members. Along with electric energy production, the association has called for highest priority in rural development; assistance to areas affected by energy developments; energy conservation; consideration of rural areas in rail abandonment decisions; low-interest loans for electric cooperatives and farmers; replacement of Locks and Dam 26 on the Mississippi River near Alton, Illinois; improved farm price support programs; tax-exempt status so rural electric systems can issue tax-exempt bonds for building new generating stations; adequate loan funds for rural telephone systems; support for agricultural research and extension by land-grant colleges and universities; keeping the Rural Electrification Administration in the USDA; a reasonable and balanced approach in selecting land for new power plants and transmission lines; and adding to wilderness areas only where multiple use is not practical. It also opposes a proposed Department of Natural Resources, severance taxes on coal that would lead to higher electricity bills, and increased prices or taxes on energy to force conservation since this would lead to more inflation.[41]

The association's 260 employees are organized into five departments that include government relations, energy and environmental policy, public and association affairs, management services, and retirement, safety, and insurance. Each department carries out matters dealing with legislation, technical information and training, overseas assistance programs, insurance and employee benefits, and publications. With sixteen registered lobbyists, the National Rural Electric Cooperative Association carries out one of the most extensive, if not the largest, legislative and lobbying effort of any organization or group with an interest in food and agricultural issues.

Farm Women as Lobbyists

Falling farm prices, rising costs, and financial stress for the farm family stimulated the organizational and legislative efforts of new and separate farm women's organizations during the mid-1970s. For many years the major farm organizations have had women's auxiliary groups, and farmwives participated. However, the emergence of the farm women's groups was influenced by the antidiscrimination efforts of other women's groups, the discrimination against farm women in the levying of estate taxes on farm property, and the women's desire to make their own organization's policies separate from those of the men. However, the farm women's groups are not registered lobbyists or part of the women's liberation movement.

American Agri-Women (AAW) is the larger of the two national farm women's groups. They have been active in testifying before the Senate and House agriculture committees. Many of their views on issues reflect the views of other farm organizations, but some feel they are more articulate in expressing them. The AAW has called for prices which provide an incentive to make a profit, freedom to produce, and tools of research and marketing as essential ingredients for success. They want to maintain conditions favorable for family farms and provide means to encourage young farmers to get started in farming. They have testified for less government regulation and more funds for land-grant colleges and universities and have opposed export limitations and restrictions on pesticides. They favor development of new energy sources for agriculture, priority in fuel allocations for agriculture, and enforcing of quality and health standards for imported foods. They approve the food stamp program for those truly in need, but oppose fraud. They call for work incentives in food stamp reform programs.[42]

Women Involved in Farm Economics (WIFE) also sent representatives to testify before the House and Senate agriculture committees in 1977 and 1978. This group supported Senator Dole's flexible parity bill in 1978, called for 100 percent of parity, wanted cotton imports restricted until the domestic price reached 100 percent of parity, favored development of gasohol, wanted vigorous promotion of exports and the same sanitary standards on imported meat as on domestically produced. It wants a larger subsidy to protect domestic sugar producers; WIFE also strongly supports the family farm and opposes efforts of foreign investors, large corporations, or investment trusts to buy and own farmland.[43]

In addition to the national groups, other state and local women's groups have organized to work for farm legislation.

Concerned Farm Wives organized in south central Kansas in March 1977. It is not affiliated with other women's groups. Its efforts were stimulated by the financial problems facing Great Plains wheat farmers during this period. It has organized letter-writing campaigns to Congress, and several women have visited Washington to talk to their congressmen.[44]

In March 1977, thirteen United Farm Wives from western Kansas appeared before the House and Senate agricultural committees. That same week, thirty-three farmers and farmwives from western Kansas and eastern Colorado, calling themselves Partners in Action for Agriculture, also appeared before these committees. They expressed concern for the financial stress resulting from low wheat prices and called for more effective price support programs, more emergency credit, enforcement of standards on imported foods, expansion of farm exports, and stopping the misuse of welfare that has discouraged migrant workers from harvesting seasonal crops for farmers. They also called for developing new uses for agricultural products such as gasohol, control of inflation, and more representation by farmers in government departments.[45]

California Women for Agriculture has grown to 8,000 members. It generated 5,000 to 10,000 letters on state and federal issues in 1978. It works with four farm groups to make sure that agriculture speaks with a united voice. It also issues a newsletter in which legislators' votes are reported on crucial farm issues.[46]

Other Producer Advocates

The American Agricultural Movement (AAM) began in Springfield, Colorado, in the fall of 1977 when a group of wheat farmers, hard hit by drought and lower prices, felt that the 1977 Food and Agriculture Act was not an adequate response to their needs. Local groups formed in other states, and thousands of farmers descended on Washington in tractors and trucks in January and February, 1978.

The movement called for Congress to require that all purchases of farm commodities be made at 100 percent of parity, that imports be restricted until prices had reached 100 percent of parity, and that an agricultural board be established which would give farmers more participation in farm policy decisions.[47] Although no legislation was passed to meet their demands, the movement resulted in the Secretary of Agriculture's setting higher target prices on wheat, and Congress did pass an emergency credit bill.

Farmers in the movement staged another "tractorcade" in January 1979, but fewer farmers participated. Demands for 90 percent of parity prices received little sympathetic hearing among Congress or government officials. Some states have organized formally, but the future of the movement and its development into another national farm organization remain uncertain.

During 1979, many local AAM groups began to promote gasohol and farm production of alcohol for fuel. A motorcade of gasohol-driven vehicles drove to Washington, D.C., in February 1980.

The National Association of Farmer Elected Committeemen is an organization of farmers who are present or past members of county, community, and state committees of the Agricultural Stabilization and Conservation Service (ASCS) of the USDA. Full-time employees of ASCS can join as associate members.

For official services to ASCS, committeemen may be paid for their services on a daily basis. Activities of the national association are on a voluntary basis, and no reimbursement from government funds is involved. The association is organized at national, state, and county levels.

As stated in their testimony, "We represent the farmers before the government and we represent the government fairly before the farmers." As farmers, usually they have been active participants in the farm price support programs. In their testimony, they have favored target prices at 100 percent of the cost of production and loan rates at 75 percent, combining disaster programs and crop insurance into a single program, no restriction on exports, transfer of the agricultural census to the USDA, increased term of storage facility loans, and a minimum funding of $500 million each year for agricultural conservation programs.[48]

The National Farm Coalition is an informal alliance of thirty-six general, commodity, and cooperative farm organization leaders. The coalition was first formed in 1970 to develop a more unified position on farm legislation among farmers. A similar coalition presented testimony in 1973 and 1977 although the groups were not all the same in each of these years. It supported target prices and loans for major commodities directly related to costs of production, mandatory loans for soybeans, standby authority for acreage adjustment, and updated acreage bases for acreage set-aside programs. It called for target prices at 90 perent of the average cost of production and loans at 80 percent. It also wanted a properly administered disaster program, extension of the Public Law 480 subsidized export program, farmer-held grain reserves, new research to help farmers improve their operating efficiency, and strengthened conservation programs.[49]

The National Organization for Raw Materials, Inc., is an informal group of persons interested in the economics of basic raw materials produced by agriculture, forestry, fisheries, and mining. In testimony it has called for full-parity prices or full costs of production for agricultural commodities and other raw materials. It wants to pay full parity for raw materials imported in exchange for full-parity prices to be paid for raw materials exported.[50]

Producer Advocates in Perspective

Lobbying is only one part of the activities of the producer advocate groups. Most are also engaged in information and educational activities for their members or nonfarmers, in sharing common interests and problems among their members, or in providing a wide range of business activities and services.

Some groups operate with registered lobbyists; others do not. Details for individual organizations are provided in appendix A.

Almost universally, these groups strongly support the concept of a family-operated farming system. In practice, the members' farming operations may be single proprietorships, partnerships, or family farming corporations. Many are farm owners who rent their land to tenants who farm it.

As farmers, members of these groups are traditionally independent and oriented toward the free-enterprise system. But they hold differing economic, political, and social philosophies which reflect the differences of policy viewpoints of the organizations. Part of these differences also reflect a short-term instead of a long-term view of certain legislative proposals, as well as the degree to which they feel government should be involved in farming and related activities.

The embargo on additional grain shipments to Russia in January 1980 presented a special dilemma for farmers and their organizations. Many farmers are traditionally conservative and patriotic. While they did not approve of the Russian move into Afghanistan, some questioned the effectiveness of a grain embargo. Most felt that farmers should not be the only group to make a financial sacrifice when foreign-policy decisions are made. So their views varied on government actions to offset the effects of the embargo.

The producer organizations are funded primarily from membership dues and business activities provided to members. Cooperatives are organized to perform business activities and are owned by the members, mostly farmers. The associations of cooperatives described in this chapter are directed by boards who represent farmer cooperative members and are managed by hired professional managers. Legislative policies and lobbying activities are determined by the boards of directors and carried out by professional staff as well as individual members.

The commodity organizations vary widely in their financial resources and legislative activity. Since they focus on a specific issue or piece of legislation, often they are effective in achieving their objectives.

With farm producers in the minority, getting legislation and regulations developed that always please producer groups cannot be expected. Even the producer groups themselves do not always agree on their policy goals. Any legislation that is developed for producers benefits will usually be accompanied by other provisions that are sought by nonproducer groups who will work for the benefit of producers to achieve their objectives at the same time.

Notes

1. A detailed discussion of the major national farm organizations appears in Ross M. Talbot and Don Hadwiger, *The Policy Process in American Agriculture* (San Francisco: Chandler Publishing Co., 1968), pp. 98-120; and in Harold G. Halcrow, *Food Policy for America* (New York: McGraw-Hill, 1977), chapter 6.

2. U.S. Senate Committee on Agriculture, Nutrition, and Forestry hearings, *State of American Agriculture*, February 27, 1978, p. 62.

3. U.S. Senate Committee on Agriculture, Nutrition, and Forestry, *General Farm and Food Legislation Hearings*, Book 2, Appendix, 1977, pp. 63-80.

4. U.S. House of Representatives Committee on Agriculture hearings, *General Farm Bill*, Part 2, March 1, 1977, pp. 87-88.

5. For more details of the early history of the National Farmers Union, see Theodore Saloutas and John D. Hicks, *Agricultural Discontent in the Middle West, 1900-39* (Madison: University of Wisconsin Press, 1950), chapter 8.

6. National Farmers Union, "1978 Policy of National Farmers Union," adopted by delegates to the 76th annual convention, Salt Lake City, Utah, March 4-8, 1978, p. 1.

7. Ibid., p. 3.

8. *National Farmers Union Washington Newsletter*, 26, 11 (March 16, 1979):1; 1979 policy of National Farmers Union adopted March 11-14, 1979, Kansas City, Mo.

9. More details about the early history are given in Saloutas and Hicks, *Agricultural Discontent*, chapter 9.

10. *American Farm Bureau Federation Newsletter*, January 29, 1979.

11. U.S. Senate Committee on Agriculture, Nutrition, and Forestry, *General Farm and Food Legislation*, Book 2, Appendix, February 23, 1977, pp. 80-84.

12. National Farmers Organization, NFO, "Historical and Background Information," Public Information Department, Corning, Iowa. No date.

13. U.S. Senate Agriculture Committee hearings, *General Farm and Food Legislation*, Book 2, Appendix, pp. 90-98; U.S. House Agriculture Committee, *General Farm Bill*, February 22, 1977, pp. 77-87.

14. U.S. Senate Agriculture Subcommittee on Agricultural Research and General Legislation hearings, *Extension of the Federal Insecticide, Fungicide, and Rodenticide Act*, June 8 and 9, 1977, pp. 227-231.

15. U.S. Senate Agriculture Committee hearings, *General Farm and Food Legislation*, February 24, 1977, pp. 245-247.

16. Ibid., March 14, 1977, pp. 874-877.

17. Ibid., February 25, 1977, pp. 297-298.

18. U.S. House Agriculture Committee hearings, *Sugar Stabilization Act of 1978*, May 25, 1978, pp. 248-262.

19. U.S. Senate Agriculture Committee hearings, *General Farm and Food Legislation*, Book 2, Appendix, February and March 1977, pp. 380-381.

20. U.S. Senate Agriculture Committee hearings, *General Farm and Food Legislation*, February 25, 1977, pp. 299-301; *State of American Agriculture*, Part III, March 1, 1978, pp. 175-177.

21. U.S. Senate Agriculture Committee hearings, *General Farm and Food Legislation*, Book 1, March 1, 1977, pp. 463-468.

22. U.S. Senate Select Committee on Nutrition and Human Needs, Committee Print, *Dietary Goals for the United States*, 95th Cong., 1st Sess., December 1977.

23. U.S. House Agriculture Committee hearings, *General Farm Bill*, March 1, 1977, pp. 38-41; Senate Committee on Agriculture, Nutrition, and Forestry hearings, *General Farm and Food Legislation*, Book 2, Appendix, February-March 1977, p. 699.

24. U.S. Senate Select Committee on Nutrition and Human Needs, *Dietary Goals for the United States*, December 1977, pp. 43-46.

25. U.S. House Agriculture Committee hearings, *Current Agricultural Situation*, February 6, 1978, pp. 162-177.

26. U.S. Senate Agriculture Committee hearings, *General Farm and Food Legislation*, Book 2, Appendix, February 28, 1977, pp. 207-210.

27. U.S. Department of Agriculture, Economics, Statistics and Cooperatives Service, "Fats and Oils Situation," July 1978, p. 6.

28. U.S. Senate Agriculture Committee, Part III hearings, *State of American Agriculture*, March 2, 1978, pp. 208-211. Telephone interview with Emmett Reynolds, April 14, 1979.

29. U.S. Senate, Agriculture Committee hearings, *General Farm and Food Legislation*, February 4, 1977, Fairfax and Ankeny, Iowa, p. 247.

30. U.S. Senate Agriculture Committee hearings, *General Farm and Food Legislation*, Book 2, Appendix, February-March 1977, pp. 440-448.

31. U.S. Senate Agriculture Committee hearings, *State of American Agriculture*, March 1978, p. 336.

32. Ibid., pp. 342-344.

33. For more detail on the history and development of farm co-operatives, see Joseph Knapp, *The Rise of American Cooperative Enterprise 1620-1920* (Danville, Ill.: The Interstate Printers and Publishers, 1969).

34. U.S. House Agriculture Subcommittee on Family Farms, Rural Development, and Special Studies hearings, *Impact of Foreign Investment in Farmland*, 95th Cong., 2d Sess., June 20, 1978, pp. 119-120.

35. U.S. House Agricultural Committee hearings, *Federal Insecticide, Fungicide, and Rodenticide Act*, March 8, 1977, pp. 118-125.

36. U.S. Senate Agricultural Subcommittee on Agricultural Production, Marketing, and Stabilization of Prices hearings, *Agricultural Transportation Problems*, July 12, 1977, pp. 16-22.

37. U.S. Senate Agricultural Committee hearings, *General Farm and Food Legislation*, March 1, 1977, pp. 431-433; U.S. House Agriculture Committee hearings, *Current Agricultural Situation*, February 8, 1978, pp. 486-496.

38. National Milk Producers Federation, 62d Annual Report, 1978, pp. 7-8.

39. U.S. Senate Agriculture Committee hearings, *General Farm and Food Legislation*, March 1, 1977, pp. 454-463.

40. James L. Guth, "Consumer Organizations and Federal Dairy Policy," *Policy Studies Journal* 6, 4 (Summer 1978):499-503. Reprinted with permission.

41. National Rural Electric Cooperative Association, 1979 resolutions adopted at 37th annual meeting, Houston, Texas, February 18-22, 1979; William E. Murray, testimony before hearings, Senate Agriculture Subcom-

mittee on Agricultural Credit and Rural Electrification, *Changes in Farmers Home Administration Loan Programs*, October 11, 1977, pp. 87-92.

42. U.S. House Committee on Agriculture hearings, *General Farm Bill*, March 15, 1977; "The New Activists Raising Responsible Hell," *Successful Farming*, November 1978, pp. 24-25.

43. U.S. Senate Agriculture Committee hearings, *General Farm and Food Legislation*, March 1, 1977, pp. 469-481; *Successful Farming*, November 1978.

44. *Successful Farming*, November 1978.

45. U.S. Senate Agriculture Committee hearings, *General Farm and Food Legislation*, March 1, 1977, pp. 481-493.

46. *Farm Journal*, January 1979, p. 40C.

47. U.S. Senate Agriculture Committee hearings, *State of American Agriculture*, Part II, February 23, 27, 28, March 1, 2, 3, 1978; U.S. House Agriculture Committee hearings, *Current Agricultural Situation*, February 15, 16, 1978.

48. U.S. Senate Agriculture Committee hearings, *General Farm and Food Legislation*, February 23, 1977, p. 194.

49. U.S. Senate Agriculture Committee hearings, *General Farm and Food Legislation*, Book 2, Appendix, 1977, pp. 47-55.

50. Ibid., pp. 681-685.

4

Merchandising the Middlemen: Advocates for Agribusiness and Free Enterprise

. . . the American public is exquisitely informed about the injustices that occur in maximum security prisons, about the psychic suffering of criminals, and the violation of the sensibilities of prostitutes and pornographers, but they are almost totally unaware of injustices to businessmen. —William E. Simon, *A Time for Truth*[a]

Agriculture in the United States has moved a long way from the self-sufficient farms and households of Colonial days. Today it is a complex industry that combines industrial inputs with advanced technology, labor, and management, superimposed on the land, to produce an estimated 90 percent of the food and fiber needs of the U.S. population.

These organizations and groups providing the inputs, marketing, and processing have certain common interests and beliefs. They believe in a system of privately owned business enterprises, operating in a setting in which market forces guide the decisions of what and how much to produce. Prices are set to cover costs of production and a profit that provides returns to stockholders and individual owners of each firm. The firms represented in the various trade and business associations have more control over the prices they receive than most farmers, but competition usually limits how high prices can be set.

Most firms recognize the important role of government to provide a stable setting, under which a capitalistic system of business can operate, and to protect public health. But they deplore the growth of government regulation that contributes little public benefit, adds costs to operating their business, and threatens the profits necessary for their survival.

The agricultural businesses and industries provide the tools and technology that help make U.S. farms some of the most productive in the world, as well as the transportation, handling, and processing services that convert raw agricultural commodities into food products that give U.S. consumers widely varied diet choices every day of the year.

The growth of government involvement in the development and use of technology, regulation of food processing and marketing, international trade, commodity price support and stabilization programs, food distribution, assistance programs, and market operations has stimulated a response

---

[a]William E. Simon, *A Time For Truth* (New York: Reader's Digest Press, McGraw-Hill Book Co., 1978). Reprinted with permission.

in the agricultural business and industrial community. Trade associations and coalitions have formed to represent their members and to keep them informed on government policy decisions and proposed legislation that would affect them. Individual firms also have established offices in Washington or employ representatives there to help keep abreast of developments in government. Coalitions have formed that may represent producers, processors, and distributors or users of a commodity. Some associations have taken stands on several aspects of food and agricultural policy decision making; others have a major, overriding single interest or concern.

For some organizations, food or agricultural issues comprise only a small part of their broad range of concerns. For others, some aspect of food and agriculture is the major thrust in their interest. The positions taken by business and industry groups may agree with the views of some producer or consumer groups, or they may be in direct conflict.

Business and industry, like other organizations, vary in their strategies and tactics. Some appear before the relevant congressional committees and subcommittees, register as lobbyists, make personal contacts with members of Congress and their staffs, and keep in touch with regulatory agencies or executive departments. At the same time, many issue newsletters and reports as part of the services to their members.

Since legislative activities may not be the major role of many trade associations and industry groups, some may register as lobbyists while others may feel no requirement to do so. The groups discussed in this chapter appear before congressional committees, register as lobbyists or as foreign agents for an agriculturally related firm or association from outside the country, or make other public comments. More detailed information about these groups appears in appendix A.

Although no two groups will have exactly the same interests, they do have some common concerns. The following categories are discussed: commodity support and stabilization programs, input regulation, commodity trading and regulation, international trade in agricultural products, food processing and distribution, and food-assistance programs.

Commodity Price Support and Stabilization

Commodity price support and stabilization programs date back to the 1930s.[1] Each program has attracted interest and concerns from those in the business community affected by it.

Grains, Livestock, and Poultry Groups

Grains, livestock, and poultry groups have a common interest in what happens to government programs that deal with grain prices and reserves. But not all agree on what the program features should be.

In its 1977 testimony, the U.S. Chamber of Commerce was represented by board member Clarence Palmby, a vice-president of Continental Grain Company, former assistant Secretary of Agriculture, and former head of the U.S. Feed Grains Council. The Chamber of Commerce favored continuation of target price and loan rates, but would like to see a provision so the Secretary of Agriculture could reduce loan rates if world prices dropped below the U.S. loan price. They favored grain reserves held by farmers with an incentive for producers to hold reserves. They recommended that the release point on grain reserves be set substantially above the acquisition price.[2]

The Chicago Board of Trade wants to maintain a daily free market in grains, oil seeds, and other commodities. They recommended that loan rates be kept low enough that market prices could perform "their traditional and essential economic function." They would prefer target prices as a means of supplementing farmers' income when prices are low. They cautioned against setting target prices so high as to be a drain on the Treasury or setting loan prices so high that the government acquires huge stocks, as it did in the 1960s.[3]

Also supporting a free-market orientation for pricing grains is the National Grain and Feed Association. They support government loans for grains and soybeans, but would keep loan rates low enough to avoid overproduction and so these crops remain competitive in the world market. They do not favor setting target prices on soybeans. They favored the idea of building a grain reserve as long as it was held by farmers and the release point was set high enough to avoid an early release of reserve stocks.[4]

In many ways the testimony given by the Chamber of Commerce, the Chicago Board of Trade, and the National Grain and Feed Association is in close agreement with the American Farm Bureau position on support prices and grain reserves.

Two industry-producer groups differ somewhat in their approach. The National Broiler Council expresses concern with government involvement in production, marketing, and price setting and opposed changes in the 1977 act in 1978. They would like to keep prices stable, however, to allow livestock and poultry industries a chance to convert grains to products that consumers can afford. Their philosophy is less interference from government, fewer burdensome regulations, and more access to world markets.[5]

The National Turkey Federation likewise opposes high loan or target prices since they affect the feed prices that turkey growers must pay. Like the National Broiler Council, it calls for appropriate programs to bring reasonable price stability to grain producers, but again cautions against artificially inflating food and feed grain prices.[6]

The Poultry and Egg Institute of America favors another approach to income support. In its 1977 testimony it called for indemnity payments for poultry and eggs when government asks that a product be removed from the market and the cause was not due to misuse or failure of the producer or processor.[7]

The National Soybean Processors Association favors soybean loan rates at 2.5 times that of corn to encourage soybean production. But they opposed target prices because they did not want to jeopardize the duty-free status of soybeans or soybean meal entering the European Economic Community. They support some form of crop insurance for soybean farmers.[8]

The National Soybean Crop Improvement Council, supported by the processors' association, calls for more research funds for soybeans and opposes federal cuts in agricultural research.[9]

Two industry groups lean more toward the consumer in their policies. The American Bakers Association's stated goal is "to maintain a low level of food price inflation and encourage full production of basic agricultural commodities." It favors abundant wheat supplies. It calls for loan programs that would provide minimum support and higher target prices that would guarantee farmers their direct costs of production. It believes it would be more prudent to support food costs through the tax system than to push up food prices through higher government loans or government commodity purchases. It favors both farmer- and government-held grain reserves.

Looking at all federal programs, the American Bakers Association would reorganize the USDA into a "Department of Food and Agriculture to establish an evenhanded policy toward all segments of the food and agriculture community."[10] In 1978 it favored retention of the 1977 Food and Agriculture Act and opposed new legislation being pushed by the American Agriculture Movement.[11]

The Independent Bakers Association supports the American Bakers Association positions. They support the idea of grain reserves; but if the carryover exceeds one year's domestic requirement, they recommend that the Secretary of Agriculture sell the surplus at the best world competitive price.[12]

Closely related to grain price support and stabilization, the Agricultural Conservation Program has also been administered by the Agricultural Stabilization and Conservation Service in the USDA. The National Limestone Institute has strongly supported these programs and urged larger appropriations when budget-cutting officials wanted to reduce payments to farmers.

Milk and Dairy Products

Milk and dairy products get involved in the political process through the support program for manufactured dairy products under the Food and Agriculture Act of 1977, preceding acts, and through the federal order program for fluid milk authorized under the Agricultural Marketing Agreements Act of 1937.

The Milk Industry Foundation represents about three-fourths of the fluid-milk processing capacity in the country. They have favored continuation of a milk support program on the grounds that it would encourage production of an adequate supply of milk. However, they did not want Congress to raise the support rate above 80 percent of parity, because they felt this level would be enough to encourage adequate production. In opposition to producers who wanted quarterly adjustments in support prices to keep pace with rising production costs, the industry groups opposed quarterly adjustments and suggested semiannual adjustments. They wanted the Secretary of Agriculture to have discretion as to whether the support rates would actually be changed at six-month intervals.[13]

The International Association of Ice Cream Manufacturers which shares a Washington office and staff with the Milk Industry Foundation also presents its policy positions jointly.

The Chocolate Manufacturers of America also watch government actions affecting the price of milk since their members claim to use about 3.5 million pounds of milk daily from 175,000 cows. They favor returns to farmers that ensure an adequate production of milk at reasonable prices for consumers. They also oppose the quarterly adjustments in price supports. The chocolate manufacturers do not want to change standards for dairy imports or add restrictions that would be a thinly disguised nontariff barrier.[14]

The National Association for Milk Marketing Reform (NAMMR) is a nonprofit association of milk processors in various regions of the country. Milk producers and cooperatives could join the association if they wished to do so. The organization was formed as a result of milk pricing arrangements under federal milk marketing orders. They are concerned about the organization of "supercooperatives," their size, and their ability to control milk supply and price. They believe prices have been forced higher than would exist under more competitive conditions. They are convinced that the "superpool" premiums, negotiated by the milk producers' cooperatives, are forcing processors to pay higher prices for milk. When they pass the higher prices on to consumers, they believe consumers in turn may buy less milk than if prices were lower. They also believe that the supercooperatives are reducing competition in the marketing of milk by leading to monopoly conditions controlled by the supercooperatives. Although the USDA is responsible for seeing that cooperatives do not unduly enhance the price of milk, the NAMMR feels that they are not really analyzing prices adequately to determine what is taking place.[15]

Cotton

Cotton has been closely involved in legislative activity since the first Agricultural Adjustment Act of 1933 was passed. For many years cotton was grown under government programs with restrictive marketing quotas, high support prices, and high costs to the Treasury. High support prices in the United States encouraged increased foreign production and development of synthetic fibers. The National Cotton Council, representing producers, ginners, cooperatives, warehouses, merchants, crushers, and manufacturers, has learned from past experiences and now wants to keep the market system operating. It wants government loans to producers to be high enough to cover the cost of production but not so high as to invite loss of the market. It does not favor a target price so high as to run up government costs. To provide price stability, it has proposed longer loan periods. It has also called for programs to expand exports and more funding for research to control boll weevils.[16]

The National Cotton Council strongly supported the Food and Agriculture Act of 1977 during the 1978 hearings when some farmers wanted to boost price supports and raise farm prices. Cotton producers have learned from experience the consequences of setting the loan rate so high that it sets the price of cotton and encourages competition from foreign cotton and manmade fiber production at home.[17]

The American Cotton Shippers Association endorses the position of the National Cotton Council and favors the concept of a price support loan based on a four-year average price for 11/16-inch, standard-length middling cotton in the United States or 90 percent of the Liverpool quotation, if lower than the U.S. price. They would favor raising the $20,000 payment limitation for price support program payments to growers "to a more realistic level" and a Commodity Credit Corporation program to encourage more exports. They do not want to see all credit for subsidized exports under Public Law 480 go to wheat and feed grains, so that cotton is excluded.[18]

The Cotton Warehouse Association is concerned about government actions that would affect the farmer's ability or willingness to grow cotton. They are also concerned about setting the crop support loan to producers that would encourage foreign competition or price U.S. cotton out of the market. Generally they support the position of the National Cotton Council.[19]

The American Textile Manufacturer's Institute also supports the National Cotton Council position. It wants efficient, profitable domestic cotton production, a permanent one-price system for U.S. cotton, expanded exports, and a stable price.[20]

Rice

Rice has been involved with political activity for many years through a price support and strict acreage control program. A new program was passed by

Congress in 1975 and continued in 1977 which lifted strict acreage controls and set up a system of loans and target prices patterned after wheat and feed grains for allotment holders. Since the change, producers and processors have debated the merits of the new program.

The Rice Millers Association and the Ad Hoc Committee of Industrial Rice Users support the program with the open production and competitive loan rates. The Industrial Rice Users see the new program as one that encourages expansion of investment in rice processing, storage, and distribution facilities. They also see the new program encouraging greater exports and helping improve the U.S. balance of payments.[21] An Ad Hoc Committee of Rice Consumers also testified to continue the 1975 act.[22]

Producers and processing and marketing cooperatives serving producers have more reservations about the new program. American Rice, a Texas cooperative representing about 2,500 growers, supported the open-production concept, but would prefer extension a year at a time until a more complete assessment of the program is possible. Riceland Foods, an Arkansas producer cooperative with about 5,000 members, supported a four- to five-year extension for the 1975 act. However, rice growers' committees of the Arkansas and Louisiana Farm Bureaus spoke out in favor of keeping the old allotment program with strict acreage controls. They are concerned that the target prices will not cover their costs of production, as the previous program with higher loan rates did. However, many growers recognized the mood of Congress in shifting to the new program and reluctantly agreed to a one-year extension.[23]

Peanuts

Peanuts and the associated government price and income support program illustrate the conflict that can develop between growers and the handlers and processors of the product. Growers, as we mentioned in chapter 3, are generally satisfied with the program which restricts acreage and gives special growing privileges to allotment holders.

The processing industry holds a different view. The processors are concerned about the peanut support program and its effect on the supply and price of peanuts. The Peanut Butter Manufacturers and Nut Processors Association and the National Confectioners Association wants an abundant supply of peanuts available and at lower prices. They see peanuts losing out in the domestic market if prices are raised or the supply is further restricted.

The processors admit that they get along quite well under the present program, since it provides them with an abundant supply of peanuts and at a stable price, except for the Virginia and Spanish types. They are critical of the program, however, because of its high cost to U.S. taxpayers; because a farmer cannot produce peanuts unless he has inherited, purchased, or leased a peanut acreage allotment; and because it has created what they believe is an artificially high price for consumers that has restricted market expansion. They believe they could sell more peanut products if the price were lower.

The processors believe Virginia- and Spanish-type peanut supplies are inadequate because of production restrictions. They would like to see acreage restrictions on these types eliminated if allotments are reduced for other peanuts.[24]

Sugar

Sugar has been described as "the most complex, devilish issue I've ever dealt with" by a top official in the Department of Agriculture.[25] For forty years until 1974, the U.S. policy was to divide up the market between domestic beet and cane sugar producers and producers in other parts of the world through an import quota system. Congress let the old law expire in 1974 because many felt that consumers were being forced to pay more for sugar than the world market price. The jockeying for shares in the import quota system to provide about half of U.S. sugar consumption also provided sizable fees for representatives of the foreign sugar-producing countries.[26]

Although some groups question why the United States should depend on domestic sugar production at all when foreign producers could supply our needs, the general agreement seems to be that a domestic sugar industry is necessary to protect the long-term interests of the U.S. consumer. Foreign sugar, produced by paying workers low wages and subsidized by the local governments, would sell for much less than the cost of domestic sugar, except for tariffs and fees which raise the price to equal domestic sugar.

On the one side of most sugar issues are the domestic producers who, producing sugar from cane or beets at higher costs than producers in foreign countries, require some form of government assistance to ensure their survival. Closely allied with the domestic sugar producers since 1974 are the corn refiners whose high-fructose corn sweetner can now compete successfully with higher-cost domestic sugar but not with lower-cost foreign sugar.

Lined up on the other side are the commercial sugar users—sugar refiners who use both domestic and foreign sugar and consumer groups. They are opposed to high price supports and import restrictions that force sugar prices higher than would otherwise prevail. They favor direct federal subsidies to U.S. producers that would not push up the price of sugar, but would subsidize growers directly from the Treasury.

Although a stop-gap sugar support program was written into the 1977 Food and Agriculture Act, it has resulted in the accumulation of deteriorating sugar stocks owned by the government, windfall benefits for importers, and what growers say is an inadequate support price to meet their rising costs.

In 1978 a congressional conference committee, in its closing hours before adjournment, failed to resolve the differences in the House and Senate bills. The bill that attempted to deal with import fees, domestic price, and use of direct payments to U.S. producers also failed to get through Congress in 1979. Also involved in resolving domestic sugar policy is the U.S. ratification of the International Sugar Agreement, which would use stockpiling and export quotas in the producing countries to support world prices at 11 cents a pound, a figure that would rise well above the U.S. support level once import costs are added.[27]

Representing the interests and concerns of the growers and processors of domestic sugar are the American Sugarbeet Growers Association, the American Sugar Cane League of the USA, the California Beet Growers Association, the Florida Sugar Cane League, the Hawaiian Sugar Planters' Association, the Rio Grande Valley Sugar Growers Cooperative, and the U.S. Beet Sugar Association.

Each of these groups has skilled, experienced professionals in Washington to represent its interests. Described as the growers' leading Washington lobbyist,[28] Horace Godfrey was administrator of the Agricultural Stabilization and Conservation Service under Secretary of Agriculture Orville Freeman in the 1960s. He is credited as drafting the 1977 de la Garza amendment (named after Congressman E. de la Garza of Texas), which created a price support loan program for sugar. For many years after leaving the USDA he represented the American Sugar Cane League of the USA, the Rio Grande Valley Sugar Growers Cooperative, and the Florida Sugar Cane League.

In 1978 Michael R. McLeod, former general counsel and staff director of the Senate Agriculture Committee, and his law partner Thomas A. Davis became representatives of the Florida Sugar Cane League; and Don Wallace Associates began to represent the American Sugar Cane League of the USA. John Bagwell, a former general counsel to the Department of Agriculture, has represented the Hawaiian Sugar Planters Association.[29]

The Corn Refiners Association supports the concept of import fees and tariffs to raise the price of foreign sugar up to a level that will enable domestic producers and corn sweetner processors to compete. They oppose direct payments that would go to the sugar processing companies and provide unfair competition to the corn refiners. They also oppose including corn sweetners in sugar legislation and dumping of foreign sugar at below production costs on the U.S. market.

The corn sweetner industry is also well represented by experienced lob-byists. Robert Liebenow, president of the Corn Refiners Association, was formerly president of the Chicago Board of Trade. The following people represent companies manufacturing corn sweetners: Herbert Waters, a former aide to the late Senator Hubert H. Humphrey and U.S. foreign aid official; Robert Best, former aide to Senator Russell B. Long of Louisiana; Joseph E. Karth, former congressman from Minnesota; Dale Sherwin, former deputy assistant Secretary of Agriculture, congressional liaison in the U.S. Department of Agriculture, and Senate Agriculture Committee staff member.[30]

Industrial sugar users and consumers are concerned with government price setting that benefits producers and processors at the expense of con-sumers. The Sugar Users Group wants a viable U.S. sugar industry and sup-ports the International Sugar Agreement. They oppose an import quota system. They do not want to see price supports set at a percentage of parity, as in the de la Garza amendment, or at a price that would result in the government's acquiring stocks of sugar as they did under the 1977 Food and Agriculture Act. They would prefer a program that holds domestic sugar prices at about 15.8 cents a pound, making direct payments to producers to make up cost differences above this price if necessary. Among those lobby-ing for the sugar users is James V. Stanton, a former congressman from Ohio,[31] associated with the law firm of Ragan and Mason.

The U.S. Cane Sugar Refiners are concerned about a government pro-gram that might price sugar out of the market in favor of corn sweetners. They would prefer a tariff rather than an international quota plan. They also opposed the report issued by the Senate Select Committee on Nutrition in 1977 that recommended a 45 percent decrease in per capita sugar con-sumption. They believe that it is impractical to include corn sweetners in a sugar act and favor the International Sugar Agreement and supplemental payments to domestic growers.

Individual sugar companies also employ registered lobbyists. The California and Hawaii Sugar Company is represented by E.A. Jaenke and Associates. Jaenke was formerly an assistant to Senator Stuart Symington of Missouri, an official in the USDA and governor of the Farm Credit Ad-ministration. Great Western Sugar Company employs the law firm of Berry, Epstein, Sandstrom & Blatchford, which also represents other agricultural clients.

At the testimony given to the Senate Agriculture Committee in 1978, the Sugar Refiners presented a study of the International Sugar Agreement prepared by Schnittker & Associates.[32] John Schnittker was economic ad-viser to Secretary Orville Freeman and later was Undersecretary of Agriculture.

The Consumer Federation of America opposes higher sugar prices and appears somewhat embarrassed at being allied with the soft drink and cookie manufacturers on the same side of the sugar price debate.[33] They were a major force in the defeat of the 1979 bill.

Organized labor has also entered the debate on development of a national sugar policy. The International Longshoremen's and Warehousemen's Union has contract agreements with fifteen sugar plantations covering 8,000 sugar workers in Hawaii. The union proudly cites the economic well-being of Hawaiian sugar workers and claims they are the highest paid cane sugar workers in the world, averaging about $6 an hour in wage and fringe benefits. They want a statement in a sugar law that would guarantee fair and reasonable minimum wages for all U.S. sugar workers.[34]

When foreign quotas were in effect in 1974 and earlier years, the congressional rules barred officials of foreign countries from appearing before congressional committees. However, the army of sugar lobbyists representing the interests of their foreign clients got special treatment from Congress. They were allowed to testify before legislative committees—a privilege routinely denied agents who serve foreign governments in other respects.[35]

Some Washingtonians willing to work as spokesmen for some of these countries included Harold D. Cooley, former North Carolina congressman and chairman of the House Agriculture Committee, who represented Thailand and Liberia; Thomas H. Kuchel, former Senator from California, who helped Colombia; Charles H. Brown, former congressman from Missouri, aided the Fiji Islands.[36]

The Philippine sugar interests, represented by John A. O'Donnell, received an extra quota under the 1965 Sugar Act, as well as the opportunity to supply almost half the deficit in the domestic quota or from other foreign suppliers. Congressman Paul Findley reported that O'Donnell was also the subject of a congressional investigation in 1963 because he distributed some $9,300 to various congressmen in the 1960 campaigns.[37] He was still registered as a lobbyist for the Philippine Sugar Commission in 1979.

Even though country import quotas no longer exist, foreign sugar producers are still represented by individuals, law firms, and consultants. Although domestic sugar and corn sweetners supply from 60 to 70 percent of the U.S. sweetner needs, the sugar market for foreign producers and the related policies that will affect U.S. imports are of keen interest to sugar-exporting countries around the world. Table 4-1 shows some of the representatives and their clients.

The law firm of Patton, Boggs, & Blow represented four sugar groups in 1978. Thomas Hale Boggs, Jr., is the son of the late Congressman Hale Boggs of Louisiana and Congresswomen Corinne Lindy Boggs.

The law firm of Doub, Purcell, Muntzing, and Hansen represents Colonial Sugar Refining of Australia. Graham Purcell was a former Con-

Table 4-1
Representatives for Foreign Sugar Interests

Representative	Country and Organization	Fees Received[a]	
Casey, Lane, & Mittendorf[b] 815 Connecticut Avenue Washington, DC 20006	South African Sugar Association	$55,000	(1976) (terminated in 1978)
Coudert Brothers[b] 200 Park Avenue New York, NY 10017	National Association of Sugar Cane Growers of Colombia	11,900	(1974) (terminated Feb. 1977)
J.M. Chambers & Co.[b] 1050 17th Street NW Washington, DC 20036	Swaziland Sugar Associates	30,000	(Apr. 1975-Jan. 1976) (terminated Mar. 1976)
Doub, Purcell, Muntzing, & Hansen[d] 1775 Pennsylvania Avenue NW Washington, DC 20006	Colonial Sugar Refining Australia	30,000	(Apr. 1978-Mar. 1979)
Hamel, Park, McCabe, & Saunders[b] 1776 F Street NW Washington, DC 20006	Belize Sugar Industries	2,500	(Aug. 1977)
	Sugar Association of the Caribbean, Trinidad	35,276.15[c]	(Jan. 1978-Feb. 1979)
	Red Path Sugars, Ltd., Canada	17,496.60[c]	(Nov. 1968 and Jan. 1979)
	La Estella Sugar Co. of South America	12,229.04[c]	
	Tate & Lyle, Ltd. (British sugar exporters)	66,932.23[c]	(Feb. 1978-Feb. 1979)
	Valdez Sugar Co. of South America		
	American Tropical Sugar of South America		
	Tababuela Industrial Sugar of Ecuador		
	National Sugar Co. of Panama		
	West Indies Sugar Association, Inc.		

Firm	Client	Amount	Dates
International Management Consultants, Ltd.[d] 1155 15th Street NW Washington, DC 20005	Swaziland Sugar Association	10,000	(May and July 1978) (latest retainer $2,500 per month)
A.S. Nemir Associates[d] Suite 1230, 425 13th Street Washington, DC 20004	Brazilian Sugar and Alcohol Institute	50,000	(Sept. 1978 and Jan. 1979)
John A. O'Donnell[d] 1001 Connecticut Avenue NW Washington, DC 20036	Philippine Sugar Commission	51,667.44[c]	(Feb. 1978-Jan. 1979)
Pendleton & McLaughlin[b] 888 17th Street NW Washington, DC 20006	Taiwan Sugar Corporation	1,208.20[c]	(Dec. 1974 and May 1975) (terminated 1975)
Paton, Boggs, & Blow[d] Suite 800, 2550 M Street NW Washington, DC 20037	Central American Sugar Council Sugar Association of El Salvador Sugar Association of Guatemala Honduras Sugar Company	64,877.47[c]	(May and Dec. 1978)
Pierson, Semmes, Crolius, & Finley[b] 1054 31st Street NW Washington, DC 20007	Mauritius Sugar Syndicate Mauritius Chamber of Agriculture	40,000	(Aug. 1975-July 1976) (terminated Dec. 1976)

Table 4-1 (*continued*)
Representatives for Foreign Sugar Interests

Representative	Country and Organization	Fees Received[a]	
Albert M. Prosterman & Associates, Inc.[b] Suite 239, 818 18th Street NW Washington, DC 20006	Madagascar Sugar Producers Paris	8,267[c]	(Dec. and June 1975) (terminated Mar. 1977)
John H. Sharon (Shaw, Pitman, Potts, & Trowbridge)[d] Suite 900, 1800 M Street NW Washington, DC 20036	Mauritius Sugar Syndicate Mauritius Chamber of Agriculture (Started January 1977)	50,000	(Aug. 1978-July 1979)
Thevenot, Murray, & Scheer (E. Wayne Thevenot, Inc.)[d] 1120 Connecticut Avenue NW Suite 1128 Washington, DC 20036	Swaziland Sugar Association	18,000	(July and Oct. 1978) ($3,000 per month)
Smathers, Symington, & Herlong[d] 1700 K Street NW Washington, DC 20006	Venezuelan Sugar Distributors Association		
Felipe J. Vicini[b] Isabel La Catolica 48 Santo Domingo, Dominican Republic	Dominican Sugar Institute		

Source: U.S. Department of Justice, *Congressional Record*, February 20, 1978, June 13, 1978, August 24, 1978, November 15, 1978, February 19, 1979.
[a]Latest year reported.
[b]Registered as foreign agent with U.S. Department of Justice.
[c]Legal or other fees, plus reimbursed expenses.
[d]Registered as foreign agent, Department of Justice; as lobbyist with Clerk, U.S. House of Representatives, for clients listed.

gressman from Texas from 1962 to 1973 and a member of the House Agriculture Committee.

Edward A. McCabe, of Hamel, Park, McCabe, & Saunders, which represents nine sugar groups, was administrative assistant to the President from 1958 to 1961 and counsel to the House Committee on Education and Labor from 1953 to 1955.

The law firm of Smathers, Symington, & Herlong represents Venezuelan Sugar Distributors Association. George A. Smathers, a firm partner, was a senator from Florida from 1951 to 1969.

Tobacco

Tobacco, although not a food crop, is one of the most controversial areas of agricultural policy and politics. Tight production controls to improve the incomes of tobacco growers have been in effect since the 1930s. Permanent legislation was first passed under the Agricultural Adjustment Act of 1938.

A farmer who wishes to grow tobacco and market it must have a government-assigned acreage allotment. Since the right to grow tobacco has value, the size of the tobacco allotment has been bid into the value of farms in the tobacco growing areas.

Continuation of price and production control and research for tobacco is supported by the American Farm Bureau Federation (AFBF). These programs also receive strong support from tobacco-state congressmen. The AFBF also opposes efforts by the Department of Health, Education, and Welfare to influence the public against use of tobacco.[38]

In the 96th Congress, the tobacco subcommittee of the House Agriculture Committee had seven members, all of whom came from states where tobacco is grown.[39] Walter B. Jones of North Carolina is chairman. In the Senate, Walter Huddleston of Kentucky is chairman of the Subcommittee on Agricultural Production, Marketing, and Stabilization of Prices which handles tobacco price support programs.

Supporters of the production control programs point out the income benefits to growers who would not be able to make as much money growing another crop. The research programs supported with state and federal funds have aimed to produce varieties with less tars and nicotine and improve growing and marketing practices.

Ever since the Surgeon General's Report on Smoking and Health linked smoking to lung cancer in 1964, the tobacco industry has been active in defending people's right to smoke, watchdogging the federal regulatory agencies involved in tobacco advertising, warning labels, and educational efforts to discourage smoking.

The Tobacco Institute, described by one health advocate as "one of the most lethal trade associations going,"[40] is the tobacco industry's eyes, ears, and voice in Washington and across the nation. It keeps in touch with members of Congress and the regulatory agencies. Its president, Horace Kornegay, was a four-term member of the House of Representatives from North Carolina from 1961 to 1969. Earl C. Clements, one of its registered lobbyists, was a former governor of Kentucky, senator, and past president of the institute. Two of its attorneys are Marlow Cook, former senator from Kentucky, and David Henderson, former congressman from North Carolina from 1961 to 1973.[41]

The Tobacco Institute prepares publications which report the taxes contributed to federal, state, and local governments by the sale of tobacco products; the exports which contribute to foreign exchange; the industry's views on health issues; and the employment provided by the tobacco industry. The institute has made grants for research to universities and medical schools to study tobacco and the associated health issues.

One of their biggest efforts in recent years has been opposition to campaigns by states and municipalities to limit or restrict smoking. The arguments against such restrictions, which were successful in California and Florida, center on maintaining personal rights and freedom of individuals to choose whether they wish to smoke.

Futures Trading

Futures trading of agricultural and other commodities is regulated under the Commodity Futures Trading Commission Act of 1974 (Public Law 93-463). It established the Commodity Futures Trading Commission (CFTC) as an independent agency to regulate trading in commodity futures. Previously futures trading was regulated by the Commodity Exchange Authority, an agency in the Department of Agriculture.

At issue is whether the Commodity Futures Trading Commission should continue to function as a separate agency, whether to shift its regulatory functions back to the Department of Agriculture or to the Securities and Exchange Commission, which regulates trading in the securities markets. After hearings in 1978, Congress voted to extend the independent status of the CFTC. Supporting extension were the Futures Industry Association, the New York Cocoa Exchange, the New York Coffee and Sugar Exchange, Inc., the New York Cotton Exchange, the National Grain and Feed Association, and the American Cotton Shippers Association. The Chicago Mercantile Exchange urged reauthorization as an independent agency, but wanted the CFTC to recognize its statutory limitations.[42]

The Kansas City Board of Trade supported the basic structure of CFTC, but opposed the idea that it should be self-funding through transaction fees. It also did not want the CFTC to review the denial of membership applications to the various commodity exchanges.

The Minneapolis Grain Exchange favored continuation of the CFTC, but wanted it to establish detailed and appropriate objectives. It was critical of the CFTC because it was "top heavy with lawyers who have little, if any, experience or no understanding of the commodity market's function."[43] Those who favored a return of CFTC functions to the USDA included Agri-Businessmen, Inc., the Chicago Board of Trade, and the Board of Trade Clearing Corporation.[44]

The American Feed Manufacturers Association requested that the act be amended to exclude feed companies that provided information to their dealers and customers regarding outlook for feed, livestock, and poultry prices from being required to register as commodity trading advisers.

Input Suppliers, Manufacturers, and Distributors

Input suppliers, the manufacturers and distributors of pesticides, fertilizers, feeds, and feed additives, have special concerns with government regulations and the administration of laws and regulations that affect their businesses. Some of the most serious conflict between private industry and government over a public policy issue has been the administration of the Federal Insecticide, Fungicide, and Rodenticide Act (FIFRA), which came under the jurisdiction of the EPA in 1970.

Behind the shift to the EPA from the Department of Agriculture was the feeling that the USDA was biased toward the benefit side of pesticides and their usage and too little concerned for the possible risks involved. The EPA was believed to be in a better position to regulate pesticides with a proper balance of benefits versus risks.[45]

However, the National Agricultural Chemicals Association sees the EPA taking a primary mandate to protect human health and the environment from unreasonable, adverse effects of pesticide use with "an ever increasing bias toward risk with too little concern for the known benefits." They see the EPA bias as greater than the reverse bias of which USDA was accused.[46]

Millions of dollars are involved in developing new chemicals for use in pesticides. The manufacturers are concerned with their property rights in such investments and with keeping this information confidential when these technical materials are registered for use in pesticides. They believe that registrants should have the right to give consent for use of their data and should have the final decision about the price to be paid by others for such use.

The Pesticide Formulators Association has also expressed concern about the administration of FIFRA, the delays in getting registration approval of new products, and the capability of EPA to administer the act. They believe that trade information should be kept private, but see the need for more flexibility in supplying data for pesticide registration. They view as unfair competition the restriction on use of data that would make it possible to get more rapid registration of new pesticide formulas. They have complained of long delays for new registrations when other companies had the same products registered and were selling them.[47]

As users of pesticide materials, the National Food Processors Association also expresses its concerns. They believe Congress did not intend to bind uses strictly to labeling directions except where necessary to prevent unreasonable adverse effects on the environment. Yet, they see the EPA as saying that in the absence of any clear definition, use of pesticides should be used only as affirmatively directed by the labeling. The concern, then, is that many unregistered pesticide uses commonly practiced before October 1972 are deemed illegal, and the EPA can take action against such illegal uses. Relief from these strict regulations is provided only by gradually reregistering all pesticides, which will take several years. And the food processors fear that not all the commonly used practices important in fruit and vegetable production will be legalized by the label changes.[48]

Recognizing the problem, the EPA issued Pesticide Enforcement Policy Statements (PEPS) which permitted certain violations of the strict label requirements and agreed not to prosecute anyone for such violations. The food processors wanted more specific language written into the law that would permit more flexible use of pesticides.

The Society of American Florists and Ornamental Horticulturists is concerned about FIFRA because it affects specialized uses of pesticides in floriculture and ornamental plant production. They see the new regulations as forcing growers to use less effective pesticides, and not all brands list the same uses. They also see the need for more flexibility in interpreting the label directions; otherwise many producers of flowers and ornamental plants could be forced out of business.[49]

The National Pest Control Association opposes the interpretation that pest control applicators are selling pesticides and should be regulated as other dealers of pesticides. They would like to see competent, trained, experienced specialists in pesticides involved in the regulation decision-making process and "limit lawyers to their important role in interpreting laws and representation of the EPA in legal proceedings."[50]

Affected by the use of pesticides, the National Fisheries Institute expresses its concerns about the effects of pesticides on fish and seafoods. It would like to see the National Marine Fisheries Services and the USDA on the scientific advisory panel to the EPA. It wants a list of pesticides recognized as sensitive to runoff that may kill fish.

Representing the fertilizer industry, the Fertilizer Institute expresses its concerns on transportation issues. It would like to see railroads operate more efficiently, but also opposes closing of branch lines that serve as vital links for moving fertilizers to dealers and farmers in agricultural areas.[51]

The Fertilizer Institute, the National Council of Farm Cooperatives, and the American Feed Manufacturers Association all oppose deregulation of railroads that would give railroads more choice of frequency of service and rates charged. Although supporters of deregulation say ensuing competition would benefit consumers by cutting transportation costs, the opponents fear that rural areas would be abandoned or rates would go up. Farmers could lose outlets to market their products, and farm input suppliers could face higher costs in moving their goods.

The National Agricultural Aviation Association, representing operators of aerial spraying equipment and also large farmers, has concerns about low farm prices and their effects on their members. They favor setting minimum prices for commodities that undergo further processing and controlling costs of production. They would also like to see a moratorium on regulation writing and enforcement. However, they see a need for regulations based on scientific knowledge instead of use of fear and emotion.[52]

The American Feed Manufacturers Association conducts a broad program of monitoring and commenting on government regulations that affect its members. Major issues include regulations dealing with medicated feeds, safety recommendations under the Occupational Safety and Health Administration (OSHA), environmental controls in feed manufacturing plants, and wage and price controls. They also have a vital interest in maintaining a viable transportation system in moving feeds to their customers and securing the raw materials used in their manufacturing operations.

With much of the equipment and supplies to run a modern farm coming from sources off the farm, agricultural credit becomes another important input, along with seed, feed, and fertilizers. The American Bankers Association operates an agricultural bankers division which conducts legislative and educational programs dealing with agricultural credit. It has expressed concern that farmers be able to get adequate credit, and especially those young people who want to get started in farming. Where government-guaranteed loan programs are operating, it favors raising the size of these loans for individual farm operators and owners and limiting loans to family partnerships and family farming corporations.

The Independent Bankers Association, representing smaller rural banks, wants adequate credit available for rural areas. It supported the

Rural Development Act of 1972 and the Farmers Home Administration guaranteed loan program.

International Trade

International trade in U.S. agricultural products exceeded $30 billion in 1979; U.S. agricultural imports totaled about half this amount. Producers and businessmen directly involved in exporting and importing have interests and concerns about government policies that will affect these movements of agricultural products.

The Agricultural Trade Council testified for expanded export programs which establish a farmer-held grain reserve and give producers an incentive to store grain. But they opposed an international grain reserve program. They favored expansion of Public Law 480 to include other countries, raising the income per capita limits from $300 to $500 so more countries would be eligible, and lending portions of the funds received under these subsidized exports so that developing countries could buy agricultural equipment and other capital developments and technical services. They opposed any kind of export embargoes except for military and strategic goods.[53]

The North American Export Grain Association has as its major purpose the expansion of grain exports. They opposed increased loan rates on grains in the 1977 Food and Agricultural Act since they felt this could create trade problems. They also oppose government regulation at export points, which slows movement of grains. They see a proposal to limit imports as inconsistent with a program to expand exports. They oppose efforts to link export goals with political goals, such as human rights, since these result in an impediment to export expansion. They viewed the American Agriculture Movement proposals as promoting inefficiency and inconsistent with a policy to promote competition in production and marketing of farm products.[54]

The operation of Public Law 480, the subsidized export program first authorized in 1954, concerns several organizations. The U.S. Chamber of Commerce favors expansion to include more countries than would be eligible if the $300 income per capita limitation were maintained.[55] The Chicago Board of Trade proposed modifying the requirement that not more than 75 percent of sales under this program be made under Title I—sales made under long-term loans at low interest. The National Grain and Feed Association also opposed the 75 percent limit on Title I sales.[56] The American Cotton Shippers Association wants more flexibility in allocations under the program, so that not all credit is used for wheat and feed grains, with cotton excluded.[57]

The large volume of imported food products creates interest in issues relating to trade barriers, quality and inspection standards, and competition from the foreign products that affects domestic producers.

Questions about competition from and quality and inspection of fresh fruit and vegetable imports from Mexico have been aired at Senate Agriculture Committee hearings. The West Mexico Vegetable Distributors Association at Nogales, Arizona, is engaged in handling the Mexican production. The Southwest Florida Winter Vegetable Growers Association, Palm Beach-Broward Farmers Committee for Legislative Action, Inc., South Florida Tomato and Vegetable Growers Association, Florida Fruit and Vegetable Association, and Florida Tomato Exchange represent the views and concerns of Florida producers.[58]

Meat imports raise policy questions from U.S. producers, importers, and exporting interests in foreign countries. The Meat Importers Council of America, Inc., carries out an educational program about the role of imported meat.[59] Washington representatives are employed by meat, fish, wool, and dairy exporting organizations in New Zealand, Japan, Austria, Denmark, France, Argentina, Switzerland, and Australia. Details are shown in table 4-2.

Some organizations promote trade interests on a broad scale that includes agricultural products as well as many other goods. The United States-Japan Trade Council is funded by the Japanese Foreign Ministry, but does not officially represent the Japanese government. It does not testify before congressional committees or regulatory agencies. Its main function is to present in an analytical way the facts and issues. Publications are sent to members of Congress, staff members, and others interested. The council also sponsors conferences dealing with U.S.-Japanese trade relationships.

Food Processing and Distribution

A number of associations and organizations have direct concerns related to issues involving food processing and distribution. The Grocery Manufacturers of America, Inc. (GMA), with 140 member companies, represents almost all the major processors and manufacturers of grocery products. Its Washington representation includes directly employed professional staff and legal and other counsulting firms. Its major objective is to solve for member companies those problems for which group action is more effective than action by companies working individually or through other associations.

Combining member-company participation with Washington staff, the GMA operates through committees and task forces. Its task forces have dealt with issues related to health, safety and quality of foods, regulatory reform, freedom to advertise, antitrust matters, pesticide registration and usage, and consumer protection. It supported a moratorium on the saccharin ban.[60]

Table 4-2
Representatives for Foreign Agricultural and Food Associations (Other than Sugar)

Representative	Country and Organization	Fees Received[a]	
Arent, Fox, Kintner, Plotkin & Kahn 1815 H Street NW Washington, DC 20006	Potash Corporation of Saskatchewan	$52,275.38	(Feb. 1978-Feb. 1979)
Arnold & Porter 1229 19th Street Washington, DC 20035	London Commodity Exchange Co.	20,255	(June and Aug. 1978)
	Swiss Cheese Union	40,850	(Feb., Apr., and Nov. 1975)
	West Mexico Vegetable Distributors Association		
	International Commodities Clearinghouse, London		
	Switzerland Gruyere Processed Cheese Manufacturers Association		
Barnes, Richardson, & Colburn 1819 H Street NW Washington, DC 20006	Australian Wool Corporation	57,964.97[b]	(Aug. 1978 and Jan. 1979)
Berry, Epstein, McIlwain, & Finney 1700 Pennsylvania NW Washington, DC 20006	Danish Cake and Biscuit Alliance	3,709.59	(Nov. 1978-Apr. 1979)
	Austrian Food Center Corporation		(terminated Mar. 1979[b])
	French Dairy Association	9,006.64	(Feb. 1979)
	CNCF Mexico (Trade promotion)	36,722.95[b]	(Dec. 1978 and Apr. 1979)
Bronz & Farrell 888 17th Street NW Washington, DC 20006	New Zealand Dairy Board	15,107.76[b]	(1978)
	New Zealand Meat Products Board	29,035.56[b]	(Dec. 1977-Nov. 1978)
Clifford, Glass, McIlwain, & Finney (Clifford & Warnke since Mar. 1979) 815 Connecticut Avenue NW Washington, DC 20006	Australian Meat & Livestock Corp.	160,000	(retainer)
	Australian Meat Board	16,953.50	(reimbursed expenses, Jan. 1978-Jan. 1979)

Agency	Client	Fee	Dates
Chapman, Duff, & Paul 1730 Pennsylvania Avenue Washington, DC 20006	Taiyo Fisheries (Japan)	5,000 on hourly basis; then 12,000 per year retainer	(beginning Jan. 1979)
	Japan Fisheries	20,000 fee plus 511.90 expenses	(Aug. 1977-Aug. 1978)
Daniels, Houlihan, & Palmeter 1819 H Street NW Washington, DC 20006	Japan Lumber Importers Association	23,996 fees, 2,713.76 expenses	(Feb. 1978-Jan. 1979)
	Japan Woolen and Linen Textile Exporters Association	12,000 fees, 7,671.72 expenses	(Mar.-Dec. 1978)
	Haitian Textile Exporters	5,200 fees, 926.35 expenses	(Feb. 1978-Jan. 1979)
	Korean Textile Export Association	40,000	(Mar. and July 1978)
	Micam-Anci (Italian footwear)	1,800 fees, 20.08 expenses	(Mar. 1978)
Doyle Dane Berback 437 Madison Avenue New York, NY 10022 (Advertising agency)	National Federation of Coffee Growers of Colombia	1,502,196.60[b]	(advertising, Mar. 1978-Mar. 1979)
Fraser Associates Suite 1006, 1800 K Street NW Washington, DC 20006	Japan Fisheries	4,600.03 800 per month retainer	(Dec. 1977 and Mar. 1978)
	Ajinomoto Co., Japan (Monitoring and research on food additives)	70,649[a]	(Dec. 1977-Dec. 1978)

Table 4-2 (*continued*)
Representatives for Foreign Agricultural and Food Associations (Other than Sugar)

Representative	Country and Organization	Fees Received[a]	
E.A. Jaenke & Associates 1735 I Street NW Washington, DC 20006	Australian Wool Corporation	60,000 fees, 476.82 expenses	(Jan. 1978-Jan. 1979)
Modern Talking Picture Service, Inc. 45 Rockefeller Plaza New York, NY 10020 (Film distribution)	Ontario Rutabaga Council Danish Agricultural Council	877.60[b] 5,575.17[b]	(1978) (1978)
O'Connor & Hannan 1747 Pennsylvania Avenue NW Washington, DC 20006	Argentine Meat Board	12,000	(Dec. 1978-Apr. 1979) ($25,000 per year beginning Oct. 6, 1978)
Pendleton & McLaughlin 888 17th Street NW Washington, DC 20006	Canned and Cooked Meat Importers Association, Argentina	8,405.15[b]	(Dec. 1974-Nov. 1975)
Albert M. Prosterman & Associates 818 18th Street NW Washington, DC 20006	Inter-African Coffee Organization (Paris)	14,853.21[b]	(1975) (terminated 1976)
Peter Rotholz Associates, Inc. 380 Lexington Avenue New York, NY 10017 (Marketing and promotion)	Italian Wine Promotion Center	26,500[b]	(Apr.-Aug. 1978)
Shea, Gould, Climenko, & Casey 330 Madison Avenue New York, NY 10017 (Public relations and information)	New Zealand Wool Board		

Samuel E. Slavisky & Associates 1100 17th Street NW Washington, DC 20036	Brazilian Coffee Institute	120,000 1979: 120,000 plus expenses (operation of World Coffee Information Center)	(1978)
J. Sutherland Gould Associates 1212 Sixth Avenue New York, NY 10036 (Public relations and promotion)	Switzerland Cheese Association	4,000	(1978) (terminated July 1978)
H. William Tanaka 1819 H Street NW Washington, DC 20006	Japan Fisheries	10,000 3,000	(Mar. 1978) (Aug. 1978-July 1979)
Tea Council of USA, Inc. 230 Park Avenue New York, NY 10018 (Promotion)	Tea Councils of Sri Lanka, India, Indonesia, Kenya, and Tanzania	200,745	(1978)
Leonard Warner, Inc. (Warner & Harris) 1030 15th Street, Room 840 Washington, DC 20006	Australian Meat and Livestock Corp.	126,279[b]	(1974) (terminated Dec. 1974)
Williams & King 1620 I Street NW Suite 800 Washington, DC 20006	Australian Canned Fruits Board	3,700 fee $100 expenses	(1978)
	Australian Dairy Corporation	9,525 fees 1,207.72 expenses	(1978)

Source: U.S. Department of Justice, *Congressional Record*, February 20, 1978, June 13, 1978, August 24, 1978, November 15, 1978, February 19, 1979.

[a] Latest year reported.

[b] Fees plus expenses reimbursed.

The GMA filed a lawsuit in U.S. district court in 1978 charging Assistant Secretary of Agriculture Carol Tucker Foreman with conflict of interest regarding the awarding of the USDA net-weight study contract to Consumer Federation of America. The suit was later dismissed.[61]

One of its registered lobbyists is Robert Taft, Jr., former senator from Ohio, whose law firm represents several clients on legislative matters.

The American Meat Institute (AMI) has been most concerned about the threat to ban nitrite from meat processing and curing. The AMI has defended the use of nitrite, citing its natural occurrence in vegetables, water, and soil; its use for thousands of years in small amounts to preserve and cure meat products; and its effectiveness in preventing botulism (a deadly form of food poisoning). It criticized the nitrite study by Dr. Paul Newberne at Massachusetts Institute of Technology, citing the Food and Drug Administration report of sloppy laboratory conditions and inconclusive and questionable data.[62]

The AMI has also been involved with proposed changes in net-weight labeling regulations. The AMI believes that the best point for regulating net weight is in the manufacturing plant. The USDA wanted to check net weights of packages in the stores. The AMI supported the General Accounting Office (GAO) report which concluded that the USDA did not have sufficient data to justify changing the regulations on how to deal with moisture loss after the product has been packaged and shipped or to assess the impact on food prices if proposed changes were made.[63]

Richard Lyng, president of American Meat Institute from 1973 to 1979, was assistant Secretary of Agriculture from 1969 to 1973.

The Institute has watched closely USDA regulations dealing with meat substitution in school lunch programs. Regulations issued in August 1978 permitted use of certain alternatives such as dry beans and peas, peanut butter, eggs, and cheese in place of the meat requirement in school lunches.

The National Independent Meat Packers Association (NIMPA) has major interests in beef and processed meats. It provides educational and information services to its members and keeps members of Congress and government agencies informed of its interests and concerns affecting the packing industry. It opposed the proposed ban of nitrite in meat processing and supported the USDA in its position that the USDA had sole control over food additives in meats, not the Food and Drug Administration. Efforts to merge NIMPA with the American Meat Institute had not succeeded by mid-1979.

Transportation issues also concern the food processing industry. The Food Marketing Institute, in its attempt to reduce costs for its members, called for discounts for backhauls by customers in their own trucks, an end to Interstate Commerce Commission (ICC) restrictions on hauling among subsidiaries and the parent company, single-trip leases where a thirty-day minimum was permitted, fewer restrictions upon becoming a regulated truck carrier, fewer restrictions on the area to be served by a contract carrier, and more dependable rail service for perishable goods from coast to coast.[64]

The United Fresh Fruit and Vegetable Association wants to see a greater proportion of traffic move by rail with dependable schedules, competitive rates, but with the agricultural exemption in the Interstate Commerce Act preserved.[65]

Food-Stamp Program

The food-stamp program creates special interests and concerns among several groups. The National Association of Retail Grocers of the United States favors keeping the food-stamp program, with the current definitions of eligible food stores, and has promised its help to run the program properly and without fraud. It supports legislation to define store disqualifications and opposes the proposed requirement that food stamps have to be signed by the user.[66]

The National Nutritional Foods Association wants the definition of food changed in the food-stamp legislation to include any food product, vitamin, mineral, or other nutrient for home consumption. The USDA has excluded vitamin and mineral products and nutrient supplements from the list of products which could be purchased with food stamps.[67]

The National Federation of Independent Business (NFIB) has taken a direct interest in reform of the food-stamp program. The reports of their members given in congressional testimony reveal a different perspective from that of the groups who strongly support food-stamp programs.[68]

Margaret Sloss, Bowling Green, Kentucky, wrote, "No humane person would wish to deny help to the truly needy or disabled—but daily the ones of us who work and support our 'give away' system see evidence of extravagance and waste and unwillingness to help themselves by too many of the recipients of these programs. Either qualification requirements are too lenient or those approving are not screening properly—probably a mixture of both."

Mr. and Mrs. Pat Pattison, owners of the Town and Country Market, Inc., in Nebraska had this to say: "Something has to be done with the food-stamp program. I am in the grocery business and when three couples (all having food stamps) pull up in a new Winnebago and are on vacation and shave their food expenses with food stamps and ask where the liquor store is so they can buy beer with a roll of $20 bills, it's a little irritating to the working people who are footing their vacation."

Mr. and Mrs. Norman Craig, Craig's Harbor Store, North Hero, Vermont, wrote, "We have expensive ($20,000) class sailboats arrive and stock up with high priced meats using food stamps. A car arrived (a late model Cadillac) and well-dressed apparent owners purchased steaks, honey, maple syrup, etc. with food stamps. They then paid cash for about $30 worth of good wine. We feel that better than 50 percent of the users eat better than we do."

The NFIB favors limiting food stamps to those with incomes below the poverty index, requiring search for employment by qualified food stamp recipients, and limiting stamp disbursement based on personal and real estate assets.[69]

The National Labor Management Foundation expresses its concern about food stamps being supplied to strikers as well as other program abuses. They see union officials wanting their members to continue high living standards during a strike. As they see it, union strike benefits have fallen, so the practice of providing public assistance to support persons on strike is rapidly becoming traditional. They advocate taking away food stamps from persons on strike not otherwise eligible to receive them.[70]

The National Association of Manufacturers hired a professor of management from the University of Maryland to speak in their behalf at hearings dealing with food stamps in 1977. They see stamps being provided to persons on strike as a direct benefit for unions who do not have to provide as much for members' needs. They do not see denial of food stamps as a tool for management; rather, denial would rectify an imbalance and return collective bargaining to neutral. They suggested a ninety-day moving average income base as a way to make stamp distribution more equitable.[71]

The U.S. Industrial Council has broad concerns with legislation that would "weaken or tend to undermine the free enterprise system." Specifically they call for tightening eligibility for food stamps, and no stamps for strikers, students, or the voluntarily unemployed. They propose tightening work rules, training, and registering for employment for food stamp recipients. They oppose cash payments in lieu of food stamps and propose photograph identification cards with countersignatures at the time of cashing food stamps.[72]

The Calorie Control Council has taken an active role in the controversy surrounding the proposed ban on saccharin. It has submitted proposals, research reviews, and arguments to support a moratorium on any ban on saccharin to scientific and regulatory agencies in the federal government, to Congress, and to the general public.

Foreign Agents

Federal law requires that U.S. citizens representing the interests of a foreign government or organization register with the Department of Justice. In the food and agriculture arena, these agents are employed by associations or firms who want to sell their products or services in this country. Individuals and firms representing foreign sugar interests were shown in table 4-1. Others representing foreign agricultural and food interests are shown in table 4-2.

Foreign food suppliers have a vital interest in tariff and trade regulations, meat and dairy import quotas, quality and grading standards, labeling requirements, and any other government regulations that would affect importation and sale of their product. Their representatives provide an important service to the home office overseas and to the buyers and consumers of the products in this country.

Members of firms representing foreign clients also include some former high government officials, although these individuals may not be directly involved in servicing the foreign accounts. David S. King, of Williams & King, was a former member of the House of Representatives and former ambassador to Malagasy Republic and Mauritius. Clark Clifford, of Clifford, Glass, McIlwain, & Finney, was Secretary of Defense in 1968-1969 and Special Counsel to the President from 1946 to 1950. E.A. Jaenke was a former USDA official and governor of the Farm Credit Administration.

Multiple Representation

Lobbying and representing companies, associations, and organizations in Washington is a professional business. Many companies and associations hire staff who work full time for one employer. Others located away from the Washington area may hire a representative who serves several clients. Some Washington-based associations employ special legislative or legal services in addition to their own staff.

These representatives may be law firms, public relations firms, or management or marketing consultants. They may represent a client for many years or perform services for only a few months. Some representatives specialize in matters dealing with food and agriculture. Because of the flexible and often confidential nature of such services, a complete, up-to-date list of all firms serving more than one client with food and agricultural interests is nearly impossible. However, at least fifty-seven registered lobbyists carry out multiple representations for clients with major agricultural and food interests.

Some serve both individual firms and trade associations. Some are registered lobbyists; others are not. Some serve both domestic and foreign clients. Some specialize in service to commodity producer-marketing groups, futures contract markets, farmers' insurance companies, professional groups, American Indian tribes, or commodity brokers. For the small company or trade association that cannot afford the high cost of a

Washington office, these representatives, who divide their time among several clients, perform a valuable service at a lower cost than a firm would pay to employ a full-time person.

Serving clients with food and agricultural interests is only part of the services rendered by many of the larger legal and public relations firms in the Washington area. For some clients, attention to matters relating to food and agriculture may be only part of the services they receive from their Washington representative.

In terms of clients, a few firms stand out in their food and agricultural specializations. The following Washington representatives were registered lobbyists for five or more clients with food and agriculture interests during 1978: Arnold & Porter; Berry, Epstein, Sandstrom, & Blatchford; Clifford, Glass, McIlwain, & Finney; Covington & Burling; Davis & McLeod; Doub, Purcell, Muntzing, & Hansen; Hamel, Park, McCabe, & Saunders; E.A. Jaenke & Associates; O'Connor & Hannan; Patton, Boggs, & Blow; Sutherland, Asbill, & Brennan; Williams & Jensen.

During 1978, Sutherland, Asbill, & Brennan registered as lobbyists for nine Farm Bureau insurance companies in Kansas, South Carolina, Mississippi, Indiana, Georgia, and Arkansas. About this time the Department of Agriculture sent a proposed new plan for all crop risk insurance to Congress. A major issue in revising government crop insurance is the role of the established private insurance companies.

Many Washington firms are not required to register as lobbyists since they do not perform services directly related to legislative activity. Such services may include legal, advertising, marketing, promotion, public and press relations, conference planning and organizing, and preparation of newsletters and publications for use by client organization members or the general public. In performing such services, the multiclient representative, either individual or firm, may not contact members of Congress or top agency officials, but observes their actions and activities very closely.

Summary and Conclusions

Agricultural business and industry provide the tools and technology that make possible the productivity record of U.S. farmers. It also provides the link to transport, process, and distribute the products from nearly 3 million farms to more than 200 million consumers.

One of the key issues has been what role government should play in stimulating, facilitating, and regulating the production and marketing processes. Consumer, environmental, and minority groups have criticized agricultural and food-industry groups. The result is stimulated legislative and lobbying activities by agricultural and food-industry groups.

Government regulations dealing with manufacture and distribution of pesticides, international trade in agricultural products, domestic food assistance programs, futures contract trading, occupational safety and health, and farm commodity support programs affect agricultural business and industry groups. Many times they add costs that are passed on to consumers and contribute to inflation.

The business and industry groups provide a communications link between their members and government activity, as well as a voice by which they seek to protect and defend themselves from the consequences of government regulation and control.

Notes

1. For a history of price-support programs see Wayne D. Rasmussen and Gladys L. Baker, *Price-Support and Adjustment Programs from 1933 through 1978: A Short History*, Agricultural Information Bulletin No. 424, Economics, Statistics, and Cooperatives Service, U.S. Department of Agriculture, February 1979.

2. U.S. Senate Committee on Agriculture, Nutrition, and Forestry hearings, *General Farm and Food Legislation*, February 24, 1977, pp. 229-235.

3. U.S. House Committee on Agriculture hearings, *General Farm Bill*, Part 4, March 15, 1977, pp. 19-24.

4. U.S. Senate Agriculture Committee hearings, *General Farm and Food Legislation*, February 25, 1977, pp. 309-313.

5. U.S. Senate Agriculture Committee hearings, *State of American Agriculture*, March 7, 1978, pp. 56-57.

6. Ibid., pp. 58-61.

7. U.S. Senate Agriculture Committee hearings, *General Farm and Food Legislation*, Book 2, Appendix, February-March 1977, pp. 677-678.

8. U.S. Senate Agriculture Committee hearings, *General Farm and Food Legislation*, February 24, 1977, pp. 236-240.

9. Ibid., March 7, 1977, pp. 581-585.

10. Ibid., Book 2, Appendix, February 25, 1977, pp. 184-190.

11. U.S. Senate Agriculture Committee hearings, *State of American Agriculture*, February 28, 1978, pp. 98-99.

12. U.S. Senate Agriculture Committee hearings, *General Farm and Food Legislation*, February 25, 1977, pp. 296-297.

13. Ibid., March 1, 1977, pp. 407-416.

14. Ibid., Book 2, Appendix, March 16, 1977, pp. 301-302.

15. Jack C. Pearce, "What Are the Purposes and Goals of the National Association of Milk Marketing Reform?" *Proceedings*, 1975 Dairy Marketing Forum, Department of Agricultural Economics, University of Illinois, AE 4382, February 1976, pp. 14-24.

16. U.S. Senate Agriculture Committee hearings, *General Farm and Food Legislation*, February 28, 1977, pp. 343-348.

17. Ibid., pp. 396-402.

18. Ibid., pp. 366-369.

19. U.S. Senate Agriculture Committee hearings, *State of American Agriculture*, March 3, 1978, pp. 243-248.

20. U.S. Senate Agriculture Committee hearings, *General Farm and Food Legislation*, February 28, 1977, pp. 402-405.

21. Ibid., March 3, 1977, pp. 519-522.

22. Ibid., pp. 530-531.

23. Ibid., pp. 524-530, 540-541.

24. Ibid., March 10, 1977, pp. 742-753.

25. Seth S. King, "Carter's Watchman over Sugar Policy," *The New York Times*, January 15, 1979.

26. William Robbins, "Lobbyists Worked Off Stage to Shape Sugar Laws," *The New York Times*, January 15, 1979.

27. Douglas Martin, "Administration Working on a Sugar Bill Tailored to Block Push for Big Price Rise," *Wall Street Journal*, January 16, 1979, p. 30.

28. Robbins, "Lobbyists Worked Off Stage."

29. "Sugar Legislation's Rapidly Revolving Door," *The New York Times*, January 16, 1979.

30. Ibid.

31. Ibid.

32. U.S. Senate Agriculture Committee, *State of American Agriculture*, February 28, 1978, pp. 139-141, 397-400.

33. William Robbins, "Powerful Rivals Clash over Sugar Price Supports," *The New York Times*, January 16, 1979, p. D-11.

34. U.S. House of Representatives Committee on Agriculture hearings, *Sugar Stabilization Act of 1978*, June 1, 1978, pp. 471-475.

35. Paul Findley, *The Federal Farm Fable* (New Rochelle, N.Y.: Arlington House, 1968), p. 137.

36. Seth S. King, "Sugar Price Supports: Sweet Deals for Lobbyists over the Last Four Decades," *The New York Times*, January 14, 1979, p. 49.

37. Findley, *The Federal Farm Fable*, p. 138.

38. *American Farm Bureau Federation Newsletter* 58, 18 (May 7, 1979):95.

39. Chris Connell, "Stop Smoking Effort Has Steady Foe in Tobacco Lobby," Associated Press, *Champaign-Urbana News Gazette*, January 7, 1979.

40. Ibid.

41. In addition to Walter Jones of North Carolina who served as chairman, the tobacco subcommittee members in 1979-1980 were Charles

Whitley, North Carolina; Dawson Mathis, Georgia; Charles Rose, North Carolina; Alvin Baldus, Wisconsin; Richard Kelly, Florida; and Larry J. Hopkins, Kentucky.

42. U.S. House of Representatives Committee on Agriculture, Subcommittee on Conservation and Credit hearings, February 22, 1978, pp. 284-293.

43. Ibid., pp. 306-310.

44. U.S. House Committee on Agriculture hearings, *Extend Commodity Exchange Act*, February 21, 22, 23, April 11, 1978.

45. U.S. House Committee on Agriculture hearings, *Federal Insecticide, Fungicide, and Rodenticide Act*, March 9, 1977, p. 231.

46. Ibid., p. 231.

47. U.S. Senate Agriculture Committee hearings, *General Farm and Food Legislation*, Book 2, Appendix, March 11, 1977, pp. 525-527.

48. U.S. House Agriculture Committee hearings, *Federal Insecticide, Fungicide, and Rodenticide Act*, March 8, 1977, pp. 90-98.

49. Ibid., March 7, 1977, pp. 50-53.

50. Ibid., March 8, 1977, pp. 100-105; U.S. Senate Agriculture Committee hearings, *General Farm and Food Legislation*, March 11, 1977, pp. 842-844.

51. U.S. Senate Agricultural Subcommittee on Agricultural Production, Marketing, and Stabilization of Prices hearings, *Agricultural Transportation Problems*, July 15, 1977, pp. 82-86, 128-131.

52. U.S. House Committee on Agriculture hearings, *Current Agricultural Situation*, February 8, 1978, pp. 539-541.

53. U.S. Senate Agriculture Committee hearings, *General Farm and Food Legislation*, March 4, 1977, pp. 562-566.

54. U.S. Senate Agriculture Committee hearings, *State of American Agriculture*, March 1, 1978, pp. 161-167.

55. U.S. Senate Agriculture Committee hearings, *General Farm and Food Legislation*, February 24, 1977, pp. 229-230.

56. Ibid., February 25, 1977, pp. 309-313.

57. Ibid., February 28, 1977, pp. 396-402.

58. U.S. Senate Agriculture Subcommittee on Foreign Agricultural Policy hearings, *Inspection Standards of Vegetable Imports*, March 22, 1978.

59. Meat Importers Council of America, Inc., "The Facts: About Imported Lean Beef," January 1978.

60. Grocery Manufacturers of America, Inc., "1978-79 Directory, A Guide to the Grocery Manufacturers of America, Inc.," Washington, D.C.

61. American Meat Institute, *Newsletter* 12, 51 (December 1, 1978):2.

62. U.S. Senate Agriculture Subcommittee on Agricultural Research and General Legislation, *Food Safety and Quality: Nitrites*, September 15, 1978, pp. 1-2.

63. American Meat Institute, *Newsletter* 12, 54 (December 21, 1978):1-2.

64. U.S. Senate Agriculture Subcommittee on Agricultural Production, Marketing, and Stabilization of Prices hearings, *Agricultural Transportation Problems*, July 15, 1977, pp. 60-71.

65. Ibid., pp. 32-37.

66. U.S. House Agriculture Committee and Subcommittee on Domestic Marketing, Consumer Relations, and Nutrition hearings, *Food Stamp Program*, March 25, 1977, pp. 700-705.

67. Ibid., April 5, 1977, pp. 645-647.

68. U.S. Senate Agriculture Committee hearings, *General Farm and Food Legislation*, Book 2, Appendix, March 8, 1977, pp. 411-413.

69. U.S. House Agriculture Committee hearings, *Food Stamp Program*, February 28; March 21-25; April 5, 1977, pp. 645-647.

70. U.S. Senate Agriculture Committee hearings, *General Farm and Food Legislation*, Appendix, Book 2, March 8, 1977, pp. 416-422.

71. Ibid., pp. 422-429.

72. Ibid., pp. 712-715.

Citizen, Consumer, and Specific-Interest Advocates: Lobbying for the "Public Interest"

We need more than individual value systems; we need a shared vision. A nation is held together by shared values, shared beliefs, shared attitudes.
—John Gardner

Citizens' Groups Defined

The citizens', consumers', and other groups with interests in food and agriculture have a broad range of concerns. Some may focus their entire efforts in the food production or distribution area. These groups, presenting views on food and agricultural issues from outside the traditional established producer, business, industry, professional, and institutional groups, have also been called "public" interest groups.[1] However, as one Senate Agriculture Committee staff member points out, no single group can represent the public, because there are too many different points of view among the 200-million-member U.S. public. He suggests they be called special-interest groups because they do present a specific viewpoint. The extent to which they represent a majority in the United States is uncertain.

Citizen and consumer groups also vary from the farm producer and buisness groups in their membership status. The producer and business groups discussed in earlier chapters are comprised of individuals or firms who pay a fee for membership and who usually expect direct benefit from such membership. Lobbying and legislative activity is usually only one part of the activity and purpose of these organizations.

The citizen and consumer groups described in this chapter often are not really membership organizations. One estimate suggests that 30 percent of these groups do not have individuals or groups as members.[2] Such groups that do not have memberships are supported by private foundations, contributions of individuals, or grants and contracts from federal agencies. These groups use the money to try to develop latent interest among certain segments of the population for which the grants were intended and to persuade Congress, government agencies, and the courts to make decisions considered to be in the public interest or in line with the intent of the law.

The lobbyists for citizens' and consumers' groups are usually considered to be working for a collective good which, if achieved, would not selectively or materially benefit the membership or the activists of that organization. The nature of their lobbying efforts and other activities also affects how they are treated under the Internal Revenue Code. If it devotes a substantial amount of its activities to lobbying openly and with members of Congress, the group does not qualify for exemption from income tax, and individual contributions to these groups are not tax deductible for the donors.

Under section 501(c)(3) of the Internal Revenue Code (IRC), tax-exempt groups could not lobby in Congress, but they were able to advocate positions before administrative agencies, initiate litigation, and also receive foundation grants.[3] However, under section 1307 of the Tax Reform Act of 1976 the Internal Revenue Code is amended with two sections—501(h) and 4911. The new IRC sections enable eligible 501(c)(3) organizatons to elect to replace the substantial-activity test for lobbying activities with a specified limit defined in terms of dollar amounts spent for influencing legislation. The effect of these provisions is to set forth explicit standards governing the amount of lobbying activity that eligible 501(c)(3) organizations can undertake without fear of losing tax-exempt status.

The permitted level of such expenditures (called the "lobbying nontaxable amount") for each year is 20 percent of the first $500,000 of the organization's "exempt-purpose expenditures" for the year, plus 15 percent of the second $500,000, plus 10 percent of the third $500,000, plus 5 percent of any additional expenditures.[4] See table 5-1.

In order to conduct lobbying efforts, register as required, yet also get the benefit of tax-exempt status for educational and litigation activities, some organizations have formed affiliate foundations. Groups that have taken this route include Bread for the World, Environmental Action, Sierra Club, Friends of the Earth, National Land for People, and Friends of Animals.

Continued financing of activities may be one of the major problems for the citizens' and consumers' groups dependent on foundation and grant support. Foundations often provide initial grants to get an organization started, but do not plan to provide permanent funding. When the grants run out, the group must turn to other sources of funding, solicit general contributions or membership fees, or phase out its activities. The Agribusiness Accountability Project, which published *Hard Tomatoes, Hard Times* in 1972 and received wide attention for its criticisms of the land-grant universities, eventually ran out of funding, and no supporting constituency had been developed. Its staff moved into other employment.

The staff and participants in the citizens' and consumers' groups usually are younger and have fewer years of work experience than those active with other lobby groups. They are intensely dedicated to their work, usually hold one or two college degrees, receive relatively low salaries, and may not be sympathetic to the established institutions in the agricultural and food system. Often they have empathy for family farms and rural life, but grew up in large cities.

**Table 5-1
Lobby Expenditure Limits**
(*dollars*)

Examples of the Percentage Limitations on Lobbying Expenditures

Annual "Exempt-Purpose Expenditures"	*"Lobbying Nontaxable Amount"* (An organization may spend up to the following amounts without being subject to the 25% penalty excise tax):		*Possible Loss of Exemption* (An organization risks losing its tax exemption if, on average, it spends more than the following amounts each year over a four-year period):	
	All Lobbying Activity, Including Grass-Roots Lobbying	*Grass-Roots Lobbying*	*All Lobbying Activity, Including Grass-Roots Lobbying*	*Grass-Roots Lobbying*
200,000	40,000	10,000	60,000	15,000
500,000	100,000	25,000	150,000	37,500
1,000,000	175,000	43,750	262,500	65,625
1,500,000[a]	225,000	56,250	337,500	84,375
3,000,000[a]	300,000	75,000	450,000	112,500

Source: Economic Development Law Project Report, May-June 1977.

[a]If an organization's annual "exempt-purpose expenditures" are more than $1,500,000, its "lobbying nontaxable amount" is equal to $225,000 plus 5 percent of the excess exempt-purpose expenditures over $1,500,000.

The Issues and the Players

Some citizens' and consumers' groups participate in a broad range of food production and marketing issues. Others concentrate their efforts on food additives and nutrition, domestic food-assistance programs, food assistance and international development, environmental concerns and pesticide use, conservation and wildlife protection, humane treatment of animals, or rural and community development.

The 1977 hearings held before passage of the Food and Agricultural Act of 1977 provided the stage for all groups interested in food and agricultural issues to make their views known.

Farm Production and Food Marketing Concerns

The Coalition of Consumer Organizations, representing the Consumer Federation of America, Community Nutrition Institute, Center for Science in the Public Interest, National Consumers Congress, The Consumer Affairs Committee of the Americans for Democratic Action, and Public Citizen Congress Watch, presented joint testimony to both the Senate and House committees.

The coalition called for a grain reserve to provide stable supplies, price support loans to cover farmers' out-of-pocket costs, increased funds for nutrition and food-related research with a users' advisory board of bona fide consumer representatives, increased funds for direct farmer-to-consumer marketing programs, continued commitment to food aid under Public Law 480, and elimination of the purchase requirement for food stamps to increase access to the program for the lowest-income people.[5]

The Consumer Federation of America (CFA) in its statement expressed further concern with linking target prices and loan rates to the value of land, believing that would increase land values and force price and loan rates up further. The CFA sees the grain reserve as an emergency supply for shortages or famine relief at home and abroad, as well as a means to prevent delays or cutbacks in Public Law 480 shipments should domestic supplies decrease. They see a system for storage and release of reserves as a stabilizing force on food prices.

They favored reserves being substantially owned and held by farmers. If market prices were to soar to a certain level above the loan rate, then they would want authority for USDA to stimulate release of reserves by canceling loan contracts or decreasing storage payments. The effects of such moves would be to encourage grain to be brought into the market. If such moves did not curtail the rise in price, then government-owned reserves would be released to moderate prices. Such a system of farmer-held stocks would protect consumers and farmers alike from instability of food prices.[6]

The CFA also called for increased nutrition and food-related research, taking control of such research away from "the Agricultural Research Service, Assistant Secretary, land grant school relationship." They favored an advisory committee composed of consumers and experts in fields related to food and nutrition independent from USDA to set policy and direction in research. They also suggested a Users Advisory Board which has policy-making input, the majority of which are bona fide consumer representatives. A bona fide consumer representative is a person who is neither employed by nor the recipient of a significant amount of investment income from the industry whose activity is under consideration.

In its final form, the Food and Agricultural Act of 1977 included new features that matched closely with the Consumer Federation of America's testimony. A farmer-owned reserve was created with a mechanism for release of reserve when prices rise. The USDA also has authority to sell its own reserves when prices reach a certain level. The target price is tied to a cost of production, but excludes the cost of land. The food stamp purchase requirement was eliminated, and a Research and Extension Users Advisory board was created that includes consumer representation. A reorganization of the USDA in 1977 and 1978 shifted more research funds from the traditional formula grants for land-grant colleges and universities to competitive grants with other universities and research institutions outside the land-grant system eligible to apply.[7]

In its 1978 annual resolutions, the CFA continued to present its views on food and agricultural policies. It called for a comprehensive land-use policy and protection of prime farmland. It also called for a national food budget to hold food inflation to a tolerable level by ensuring food supplies sufficient to meet domestic nutritional requirements, food assistance needs, and institutional demands; provide for commercial exports; supply foreign assistance commitments; and maintain both domestic and world food reserves. However, it also supports price stabilization programs which provide for production expenses and a reasonable return for family farmers and ranchers as well as low-interest credit for young family farmers to get started. It also supports a strategy to decentralize production and economic concentration in food processing, distribution, and retailing; to increase the efficiency of the marketplace; and to assist family farmers and consumers in the formation of cooperative marketing and retailing activities in local communities. The CFA supports the efforts of farm workers to organize to promote their rights to decent earnings and working conditions.

They called upon Congress to investigate the degree and nature of corporate concentration within the food industry, including the non-competitive impact of advertising, vertical integration, and the increase in the number of conglomerates in the food industry. They also urge a review of agricultural marketing orders and marketing agreements and a reexamination of the adequacy of the Capper-Volstead Act to protect and regulate agricultural marketing cooperatives.

The CFA encourages the continuing efforts of the USDA to become a Department of Food which is responsive to the needs of all those affected by the food system. It wants to see meat and poultry inspection programs maintained in the USDA rather than shifted to the Food and Drug Administration.

The CFA advocates a national commitment to domestic and foreign aid programs to prevent hunger and malnutrition and supports the principle that every person in this country and throughout the world has the right to a nutritionally adequate diet and this right should be recognized as a cornerstone of U.S. policy.[8]

In 1979 the CFA opposed sugar interests that wanted to raise sugar support prices each year and which would also raise retail sugar prices.

What is the background of an organization that apparently exerts a major influence on the nation's food and agricultural policy? How does it operate and how are its policies determined? The Consumer Federation of America was organized in 1968 following two years of meetings by the Consumer Assembly, in which state and local consumer groups expressed the need for a Washington clearinghouse for information and services.

Since that time the CFA has established itself as an important and successful advocate for the consumer in Washington and on Capitol Hill. In the food and agriculture area, it cites among its successes the Federal Meat Inspection Act Amendment of 1970, the Egg Products Inspection Act of 1970, the Agriculture and Consumer Protection Act of 1973, and the Farmer-to-Consumer Direct Marketing Act of 1976.[9]

It joined with a number of farm groups to support the Emergency Farm Act of 1975 that would have raised target and loan prices. Although passed by Congress, the act was vetoed by the President, and Congress sustained the veto. It supported a Consumer Protection Agency which Congress rejected in 1978.

As with any new organization, some financial problems have occurred. Deficits threatened the survival of the organization in 1971 and 1972,[10] but increased dues produced a balanced operating budget in 1975 and 1976.[11] The annual budget of $90,000 in 1972 had increased to $300,000 in 1975.[12] The CFA research unit, the Paul H. Douglas Consumer Research Center, received a grant of $110,538 from the Office of Consumer Education (HEW) in 1976. A research contract for $23,000 from USDA to study regulations on net-weight labeling in 1978 was desribed by one informed official as "not reaching the bottom line." Uncertainty of funds threatened the future of the research unit in 1979.

The CFA, chartered under the New York Membership Corporation law, operates as a tax-exempt corporation under section 501(c)(4) of the Internal Revenue Code.[13] The federation has about 220 national, state, and local organizations as members. Membership is not open to individuals. The amount of dues that each contributes varies with its size as well as its ability and willingness to pay. Two types of membership are provided for in the charter. Consumer group membership includes any city, county, regional, state, or national consumer association which supports the programs and objectives of the organization. Supporting group membership includes national organizations sympathetic to the work of the CFA with a strong secondary interest in consumer issues. The supporting groups pay the bulk of CFA's bills.[14] But the consumer group members, which may have up to ten votes depending on their size, have more voting power than the supporting group members that have only one vote each.

The largest contributor to the CFA budget in 1976 was Consumers Union, publisher of *Consumer Reports*, which provided about $34,000. Total support from labor organizations was about $40,000, including $7,500 from the Industrial Union Department, AFL-CIO, and $5,000 from the AFL-CIO.[15] Bristol Myers Corporation contributed $5,000. National Rural Electric Cooperative Association and American Public Power Association each contributed $4,500. Rural electric cooperatives contributed a total of about $12,500, and state and local consumer organizations gave about $5,000.[16]

The board of directors, drawn from CFA affiliates, meets four times a year and governs the CFA between annual meetings.[17] The executive committee of twelve members, including seven officers, meets once a month. The president in 1978 and 1979 was Ellen Haas, director of the Consumer Division of Community Nutrition Institute and founder of the Maryland Consumers Council.

The success or failure of CFA operations really lies with its executive director. The number two job is the more powerful.[18] Erma Angevine, the first executive director from 1968 to 1973, is credited with establishing the CFA as a voice of consumers in Washington and serving as a national representative for consumers. Previously she had worked with the National Rural Electric Cooperative Association. Carol Tucker Foreman, the second executive director, became Assistant Secretary of Agriculture in 1977. Her successor, Kathleen O'Reilly, gained her first experience as a consumer activist with Ralph Nader's organization. At the CFA she has maintained a fast pace, presenting the CFA's positions on a broad range of public issues to congressional committees and regulatory agencies.

Through the years some consumers' groups have expressed concern that the large supporting groups members—the labor unions, rural electric cooperatives, and public power groups—dominate the federation's policies. Officials close to the operation do not believe that this happens. Internal differences do occur. The National Farmers Union, which has served on the board of the CFA almost continuously since the beginning, has disagreed at times with other board members on views toward farm price supports.

Although it conducts some educational and research efforts, the Consumers Federation of America is mostly a lobbying organization covering a

wide range of issues, including food and agriculture. About 90 percent of
the staff effort is devoted to lobbying efforts to serve the needs of its constituency—the member organizations. The CFA board sets the policy for
the staff to carry out. The executive director and the small and changing
staff face a wide range of issues on which to present the CFA's positions,
which makes it difficult to go into much depth or follow through on every
issue. The 1979 policy resolutions covered antitrust, communications, consumer education, corporate accountability, credit and the financial system,
energy and natural resources, environment, food and nutrition, government
reforms, the handicapped consumer, health care, housing, insurance, low-
income consumers, transportation, and general resolutions on the conduct
of government.

The Exploratory Project for Economic Alternatives devoted some attention to food and agricultural policy in 1976, but has been more active in
studying other public issues since that time. The preface to its report
"Toward a National Food Policy" stated that "many of our most fundamental economic institutions are no longer adequate to meet the dangers
and opportunities ahead." The summary statement concluded that "low
stable food prices, a secure income for family farmers, and shift away from
agribusiness must be the heart of a new American food policy for the coming decades." The first goal calls for a new direction in agriculture—a pricing plan that protects both the family farmer's income and the consumer's
pocketbook. The report suggests that the key to accomplishing this goal lies
in establishing food reserves and managing supplies in the consumer's interests. Such a stabilization program would include public control of food
exports and imports.

The report sees direct payments to producers as far more equitable and
less inflationary than the traditional approach. It also approves of
assistance to the consumer and family farmer through tax policies, antitrust
action, and payment limits that "break the hold of agribusiness and its
government allies over production itself, over agricultural research, farm
cooperatives, the supply of the farmer's necessary inputs and food distribution."

The third goal is to develop nationwide production of most crops on
small, multicrop farms. They see decentralization of farming as a means of
energy saving in food processing, packaging, and transportation, greater
consumption of fresh foods grown with a minimum of chemicals and
hauled minimum distances from farms where they were produced to the
cities where they are consumed. Although the report disclaims to be the official position of the Exploratory Project, it was prepared in "the hope that
it would help stimulate further debate and clarify fundamental issues."[19]

The Friends Committee on National Legislation (FCNL) called for setting price supports to consciously accumulate reserves. They favored setting

a limit on the amount of production eligible for support according to the size of the producer. They favor Congress's taking a look at tax incentives that affect production decisions, limiting use of the cash accounting system for federal income taxes to smaller farms, and shifting the Public Law 480 subsidized export program to more emphasis on human needs and almost exclusively encouraging food-producing capability in developing nations.

They endorse more "people-oriented" research, more study of energy-saving alternatives and the effects of food systems on people, and the presence of more social scientists on research advisory boards. The FCNL believes that there is a size of farm beyond which there is little or no justification for public policies that encourage or subsidize further growth. Social and community values should become more important considerations in determining federal farm policies.

The FCNL also favored elimination of the purchase requirement for food stamps and retaining of commodity assistance programs for American Indians since food stamps do not work well for them.[20]

The National Catholic Rural Life Conference (NCRLC) and the U.S. Catholic Conference believe that in determining moral content of U.S. policy, we should weigh and relate our responsibilities to farmers, consumers, our allies, our adversaries, and food-deficit developing countries. They believe that farmers should be guaranteed a just and adequate income and consumers a stable supply at a reasonable price. They favor grain reserves held by both farmers and government, coordinated as part of an international system. They favor dispersing farm ownership and production, conservation, and protection of prime agricultural land from unnecessary nonfarming development. They want more production research for small farm producers.

The NCRLC would like to see more Public Law 480 exports shifted to "include needs of the hungry as part of our responsibility," not leaving such a decision to "the random chance of a surplus market." The NCRLC also favored eliminating the purchase requirement for food stamps, providing a standard deduction, basing eligiblity on current income, and no limitations on aliens.[21]

Congress Watch, the lobbying arm of Ralph Nader's Public Citizen, called for a grain reserve to meet both domestic and international needs. They see a reserve as a means to reduce price instability such as experienced in the early 1970s. They also favored reserves being held by farmers as the lowest cost method, but would also like to see emergency reserves owned by the government to be released only in times of crises such as droughts, famines, and floods.[22]

Some misunderstanding of how farm prices are determined seems evident in the testimony favoring reserves to maintain price stability. Frances Zwenig stated, "Unstable supplies will cause livestock and poultry producers to increase their margins to insure against potential losses that would not arise under stable supply conditions."[23] Few, if any, producers can set the price and the margins they receive for their livestock and poultry because of the competitive market conditions under which such prices are established.

Consumers for World Trade became interested in food and farm policies as part of their total concern about special interests lobbying for protection from imports. They have actively opposed measures limiting imports of beef, sugar, textiles, and copper and supported efforts to reduce trade barriers through multilateral trade agreements negotiated in the "Tokyo Round" of trade negotiations. The organization claims endorsement from Arthur Burns, Paul McCracken, Dean Rusk, George Schultz, and Cyrus Vance, which suggests a bipartisan support for their views.

Consumers Opposed to Inflation in the Necessities (COIN), comprising a coalition of sixty consumer and labor groups, mounted a campaign in 1979 as rapid inflation of prices created serious concerns. The food task force, chaired by Ellen Haas and Tom Smith from the Community Nutrition Institute, included representatives from National Consumers League, Center for Science in the Public Interest, Congress Watch, Virginia Citizens Consumer Council, and the Food and Beverage Department of AFL-CIO.

In their June 1979 testimony before the Joint Economic Committee, the task force called for Congress to turn back "unnecessary increases in dairy and sugar support prices"; allow greater amounts of beef imports when domestic supplies are very tight; permit sale of lower-cost reconstituted milk; allow continued unrestricted imports of Mexican vegetables; encourage competition among and eliminate restrictions on trucking agricultural commodities; reform meat pricing by requiring use of more than one reporting sheet in all meat transactions, mandatory reporting of each transaction, and USDA licensing of reporting agencies; reform fruit and vegetable marketing orders; and encourage consumer food co-operatives that would reduce marketing costs.

The task force also called for urgent exploration of "fast-hitting anti-inflationary rebates or subsidies in the food sector" that might include selective subsidies or rebates on key food items of special significance to a majority of families, temporary across-the-board reductions of food prices applied at the wholesale or retail level, and tax incentive programs at the retail level that would show up in direct reduction of retail prices. They expressed concern with the concentration in food marketing, and they favor legislation that would overturn the Supreme Court's Illinois Brick decision, a law designed to enable consumers to recover damages from manufacturers, wholesalers, and retailers for antitrust violations. They also called for reorganization of antitrust laws that would permit more effective enforcement against "large scale horizontal, vertical, and conglomerate concentration.'' They favor restrictions on franchising among processors, wholesalers, and retailers that give exclusive territorial allocation.[24]

Nutrition and Food Additives

Some of the most direct conflicts and confrontations among consumers, producers, and industry occur over issues relating to nutrition and food additives. Citizens' and consumers' groups most directly involved include the Community Nutrition Institute, Center for Science in the Public Interest, the Health Research Group of Public Citizen, and Congress Watch.

In its 1977 testimony, the Community Nutrition Institute called for more food and nutrition research because "the food system lacked the standards and techniques which would enable consumers to relate dietary needs to the food system." They also stated that part of the problem was placing responsibility for consumer education on the Extension Service, which was criticized for being ineffective in urban areas.[25]

Congress Watch also called for an agricultural and nutrition advisory council independent of the Agricultural Research Service and the land-grant college system.[26]

The Health Research Group of Public Citizen, headed by Dr. Sidney Wolfe, has been concerned with safety of food additives. They have proposed (1) that all coal-tar dyes be removed from the market since they are "either clear-cut or suspect cancer-causing chemicals aside from having other health risks"; (2) that the present concept of "generally recognized as safe" (GRAS) substances should be considered potentially dangerous until complete and adequate tests prove otherwise; (3) the marketing of any new food additive not be permitted unless it has been thoroughly tested, has evidence of more than a cosmetic benefit to food, and is better than an existing food additive of the same category; (4) further testing of food additives by industry be shifted to academic centers; and (5) a housecleaning at the Food and Drug Administration Bureau of Foods be done by replacing them by people with more critical scientific faculties.[27]

The most controversial food additive issue since 1977 has centered on nitrites and their use in processing and preserving meats. In defending nitrite use, the American Meat Institute cites research studies in Holland and Denmark where there were two lifetime rat-feeding studies of nitrite-cured meats containing up to 5,000 parts per million of nitrite and no resulting cancer formation, and a similar study of fried bacon in Canada with negative findings on the cause of cancer. They also point out that the study contracted by the Food and Drug Administration and carried out by Dr. Paul Newberne at Massachusetts Institute of Technology was faulty and invalid and should not be used for a decision on any regulation. Food and Drug Administration investigators discovered a diet mixup with an animal caretaker feeding the wrong diet to a group of rats, scales which were not capable of accuracy in weighing the amount of nitrite mixed into various diets, and other problems that may have prevented accurate measurement of results.[28]

Newberne, in responding to Food and Drug Administration auditors, explained that his laboratory performs research and does not function like a commercial testing laboratory with a quality assurance unit. But he also stated that the data came from a reliable strain of rats and that the findings were sufficient to justify a considerable concern and a need to reduce nitrites.[29]

Michael Jacobson, executive director of the Center for Science in the Public Interest, has called for elimination of nitrite as an additive in baby foods and in smoked fish where it seems entirely unnecessary. For other meat products he believes other chemicals or processes should be tested and evaluated to reduce or eliminate the need for sodium nitrite in processing.[30]

Ellen Haas, speaking for Community Nutrition Institute (CNI), called for phasing out the use of nitrite over as short a period as possible, and she claims that this task is reasonable and feasible, despite the dangers of botulism.[31]

In a further argument against nitrite, Thomas B. Smith of CNI concluded that "substantial scientific evidence confirms the carcinogenic [cancer-causing] hazard of nitrite and its metabolic derivatives; nitrite is not essential as a food additive, current efforts by the U.S. Department of Agriculture to reduce but not eliminate the cancer hazard stemming from nitrite use do not adequately address the substantial health risk, and food safety laws for the prohibition of nitrite from use as a food additive must be taken quickly to guarantee the safety of now-hazardous meats."[32]

Eleanor Seiling, president of United Action for Animals, shares the public's concern about possible hazardous effects of chemicals in our food supply, but she also questions the appropriateness of the currently used animal tests to evaluate the potential carcinogenicity of chemicals, "not only because of the suffering of the animals but because our research shows that the methods used today in cancer bioassays were developed at the turn of the century and probably before."[33]

With wide differences of opinion, there is no easy solution. As Senator Lugar concluded, "The question revolves back to how in public policy, nitrite can be reduced without other difficulties from which consumers may suffer."

Behind this testimony attempting to influence significant food policy decisions are four citizen and consumer advocate organizations that did not exist before the 1970s. They are identified as nonprofit, public interest groups, and none has members in the same sense that traditional farm and business groups have dues-paying members and a board of directors that establish the policies of their organizations.

The Center for Science in the Public Interest was established in 1971 by Michael F. Jacobson. He was previously employed by the Salk Institute for Biological Studies and obtained the Ph.D. in microbiology from Massachusetts Institute of Technology in 1969. As director, Jacobson has investigated, publicized, and testified on food and nutrition, consumer, and environmental problems. He has written books and articles, and he serves as executive director of *Nutrition Action*, a monthly magazine that deals with nutrition and food problems at home and abroad. He directed a Food Day annual program for several years which sought to bring public attention to what he believed to be the most pressing food and nutrition issues. He has spoken out against high food prices, monopolies in the food industry, corporate investment in agriculture, conflicts of interest between industry and government, and low-nutrition processed foods. Support for the center has come from foundations, contributions, and sale of publications.

In its October 4, 1978 issue *Medical Tribune* commended the efforts of the Center for Science in the Public Interest for "bringing to consumer advocacy good health perspectives and priorities, a sense of responsibility and sensitivity to the needs of the public . . . its integrity, its ability to uncover important problems, its efficient use of very limited resources and its remarkable effectiveness."

Community Nutrition Institute (CNI) was founded in 1970 by Rod Leonard. He had served as assistant to the Secretary of Agriculture for press relations from 1961 to 1966, deputy assistant Secretary of Agriculture, and administrator of the Consumer and Marketing Service in the U.S. Department of Agriculture from 1966 to 1969. Its efforts have centered on development of food and nutrition policy at the community level. Educational efforts target both the general public, through newsletters and publications, and low-income people, through training and advocacy programs. It publishes a weekly newsletter and publications on specific topics, contracts for research and training programs with state and federal agencies, and sponsors and conducts conferences on various aspects of food and nutrition. A 1979 conference on nutrition guidelines, toward a national strategy, was held in cooperation with Food Marketing Institute and *Family Circle* Magazine. Its staff testified before various congressional committees relating to food and nutrition. Rod Leonard, director, took leave in 1978 and 1979 to work as assistant to Esther Peterson, the President's advisor on consumer affairs.

The CNI has no members but has an appointed advisory board comprised of representatives from consumer groups, churches, nutritionists, community, senior citizens, and welfare rights groups. Final policy decisions on the positions to be presented in hearings and publications are made by the director and staff.

Major funding in recent years has come from grants and contracts from Community Services Administration and other units in the Department of

Health, Education, and Welfare; USDA; foundations; and sales of newsletters and other publications. A significnat part of the CNI administrator's time must be devoted to cultivating future grants and contracts to keep funds flowing for CNI projects and to keep staff employed.

Ellen Haas, the director of the CNI Consumer Division, also serves as president of the Consumer Federation of America. She holds the B.A. degree in history from the University of Michigan, was founder and first president of the Maryland Citizens Council, worked at one time for National Consumers League, and also serves on the National Agricultural Research and Extension Users Advisory board.

Health Research Group, headed by Dr. Sidney Wolfe, is a part of Public Citizen, founded by Ralph Nader. Wolfe received the M.D. degree from Cleveland's Western Reserve University and worked for the National Institutes of Health before joining Ralph Nader and establishing the Health Research Group in 1971. Wolfe has worked to correct a variety of health hazards, only some of which relate directly to food and agriculture. He is credited with the Food and Drug Administration's ban on use of red dye no. 2 as a food coloring and the removal of chloroform from cough medicines and toothpaste in 1976. He has also been involved with an antismoking campaign and use of DES, a drug once given to pregnant women.[34] His efforts to change policy have concentrated more on persuasive tactics with agency heads and executive departments than on congressional testimony. Funding for the group is allocated from Public Citizen, through donations and other income received.

Congress Watch is the branch of Public Citizen that watches actions by Congress on food and other issues. A staff of registered lobbyists presents testimony and makes contacts with staff and members of Congress. Like the Health Research Group, the organization has no members as such. However, Frances Zwenig, coordinator of food and agricultural issues, played an important role in rounding up opposition to the Agricultural Act of 1978. The House of Representatives defeated the bill by more than 100 votes, bringing strong resentment and disappointment by farmers in the American Agricultural Movement who sought higher levels of price support.

Special citizens' interest groups such as Ralph Nader's Public Citizen do face limitations in trying to represent all citizens in class-action suits. United States District Judge John Sirica ruled that consumer groups with nonelected leadership cannot claim to represent the public at large in filing lawsuits. In a suit filed by Ralph Nader's Public Citizen and the Health Research Group, the judge noted that the Nader groups have no dues-paying members and no elected officers. Nader would hardly be in a position to seriously argue that his contributors or supporters exercise to any substantial degree even indirect control over his organizations. Judge Sirica stated that only a democratically organized group with dues-paying members and elected officers would have a legitimate right to sue.[35]

The controversies involving food additives, pesticides, drugs, and other health issues brought about the establishment of the American Council on Science and Health in 1978. It is described as an educational association promoting scientifically balanced evaluation of chemicals and human health. Its executive director, Elizabeth M. Whelan, is associated with the Harvard School of Public Health. Its board of advisors includes distinguished scientists from universities, industry, and professional associations. Although not a lobbying organization, it plans to serve as a voice of national public health policies based on reasonable assessment of benefit and risk. It points out that it is free from financial ties, with interest groups being funded by contributions from individuals, foundations, government, and community agencies.

Federal Government and Domestic Food Programs

With the growth of domestic food assistance programs through food stamps; school lunches; school breakfasts; and the women's, infants', and children's (WIC) programs has also come the growth of citizen and community groups seeking to influence the direction of these programs.

Domestic food programs in 1978 cost an estimated $8,054 million, more than half of the total USDA budget.[36] And no matter what the official name, the federal government operates a Department of *Food* and Agriculture.

Recognizing the rising costs of food stamps and other programs, the Department of Agriculture tried unsuccessfully to limit benefits and expenditures in 1975 and 1976. Although some reform legislation was suggested, the major changes occurred in the Food and Agriculture Act of 1977.

Citizen, consumer, labor, and welfare groups almost unanimously supported the elimination of the purchase requirement for food stamps. When the food stamp program began in 1964, most eligible persons had to spend a certain percentage of their monthly income for stamps to receive the free bonus stamps. Strong arguments were made that many eligible low-income people could not set aside money to buy food stamps, so they did not participate. Strongly supporting the elimination of the purchase requirement and expansion of the food-stamp program to more low-income people were the Children's Foundation, Food Research and Action Center, Community Nutrition Institute, Consumer Federation of America, National Child Nutrition Project, National Urban League, National Council of Senior Citizens, League of Women Voters of the United States, Women's Lobby, American Association of Retired Persons, Migrant Legal Action Program, National Association of Farm Worker Organizations, Almagamated Meat Cutters and Butcher Workers of America, Industrial Union Department of AFL-CIO, and United Automobile, Aerospace, and Agricultural Implement Workers of America.[37]

The National Congress of American Indians and the National Tribal Chairmen's Association called for expanded commodity distribution for Indian tribes since food stamps were too difficult to obtain and adequate retail food stores were often too far away. They wanted tribes to have more control over food programs, more cooperative programs with states and Indian tribes, and full payment of administrative costs by the federal government.[38]

Robert Teets, attorney for the California Rural Legal Assistance Food Law Center, argued against eliminating the purchase requirement. He believed that redefining eligibility for the program was of higher priority, and many low-income people would be eligible for stamps without making a purchase if the current regulations were properly followed. He also argued that illegal aliens should not be excluded from food-stamp eligibility.[39]

In outright opposition to the food-stamp program, the Conservative Caucus called for its elimination. Certain groups also wanted other changes. The National Council of Senior Citizens would like to have stamps mailed to recipients. The National Child Nutrition Project would like to see improved administrative efficiency in state and county offices. They would also favor cash instead of stamps for food assistance, but recognized that Congress is not yet ready to make that move. The Food Research and Action Center proposed that reimbursement to states be reduced by the amount of sales tax charged on food. The Woman's Lobby wants an additional $100 a month deduction in determining eligibility for working mothers. The League of Women Voters opposes the work registration requirement and wants eligibility based on present income—not a past period. The American Association of Retired Persons would prefer cash payments to stamps.

The Migrant Legal Action Program calls for adjustments in deductions to take into account inflation and the rising cost of living. They also favored three-month certification periods for migrant workers. The National Association of Farmworker Organizations called for a national certification process and consideration for the irregularity of migrant workers' incomes and food stamp needs.[40]

Organized labor is sensitive to food-stamp regulations that affect eligibility of persons on strike. The Amalgamated Meat Cutters and Butcher Workers do not favor a thirty-day, retroactive income accounting period for determining eligibility. They also oppose the requirement that the thrifty food plan be used in determining the amount of food stamps distributed. The United Automobile, Aerospace, and Agricultural Implement Workers call for uniform benefits across state lines, use of current income for eligibility, and no eligibility tests that require listing equity of property owned. The Industrial Union Department of AFL-CIO points out that strikers represent only 0.2 percent of food-stamp participants, and their elimination would produce negligible program savings. They have also called for eligibility to be based on current income, not the past thirty days.[41] Organized labor groups point out the need for maintaining high employment since such a policy would eliminate the need for food stamps for many persons.

Although food stamps comprise the biggest federal food program, school lunch programs were the second largest, with an expenditure of $1.8 billion in 1978.[42] In May 1979, the USDA announced that it was allocating $98,000 for a joint campaign with the National Congress of Parents and Teachers to improve and expand child nutrition programs in the schools.[43]

The Courts and Food-Policy Interpretation

The revision of the Food Stamp Act in 1971 redefined the purpose of food stamps from supplementing the food-purchasing power of low-income people to a program "which will permit low-income households to purchase a nutritionally adequate diet through normal channels of trade."[44] The result has been a shift of interpretation and rule making on certain aspects of domestic food programs from the USDA to the courts.

Behind these court decisions lie the feelings, as one judge explained, that "Our duty, in short, is to see that important legislative purposes, heralded in the halls of Congress, are not lost or misdirected in the vast hallways of the federal bureaucracy."[45]

Some court rulings that illustrate the effects on the federal food programs are described:

A group of persons living in the same household in New York, but not all related to one another, brought suit because eligibility for a household to participate in the food-stamp program had been defined as only related individuals. Congress had apparently tried to deny food stamps to "hippy" communes. The court ruled that the purpose of the food-stamp programs was to improve the agricultural economy and to alleviate hunger and malnutrition. The statuatory classification of a household was declared irrelevant and invalid under the equal-protection clause of the Constitution (*Moreno* v. *USDA*).[46]

Migrant farm workers brought suit, challenging the food-stamp regulation permitting consideration of applicants' anticipated income in the certification of eligibility. The Court held that the regulation deprived migrants of statuatory right to obtain a nutritionally adequate diet and that the USDA could not refuse food-stamp assistance on the basis of income actually available (*Gutierriz* v. *Butz*).[47]

Heads of low-income households qualifying for food stamps sued on behalf of low-income tenants of subsidized housing, challenging the instructions of the Secretary of Agriculture requiring that rent subsidies be included as income for food-stamp purposes. The plaintiffs won on the basis that the instructions had not been properly placed in the public record and in view of the impact upon certain food-stamp recipients.[48]

The USDA's use of an economy food plan for setting stamp allotments was challenged on the basis that it did not permit low-income households to purchase a nutritionally adequate diet. Allotments based on the economy food plan were upheld by the U.S. District Court, but later a three-judge appeals court indirectly overruled the U.S. District Court, invalidating the entire allotment schedule for not conforming to the Administrative Procedure Act (*Rodway* v. *USDA*).[49]

Federal court judges have also ruled that the government will have to spend the full amount that Congress appropriated for hot meals for elderly persons,[50] blocked new regulations that would have eventually removed about 1.6 million families from the food-stamp program,[51] and ordered the USDA to nearly double its spending on the special nutrition programs for mothers and infant children.[52]

These cases illustrate the significant role that the courts have taken in administration of food-assistance programs. Citizen and consumer interests are being tested in other cases outside of food assistance.

A suit filed on behalf of nineteen farm workers by a group of attorneys with California Rural Legal Assistance challenges the University of California's research to develop labor-saving harvesting machines that would displace farm workers. Action was still pending in late 1979.[53]

Food-Assistance Lobbying by Membership and Nonmembership Organizations

Each organization that is concerned with food-assistance programs has certain unique characteristics which have brought it into existence and keep it functioning. The major difference which divides them, however, is whether they are true membership organizations or have no members and receive their support from federal grants, foundations, churches, or direct contributions.

The membership organizations involved with food-assistance issues include the American Association of Retired Persons and National Retired Teachers Association; Conservative Caucus; Women's Lobby; League of Women Voters; National Council of Senior Citizens; National Urban League; the National Congress of American Indians; The National Tribal Chairmen's Association; United Automobile, Aerospace, and Agricultural Implement Workers; the Amalgamated Meat Cutters and Butcher Workers of America; and the Industrial Union Department of AFL-CIO. The National Association of Farmer Worker Organizations is really a quasi-membership organization since about 2 percent of its funds come from membership dues.

The membership organizations were established to serve certain needs of the membership. Since part of their membership had needs for, or a desire to participate in, food assistance through the federal programs, the organization established a position and made it known to Congress and federal agencies involved.

However, some of the most active groups involved in food assistance programs are nonmembership organizations. These include the Community Nutrition Institute mentioned earlier, Food Research and Action Center, the Children's Foundation, the National Child Nutrition Project, and the Migrant Legal Action Program. These groups were established by persons who believed there were people who could benefit from food-assistance programs, who needed help, and who usually did not belong to an organized group who could help them directly.

The Children's Foundation was established in 1969 "to give impoverished children and their families a voice in the nationwide effort to eliminate hunger in the United States." The Children's Foundation describes itself as "advocates for a very particular special interest, connecting the capitol with communities, translating needs into national policy, legislation into local programs." Working throughout the country, they serve as a vehicle for community organizations that seek to reform and expand the federal food assistance programs by the USDA's National School Lunch Program; School Breakfast Program; WIC program for malnourished mothers, infants, and young children; Child Care Food Program for children in day care; Summer Food Program; Commodity Supplemental Food Program; and Food-Stamp Program.[54]

The Children's Foundation operates an office in Washington and regional offices in Atlanta, Georgia, Sante Fe, New Mexico, and Pierre, South Dakota. In Washington the national staff monitors and seeks to shape food-assistance legislation, regulations, and policy. They were not listed as registered lobbyists. Barbara Bode has been president of the Children's Foundation since 1972. Previously she had directed the national school lunch organizing campaign for the Children's Foundation and had worked as field director in the South for the National Council on Hunger and Malnutrition. Her academic studies were in history and comparative literature, and she had been a university instructor. She serves on boards of directors of more than a dozen national organizaions active in child welfare, women's issues, and social change. Joan Williams, the deputy director since 1977, formerly executive assistant of the National Welfare Rights Organization, has skills in community organization, administration, and communications.[55]

The Children's Foundation has received funding from twenty-one private foundations and churches and the Community Services Administration (CSA) (HEW). The complete list appears in appendix A. Some examples of these grants are listed in table 5-2; the largest was $600,000 from CSA in 1978-1979. The large number of funding sources suggests that the Children's Foundation has done an effective job in carrying out the projects it has undertaken.

The Food Research and Action Center (FRAC) was organized in 1970 as a nonprofit law firm and advocacy center working with the poor and near-poor to end hunger and malnutrition in the United States. It works primarily with federal food programs. However, in recognizing that hunger and malnutrition are caused primarily by lack of income and are "the tragic symptoms of the maldistribution of economic resources in this country," FRAC began to expand its efforts in 1979, working as an organizing tool for poor people and their allies in the larger effort at creating meaningful social change.[56]

Their work focuses in three areas; representing the poor and near-poor in development and implementation of federal food programs and to protect their rights with litigation and legal support to local legal services offices;

Table 5-2
Grants Received by Children's Foundation

Source, Date	Amount ($)	Purpose
Arca Foundation, 1976	25,000	For cooperative effort in food- and nutrition-related issues with Center for Science in the Public Interest and Food Action Center.
Ford Foundation, 1976	43,735	To study operations in twelve state school food programs.
Goldman Foundation, 1976	40,000	To monitor and implement federal special supplemental food program for women, infants, and children of low income.
New York Foundation, 1975	10,000	To support basic program dealing with problems of hunger and malnutrition.
Rockefeller Brothers Fund, 1976	40,000	For information and technical assistance to groups working to increase availability and adequacy of federal food programs for children.
Rockefeller Foundation, 1976	75,605	For southwestern Food Rights Project to help low-income communities develop community-influenced food delivery systems.
Community Services Administration, Department of Health, Education and Welfare, 1978-1979	600,000	Training and technical assistance under community food and nutrition programs.

Source: *Foundation Grant Support Index*, Community Services Administration.

to help community groups and coalitions work to improve food programs through local organizing and advocacy efforts and to promote the development of organization among recipients and their friends to tackle food and other poverty-related issues; and to develop written materials to help people understand the food programs and national and state legislative issues around the food programs and welfare reform so they can express their views.[57]

Ron Pollock, who was the founder of FRAC, and Roger Schwartz, its present director, were the attorneys who successfully convinced the federal courts to change federal regulations in the *Rodway* v. *USDA* and *Moreno* v. *USDA* cases mentioned. They also were part of the case in 1972 which required the USDA to issue stamps retroactively to eligible households (*Bermudez* v. *USDA*) and in 1974 in the Minnesota case which required the Secretary of Agriculture to step up outreach efforts for the food-stamp program (*Bennett* v. *Butz*).[58] They also convinced federal judges to block changes proposed by the USDA in 1976 that would have reduced the number of food stamp recipients.

In 1979, FRAC came under fire from Congressman Paul Findley, sponsor of pilot workfare project legislation under the food-stamp program, because they were using federal funds in an attempt to scuttle these workfare projects.

The Food Research and Action Center has pioneered the use of the courts and legal assistance to the poor for the purpose of expanding the federal food-assistance programs. Other public service law firms, funded by foundations and Community Services Administration, have also been involved in the outreach program. Some examples of CSA support for this effort are shown in table 5-4.

The National Child Nutrition Project (NCNP) in New Brunswick, New Jersey, was established in 1972 as a nonprofit organization seeking to improve and expand federal food-program operations. Much of its support has come from the CSA and sale of publications to organizations engaged in food assistance programs. The NCNP received $10,000 in 1975 from the Meyer Foundation to complete a Washington metropolitan food stamp campaign.[59]

Its president, Lewis Strauss, served as administrator of the Food and Nutrition Service in the USDA in 1978 and 1979, and Christine Van Lenten also moved from the National Child Nutrition Project to be his special assistant.

The Migrant Legal Action Program, Inc., funded by Legal Services Corporation, provides direct assistance to legal services offices on migrant and seasonal farm worker issues and advocates directly for farm workers on national policy matters. Funding for the program was expected to increase 50 percent in 1979, to about $6.2 million. In 1976, Migrant Legal Action

Program represented farm workers in the case which challenged the anticipated income policy in the food-stamp program mentioned above (*Gutierrez* v. *Butz*). They brought suit because the anticipated income resulted in attributing to migrant households money which they did not have to spend on food. Burton D. Fretz, then employed by California Rural Legal Assistance, worked on this case and later joined Migrant Legal Action Program as their director of legislation. He was listed as their registered lobbyist in 1978.

Migrant Legal Action Program favored elimination of the purchase requirement, issuing of food stamps in the migrant camps, and in areas with concentration of Spanish-speaking recipients called for bilingual outreach staff and written notices concerning granting, denial, reduction, and termination of benefits in both Spanish and English.[60]

The National Association of Farmworker Organizations (NAFO) through its fifty-four member organizations carried out a broad program of assistance to farmworkers in employment services and training, safety and health, housing, minimum wages, child labor and crew leader abuses, insurance, hunger and nutrition, and migrant education. Its major funding for 1977-1978 came from Community Services Administration, which provided $1,500,000 of its $1,630,000 budget, or about 92 percent.[61]

About 43 percent of its expenditures in 1977-1978 went for central and regional staff salaries and travel; 35 percent for direct grants to farm worker organizations; 6 percent for board and task force travel; 6 percent for communications to the field; 5 percent for central and regional office support; and 5 percent for workshop, conference, and training and technical assistance costs.

The organization has come under criticism from Senator Gordon Humphrey (New Hampshire) and the American Farm Bureau Federation because its hotline program was being used to promote a nationwide boycott against United Brands, Inc.[62]

Among the fifty-four member organizations, about twenty are membership organizations in which farm workers are actual members of the organization. The remaining NAFO member organizations are offices in communities which serve the farm worker as a client rather than as a member.

Support for Food-Assistance Efforts by Nonmember Organizations

As reported, some of the most active advocates and legislative activity for federal food programs is carried out by nonmember organizations. Behind the activities and talents of these organizations must come funding from some source. The CSA (in HEW), with a total budget of $597.3 million in the 1978 fiscal year and $542.9 million estimated for the 1979 fiscal year, was a major source of funding for some of these groups. The Community Food and Nutrition Program was allocated $29 million in 1978 and $30 million in 1979.[63]

The programs funded to Washington-based organizations and local community groups were earmarked for nutrition access, nutrition self-help, nutrition education, nutrition crisis relief, and nutrition training, training assistance, and on-site assistance.

Some of the grantees under the CSA Community Food and Nutrition Program appeared before congressional hearings on the food-stamp program, some were legal services organizations involved in litigation on federal food programs, and three of the Washington-based groups were registered as lobbyists.

The three largest grants in the 1978 fiscal year allocations were the Food Research and Action Center, $644,615; the Children's Foundation, $600,000; and the Community Nutrition Institute, for work in three regions totaling $509,683. The National Association of Farmworker Organizations received $134,000 under the Community Food and Nutrition Program.[64] Each of these four groups appeared to testify at hearings on food stamps; FRAC, CNI, and NAFO are registered as lobbyists.

There are thirteen community and regional groups and five national organizations receiving Community Food and Nutrition Program funds from CSA in 1978 that also testified at food-stamp hearings in 1977. These are shown in table 5-3. The CSA also funded eleven legal assistance organizations under its 1978 Community Food and Nutrition Program; their locations and amounts are shown in table 5-4. The largest grant went to California Rural Legal Assistance in which $183,218 was granted for nutrition access, training and technical assistance, and on-site assistance.

The operations of some groups engaged in food outreach and advocacy have brought criticism from members of Congress. During the 1977 hearings, Senator Robert Dole of Kansas commented, "I never felt that we would get around to funding political groups with federal money, even though they might have a consumer division."[65] Congressman William Wampler of Virginia commented during the food-stamp hearings,

Part of the frustration has been many of the organizations, such as those represented by Mr. Kirsch [FRAC], who have frustrated the whole process with lawsuits. We have been unable to implement executive orders and meaningful changes. This clearly is their right. . . . But it might well be that whatever Congress decides to do legislatively will ultimately end up in litigation and frustration and we wili never get any meaningful reform in a program of this type. . . .

Last year, unfortunately, I think we reported a bill that simply put a seal of approval, or put legality on a lot of things that were transpiring that were illegal. There is a great deal of manipulation going on in the food stamp program, some illegal and some legal.[66]

Table 5-3
Community Services Administration Food and Nutrition Program Grantees[a]

Grantee and Organization	City and/or State	1978 Grants ($)
Community Development Program, National Congress of American Indians: Navajo Tribe	Arizona	290,000
Yakima Tribe	Washington	44,000
Nez Perce Nation	Idaho	64,760
Hunger Task Force, Community Council of Greater New York	New York, N.Y.	100,000
Food Law Project, Community Action for Legal Services	New York, N.Y.	176,987
Economic Opportunity Commission of Nassau County, Inc.	Hempstead, N.Y.	55,556
Champlain Valley Office of Economic Opportunity	Burlington, Vt.	26,420
Bread and Law Task Force	Montpelier, Vt.	34,297
Southeastern Vermont Community Action	Bellows Falls, Vt.	23,240
Food Law Center, California Rural Legal Assistance	San Francisco, Calif.	183,218
North Carolina Hunger Coalition	Charlotte, N.C.	59,912
Northeast Washington Rural Resources Development Association	Colville, Wash.	18,328
Georgia Citizens Coalition	Atlanta, Ga.	70,000
National Child Nutrition Project	New Brunswick, N.J.	118,514
Food Research and Action Center	Washington, D.C.	644,615
Children's Foundation	Washington, D.C.	600,000
Community Nutrition Institute	Washington, D.C.	509,683
National Association of Farmworkers Organizations	Washington, D.C.	134,000

Source: Community Services Administration, U.S. Department of Health, Education, and Welfare.

[a]Testifying or submitting statements to House Agriculture Committee or Senate Agriculture Committee subcommittee on nutrition hearings on food stamps, February, March, and April 1977.

Table 5-4

Legal-Assistance Grantees under Community Services Administration Food and Nutrition Program, Fiscal Year 1978

State and Organization	Grant ($)
Maine, Pine Tree Legal Assistance	22,365
New Hampshire, New Hampshire Legal Assistance	41,338
New York, Community Action for Legal Services	176,986
Delaware, Delaware Food Law Center Project	58,100
Virginia State Legal Aid Society	88,920
North Mississippi Rural Legal Assistance	32,000
Illinois Legal Assistance Foundation, Chicago	59,000
Indiana Legal Services Organization of Indianapolis	42,000
Ohio State Legal Services Association, Columbus	66,000
California Rural Legal Assistance, San Francisco	183,218
Alaska Legal Services Corporation, Anchorage	41,750

Source: Community Services Administration, U.S. Department of Health, Education, and Welfare.

Foreign Food Assistance and International Development

Concerns for the needs of people around the world following World War II and the famines and reduced worldwide food supplies in the early 1970s have stimulated interest in helping people in other countries to improve their food supplies and living conditions. A number of these groups are active in Washington, seeking to influence the direction of U.S. food and agricultural policies.

Bread for the World has strongly supported the grain reserve program to stabilize supply and prices as well as legislation to create an international emergency grain reserve for times of famine. It has also supported domestic food-assistance programs for those most in need, favored changes to make U.S. food assistance more effective in aiding developing countries to help themselves produce more food, and sponsored educational efforts to inform people about world hunger problems through regional seminars.

Bread for the World is one of the most respected citizens' groups concerned with hunger problems at home and abroad. Its executive director, Arthur Simon, is a Lutheran minister and a brother of Illinois Congressman Paul Simon. Its board includes leaders of various church denominations, educators, scientists, theologians, business executives, a farmer, and Senator Mark Hatfield of Oregon.

Approximately 84 percent of the organization's income comes from memberships and membership-related contributions. Membership had surpassed 25,000 by mid-1979. Its 1978 operating income was $562,536.[67] Salaries for staff are based on need rather than position, with salaries averaging about $9,600 in 1978. The majority of their work is done by volunteers across the country and by interns and others who serve in the New York and Washington offices. To separate its legislative and lobbying efforts from its educational program, the Bread for the World Education Fund was established. Its total income in 1978 was $103,538.

Supplying people in poor countries with food and other needs, CARE has a major interest in the subsidized exports under Public Law 480. It has called for expanding Title II shipments, which provide commodities for distribution by voluntary relief agencies.

The American Council of Voluntary Agencies for Foreign Service also favors specifying a minimum of 1.5 million tons of grain for distribution by voluntary agencies each year and multiyear programming, which would enable voluntary agencies to plan their efforts with more certainty.

The Interreligious Task Force on U.S. Food Policy favors establishing priority for Public Law 480 shipments to combat hunger and malnutrition and setting up a special title for development projects. The task force also supports policies that would maintain the system of dispersed family farms; more research and extension funding for small and moderate-size farms, environmental and energy problems; revision of the price support system to base benefits on financial need; and raising of price support loans to build reserves.

Church World Service and Lutheran World Relief also urge continued food aid availability under Public Law 480, focusing food aid on the neediest nations, using food aid to meet development objectives, and separating need from political considerations.

Catholic Relief Services and the U.S. Catholic Conference call for designating a specific amount of grains to be distributed by nonprofit, voluntary agencies so they can budget their staff and have some assurance that they will have commodities to distribute. They also favor a multilateral international reserve and domestic grain reserves to stabilize farmers' prices.[68]

The Overseas Development Council (ODC) has been concerned about grain reserves and world food security. It has favored government-held grain reserves and has called for a U.S. policy that would help establish a world food reserve and link food aid with development effort in the poorest countries. It would like to see Title II aid (gifts and donations) expanded, but such aid should not discourage local production in the developing countries. The ODC also favors a three-year commitment for food aid.[69]

The Environmental Fund is concerned about population growth and calls for requiring that a government do something about population growth to receive food aid. Their view is that "to supply food to those who cannot or will not stabilize their populations makes no sense whatever."[70]

The Action Center (previously Food Action Center), a project of the Institute for World Order, was concerned with the use of infant formulas in developing countries rather than encouraging breast feeding. They mounted campaigns against companies producing and marketing infant formulas in developing countries. The Action Center went out of business in 1979, probably because of a lack of funds.

Environmental Concerns and Pesticide Use

The use of pesticides and their effect on the environment have been a significant issue in agricultural and food policy discussions during the 1960s and 1970s. The concerned groups may be large membership organizations, small lobbying groups, or public interest law firms.

The Sierra Club is one of the oldest and largest organizations working to protect and conserve natural resources. It has called for expanded staff in the Environmental Protection Agency to reevaluate all test data and to test both active and inert ingredients in pesticides. It would like to have health and safety information made public. It favors more funds for research and educational efforts in integrated pest management, which would reduce farmers' dependence on "harmful" pesticides.

Friends of the Earth also favors less use of pesticides. To help farmers, it calls for every registered pesticide to be put into an integrated pest-management program. It is concerned about low returns for farmers and high profits for chemical companies who sell pesticides.[71] It has also called for stricter controls and testing, mandatory testing and licensing for homeowners who wish to use restricted pesticides, and upgrading the Food and Drug Administration monitoring program.

The Environmental Defense Fund favors making registration data dealing with health and safety available to the public and supports continued administration of the Federal Insecticide, Fungicide, and Rodenticide Act by the EPA. It has also expressed concern about the EPA issuing conditional registrations for new pesticides which must be reviewed and acted on again at a later time.[72] The National Audubon Society has presented joint testimony with Environmental Defense Fund.

The Rachel Carson Trust for the Living Environment has urged that the EPA straighten out its files, computerize them, and get qualified people to expand and speed up its testing program. It also favors more public release of health and safety data.[73]

Concerns for Conservation and Wildlife

The National Association of Conservation Districts is the most producer-oriented of the conservation groups. It calls for actions to encourage a healthy, vigorous, and prosperous agriculture; for conservationists to be represented on the research users' advisory board; for increased funds for conservation programs on agricultural lands; and for rural fire protection programs.[74]

The Natural Resources Defense Council supports repeal of the export exemption on pesticides so U.S. companies could not sell products abroad which could not be legally used in this country. It would like to see conservation practices tied to target prices and crop support loans. It wants to see forestry incentives incorporated into the price and income support program.

The National Wildlife Federation has a major interest in conservation legislation that helps protect wildlife. It would like to see multiyear set-aside programs, prohibition of haying on set-aside acres, and programs that encourage more forestry plantings. It has been concerned that Agricultural Conservation Program funds finance production-oriented practices at the expense of practices designed to enhance long-term environmental values.[75]

The Wildlife Management Institute has suggested tax credits to encourage landowners to carry out practices that protect wildlife. It supports long-term conservation contracts of ten years or longer.[76]

The Wildlife Society favors greater expenditure to establish conservation areas that would protect and encourage habitats for wildlife. It suggests a total management scheme for our nation's agriculture which includes crop production, soil and water conservation, and wildlife maintenance and enhancement.[77] Some would interpret this proposal as greater government control over land-use and production decisions.

Conservation and Environmental Controversies

The citizens' and special interest groups involved in conservation and environmental issues have created some of the sharpest controversies in food and agricultural legislative efforts. Farmers and ranchers have been annoyed, and at times infuriated, by government regulations that have restricted use of pesticides representing some of the most recent and advanced production technology. Manufacturers of pesticides, investing millions of dollars to develop new products, feel that their property rights are being threatened by proposals to let others decide how much compensation they should receive for sharing their research and test data with others who want to register similar products.

Aerial spraying in forests and public lands is considered a serious environmental hazard by some groups. However, some suspect that the efforts to restrict aerial spraying of herbicides in some Western forest lands come from groups who want to harvest marijuana growing in these areas.

Farm workers claim serious effects from exposure to pesticides used in producing various crops. On the other hand, others believe that the exposure danger to farm workers from spraying pesticides results most frequently from failure to follow the rules on reentry time after spraying and to illegal aliens hiding in the citrus groves when they are sprayed.

The efforts to set aside certain public lands as wilderness areas conflict directly with residents and landowners who want to use public lands for grazing, timber cutting, and mining. The viability of many communities in states with large public land holdings depends on use of some of these natural resources.

Many scientists who once counted themselves friends now consider themselves adversaries of such groups as Natural Resources Defense Council, the Environmental Defense Fund, and Friends of the Earth over differing interpretations of the hazards in recombinant-DNA research. The break developed when the environmental groups sought to have the federal government tighten safety measures that apply to laboratory experiments, while scientists were working to relax the rules.

Some scientists have expressed disillusionment and concluded that "some of the environmental lobbies are in business to peddle paranoia." The environmentalists have been accused of scaring the public needlessly so that the more the public worries about the environment, the more likely it is that people will keep providing them with the funds to keep their organizations growing.[78]

The scope of legislative efforts by conservation and environmental groups is broader than food and agricultural issues. In this section the groups most concerned with use of pesticides in agricultural production, acreage set-aside programs that affect wildlife survival, and other agricultural conservation programs have been identified. Groups concerned with issues dealing with wilderness areas, forest conservation, mining, and mineral development are beyond the scope of this section.

Humane Treatment of Animals

Among citizens' organizations with special interests are a group whose major concerns focus on humane treatment of animals and birds, including domestic animals and poultry used for food. Some are registered lobbyists. Others carry out research and educational efforts, and some testify before congressional committees.

Animal humane groups are philosophically opposed to the killing of animals. Through their efforts, they were able to secure enactment of the Federal Humane Slaughter Law in 1958 and the strengthening of that act passed in 1978. They have also been concerned with what they see as extreme cruelty involved in the predator control activities of the U.S. Fish and Wildlife Service.

The Humane Society of the United States supports humane slaughter methods and wants meat purchased in this country to come from animals that have been slaughtered humanely.

The Society for Animal Protective Legislation has called for increasing the coverage of the Federal Humane Slaughter Act and extending it abroad by providing stronger incentives and strict compliance through daily inspection for meat that will be imported in the United States. They support a requirement that handling of kosher slaughtered animals meet the same humane standards as all other livestock.

The Animal Protection Institute would also like to have the handling of animals before slaughter investigated.

The National Association for Humane Legislation and the Committee for Humane Legislation worked together closely in securing congressional approval for the Humane Methods of Slaughter Act of 1978. The 1958 act affected only meat packing establishments owned by firms which sell meat to federal government agencies such as the Army and Navy. The 1978 act requires that all federally inspected meat be produced from livestock handled and slaughtered in accordance with humane methods named in the 1958 act. Also foreign plants exporting meat products to this country, which also come under the meat inspection provisions, will be required to observe the same humane handling and slaughtering provisions that apply to U.S. plants. The slaughtering methods used in many foreign plants were considered extremely crude and inhumane by those supporting the new act. Congressman George Brown (California), Senator Bob Dole (Kansas), subcommittee chairman of livestock and grains W.R. Poague (Texas), and House Agriculture Committee Chairman Tom Foley were considered especially helpful in moving the bill through to passage. Mrs. Tom Foley, who serves as his legislative assistant, is cited as "actively interested in animal welfare."[79]

The meat packing industry, the USDA, and the Department of State expressed concern that requiring humane slaughter methods by foreign plants might be considered a nontariff barrier and an "exercise of extraterritorial jurisdiction" which could give rise to strong opposition from our trading partners.[80] Yet this provision remained in the bill, and the Secretary of Agriculture later issued regulations to require humane handling and slaughter domestically and in foreign plants which export meat to the United States.[81]

The Society for Animal Protection has also urged its members to protest to the Department of Interior against their "coyote-killing boondoggle known as the Animal Damage Control program." They point out that the $18 million spent in 1978 was not accompanied by any estimate as to whether the expenditure resulted in any significant impact on prevention of livestock losses by predators. They also criticized the Department of Interior for their draft environmental impact statement which did not propose any substitute plan for mass killing of coyotes or encourage livestock owners to care for and protect their own animals. It expresses great concern that "sheep and cattle do not even have to be provided with adequate food and water when they are grazing on public lands."[82] It also claims success in getting an amendment to the appropriations bill for animal health research that will allocate 5 percent of a $20 million fund for discovery and development of better animal birth-control methods.

The Committee for Humane Legislation has been concerned with federal grants to state fish and game commissions under the Pittman Robertson Act. They see the work of state game and fish commissions as favoring "game" animals over "nongame animals." They favor legislation that would take the federal government "out of the hunting-trapping propaganda business," pointing out how federal programs have greatly increased the population of deer and ducks to the detriment of all other wildlife species. The Committee for Humane Legislation and Friends of Animals successfully filed a lawsuit against the Department of Interior to force a study of the detailed environmental consequences of the Pittman Robertson Act. The suit resulted in the preparation of an environmental impact statement of the overall federal program of grants to state fish and wildlife commissions.

Other issues and concerns among humane organizations include hunting and selective slaughter of Alaskan seals, humane methods of slaughtering poultry, methods of euthanasia employed by veterinarians for small animals and pets, production practices in the poultry industry including debeaking, disposing of unwanted chicks when first hatched, and confined rearing in large buildings. Mass production of veal calves in confined conditions has also been studied and criticized because of the close confinement and the forced feeding of the calves on rations that they believe makes them anemic.[83] Promoting of vegetarianism is considered a means of promoting humaneness and reducing the number of animals used for food.[84]

Rural Development and Rural Living

The organizations concerned with improving rural communities and rural living comprise a large number of national, state, and local groups. Through a network of publications, newsletters, and personal contacts at national conferences they are working for passage of legislation and changes in regulations in federal agencies, which they hope will improve the living conditions for rural citizens of this country—particularly those with low incomes and limited economic opportunities.

A few register as lobbyists; most do not since they do not believe that the present law requires them to. They receive only part or none of their funding from membership dues. Most are funded from federal agency grants for carrying out projects established by law, from foundation grants, and from churches and individual contributions. Some see their major role as a clearinghouse for information that will be used by state and local groups in their community activities and in contacts with members of Congress and federal agencies. Lobbying and legislative activity is a more significant part of the activities of some groups. Others see their main role as working with lower-income people in rural areas to improve their incomes and living conditions.

With limited membership or constituency and limited and uncertain funding, and being relatively new, many of these organizations support and assist one another in various ways. This network of assistance and mutual help through newsletters and publications, joint testimony and writing efforts, coalitions to support legislation, and service on committees and boards is illustrated in appendix D.

Rural America emerged out of a 1975 conference on rural America in Washington sponsored by a large number of rural electric cooperatives, labor unions, churches, and rural-oriented groups. Additional funding was also received from the Clark Foundation and the Winthrop Rockefeller Charitable Trust. In 1977, Rural America merged with the Rural Housing Alliance, formed in 1966. With a membership of 2,315 in mid-1979, the receipts from membership and dues comprised about 1.2 percent of the total receipts for June 1978 to June 1979. Most of the $6.8 million funding came from the Department of Labor and CSA. Detailed funding is shown in appendix A.[85]

About three-fourths of the funds received were paid out in grants to local groups for farm worker housing, farm worker job training, and monitoring community development block grants. About one-fourth of the funds received were spent by the national office for general administration, training, and assistance under the grant programs, publications, and membership services. During 1979, the Department of Labor attempted to terminate Rural America's participation in its farm worker housing program. A compromise was worked out which shifted Rural America's role to training and technical assistance to rural housing agencies.

From January 1978 through May 1979, staff members of Rural America testified before eighteen congressional committee hearings dealing with the consumer cooperative bank, community health centers, extension of the Older Americans Act, authorizations for Farmers Home Administration, Comprehensive Employment Training Act (CETA) reauthorizations, enforcement of the 1902 Reclamation Act, farmer-to-consumer direct marketing, rural development research, rural transportation, foreign ownership of U.S. farmland, urban policy community development, farm worker housing, housing program and rural development authorizations.

Rural America's staff of eight has concentrated on action-oriented research, technical assistance, and training and information dissemination. Research is action- and policy-oriented to document needs and assess adequacy of governmental responses. It has worked for the implementation of the Reclamation Act of 1902 and supported the Family Farm Development Act.

Four national conferences were held between 1975 and 1979 in which rural advocates from all over the country shared information and mapped strategies on a variety of topics. At the 1979 "Taking Charge" conference, briefing, advocacy, strategy, and discussion sessions included the Family Farm Development Act, Agricultural Land Protection Act, Family Farm Anti-Trust Act, reclamation law in federal irrigation projects, minority access to farmland, rural housing appropriations, farm labor housing, cooperative housing between Department of Housing and Urban Development and Farmers Home Administration, rural development initiatives, community development block grant reform, Community Reinvestment Act, health planning, prepaid health plans and health maintenance organizations, national health insurance, occupational and environmental health, alternative energy for small farms, federal food programs, limited-resource farmer programs, small farm research, farmland ownership research, federal water policy, reclamation law enforcement, Forest Service policies, strip-mining regulations, self-help housing, energy alternatives for low-income rural housing, consumer cooperative bank, rural transportation, impact assistance for rural commmunities, land trusts and cooperative ownership, and labor organizing in the rural United States.

The conference included small group meetings with staff members of congressional committees, members of Congress, and federal agencies engaged in administering various rural-oriented programs of interest to conference participants.

Member organizations and the 1979 Rural America conference participants cover a broad range of specific interests and objectives. These include advocacy or high interest in small farms and development of "appropriate technology," organic farming and gardening, solar energy, land reform and land redistribution, land for minority groups, legal assistance to the rural poor, rural electrification, improved rural housing, domestic and international food assistance, rural churches, and improved rural health care. Discussion sessions revealed some sentiment against nuclear power, agribusiness corporations, the USDA, and the land-grant colleges and universities.

The forty-three-member board of directors includes nationwide representation of persons concerned with the development and progress of rural communities, consumer affairs, rural housing, education, and advocacy. The chairman of the board since January 1979 is George Ballis, also coordinator of the National Land for People, Fresno, California.

The National Rural Center (NRC) was established in 1976 as a private, nonprofit organization with Ray Marshall as president. Marshall was later appointed Secretary of Labor by President Carter. The NRC was the outgrowth of a task force on southern rural development formed in 1974 whose members represented Southern corporate, academic, government, and racial leaders. The task force, funded from the Rockefeller Brothers Fund, the Ford, and Edna McConnell Clark Foundations, produced policy recommendations in several areas including energy, agriculture, education, health, credit, manpower, and community development.

The National Rural Center's primary concerns are in the areas of employment, agriculture, health, education, economic development, and law. It deals with these fields by monitoring and evaluating federal programs, recommending new federal procedures, supporting a national network of local rural development groups, and providing up-to-date, reliable information on rural affairs to policymakers in Washington.[86]

In 1978 and 1979 it sponsored a series of conferences on small farms in cooperation with the USDA and the land-grant colleges and universities. A consortium of federal agencies funds the Center's Rural Information Outreach Service.

Network, a Catholic social justice lobby, has nationwide membership and is organized by states and congressional districts. It selects issues for its efforts through a referendum of members at the beginning of each Congress. The staff then develops position papers and distributes them through its publications or at testimony before public hearings.

Food policy, both international and domestic, is a high priority with its membership. It has supported legislation that addresses immediate hunger needs as well as opposing policies and trade patterns that "foster inequity to the detriment of the poor." To alleviate hunger and malnutrition, Network believes that basic structures of food production, processing, and distribution will need to be changed. They called upon the Presidential Commission on World Hunger to investigate how U.S. food aid, technology transfers, and trade policies "often create dependency, hinder economic development within the Third-World Countries and benefit the already wealthy."

The specific issues that they feel should be addressed include land ownership patterns to determine the extent of ownership by large corporations and foreign investors, policies to discourage the trend toward concentrated land ownership, determination of farm size beyond which there is little or no justification for policies which encourage or subsidize growth, enforcement of the Reclamation Law of 1902, promotion of the acquisition of land by young and/or beginning farmers, challenging tax laws that encourage farm investment by nonfarmers, encouraging tax code changes to zone agricultural land for agricultural use, assessing land according to its ability to produce agricultural revenue, encouraging consumer education of marketing costs, developing direct farmer-to-consumer marketing, encouraging sound conservation practices, calling land-grant colleges to "accountability" regarding research for small farmers and organic farming methods, focusing federal research on needs of small and moderate-size family farms (including ways of reversing decline in number of farms, "appropriate technology," and organic methods), and investigating approaches to decentralized food production and distribution such as community gardens and direct marketing.[87]

The Center for Rural Affairs at Walthill, Nebraska, was established as a result of efforts by the Goldenrod Hills Community Action Council. Its work has focused on improving life and living conditions through demonstrations and educational programs on small farms and rural communities in Nebraska. Along with other small farm advocates, it supported an amendment to the Agricultural Credit Act of 1978 to allocate 25 percent of the funds for farm ownership and operating loans for low-income, limited-resource borrowers. Through its newsletter, it provides information and support on small farm issues such as enforcement of the Reclamation Act of 1902, legal services to low-income farmers, and credit for limited-resource farmers.

In October 1978, through grants from the Campaign for Human Development of the U.S. Catholic Conference and the Shalan Foundation, it began a small farm advocacy project. The project will challenge small farm discrimination as found in federal and state agencies and publicly supported private organizations and will also include a smaller national effort aimed at strengthening federally financed Legal Services Corporation projects to deal with small farm issues. Since Legal Services Corporation is in the process of expanding into rural areas, they believe its local offices can provide valuable legal assistance to small farmers.[88]

National Land for People (NLP) has been described as a consumer-farmer land reform organization that undertakes legal battles and consumer education in its work to achieve "democratic land control." Its major concern has been the Land Reclamation Act of 1902, which limits ownership to 160 acres of federally irrigated land.

Their philosophy is expressed in this statement from their brochure: "Our land is the source of our wealth, the sustenance of our lives. How our land is controlled and manipulated determines the character of our society. If land control is widespread among the populace, democracy tends to flourish. With land held narrowly, freedom withers."[89]

A major victory for the NLP came in August 1976 when the U.S. District

Court for the District of Columbia in *National Land for People* v. *Bureau of Reclamation et al.* ordered the Department of Interior to initiate rule-making proceedings with respect to the criteria and procedures to be used in approving sales of excess lands under the 1902 reclamation law. In August 1977 the U.S. Ninth Circuit Court of Appeals ruled that the 160-acre limitation of the Reclamation Act of 1902 applied to the irrigated farms of California's Imperial Valley—lands that were previously considered exempt.

The Bureau of Reclamation responded with proposed rules and regulations to strictly enforce the 1902 law. The presumed economic and social consequences of putting the proposed rules into effect after seventy-six years of benign neglect were considered so large that a court-ordered environmental impact statement was required before enforcement. So several years will elapse before strict enforcement could occur.[90]

In 1979 bills requiring changes in the 1902 law were introduced. One bill backed by National Land for People, the Reclamation Lands Opportunity Act, places a maximum acreage of 640 acres on farms receiving water from federal projects, calls for a lottery to transfer excess lands, and required owners to live within fifteen miles of the farm. Another bill backed by most current owners and operators would update the law to conform to current farming practices and require few changes in current ownership and operating procedures.

One of the crucial issues in this debate over federal land reclamation policy is what constitutes an economical size unit. National Land for People claims that 160 acres can be a viable unit. But the issue is very complex, depending on the location, type of crop grown, and costs encountered.

Research done by the University of California at Davis shows that the typical crop mix of sugar beets, tomatoes, barley, and alfalfa required about 600 to 800 acres to compete with much larger farms on a unit cost and profit basis. Farms with more than 200 acres were required to break even. In the Westlands district lowest costs were achieved at around 800 to 1,000 acres.[91]

The Bureau of Reclamation in its environment assessment commented on the lottery system of selecting new owners: "The lottery could cause various economic impacts by selecting purchasers who lack sufficient assets, financing, and experience to farm successfully. Failure to organize the excess lands into economically viable units, to establish adequate criteria for eligible purchasers and to provide adequate financing and managerial training, could result in severe hardship to the new family farmers."[92]

The debate over enforcement of the Reclamation Act of 1902 is viewed by some as the first step in a land reform movement and a campaign to redistribute land from the large holder to those who have little or no land. So the outcome of the debate over water in California and other federally funded water projects will be watched closely. Others see the National

Family Farm Development Act as another beginning for land reform "that will make it impossible for our country's agriculture to be dominated by a few."[93]

George Ballis, one of the founders and the coordinator of National Land for People, is described as a farmer, holds the B.A. degree in political science and journalism from the University of Minnesota, served in the U.S. Marine Corps in World War II, and is a professional photographer. He was editor of the *Valley Labor Citizen*, a Fresno-area labor council newspaper, and a field director for the Student Nonviolent Coordinating Committee during late 1950s and 1960s.[94]

Jessie de la Cruz, described as a farm worker turned farmer, is the treasurer of National Land for People. She was a former board member of Rural America, a former migrant worker, and organizer for the United Farm Workers under Caesar Chavez. Her family owns one-fourth interest in 40 acres of land in the Fresno area.[95]

Berge Bulbulian, often referred to as president of National Land for People, was also chairman of the board of the California Rural Legal Assistance Corporation, a public assistance law firm funded by Legal Services Corporation and CSA.

The National Land for People Foundation was established as a non-profit, tax-deductible organization under section 501(c)(3) of the IRS code to receive grants and contributions that are tax-deductible. Contributions made for its lobbying efforts are not tax-deductible, placing NLP under section 501(c)(4) status under the IRS code.

National Land for People believes that the legal basis for their cause has been strongly supported by the National Farmers Union and the AFL-CIO. Key coordination work has been done in Washington by Henry Hyde at Rural America who helped organize a water-land-people clearinghouse.[96]

The Stern fund, an early supporter, made a second grant to help NLP monitor the law, to help small farmers and cooperative groups acquire land and operate successfully with appropriate marketing arrangements, and to carry out educational efforts to influence national and agricultural policy.[97]

On the other hand, the American Farm Bureau Federation has objected to the 1902 law, pointing out that water is the most critical factor and the U.S. economy is dependent on the ability of the U.S. farmer to maintain his productive capability. They see arguments favoring the 1902 law based on social philosophy rather than on economics.[98]

California Westside Farmers, which represents farmers in the reclamation project areas along the west side of the San Joaquin Valley, points out that the efforts to enforce the 160-acre limitation would cause dislocation of established farms and constitute unjust seizure of property. They believe the proposed system of small farms would have extremely unlikely chance of success in the Westlands area. They see the public advocate groups, such as

National Land for People, California Rural Legal Assistance, and others, mounting a massive lobbying campaign which has challenged the basic property rights of the people whose taxes pay for the antipoverty programs.[99] Westlands farmers and others farming in federal water projects in seventeen states formed the Farm-Water Alliance, a coalition lobbying to revise the Reclamation Act of 1902 so it is workable under present conditions.

California Rural Legal Assistance (CRLA), although operating primarily in California, has become involved in activities that affect national food and agricultural policy decisions. Operating with a grant of $2,584,564 from Legal Services Administration and $183,218 from CSA in fiscal year 1978, it would appear to be the largest public interest law firm funded to serve rural clients.[100]

The Food Law Center of CRLA is involved with federal food programs. Robert M. Teets, Jr., who testified on food-stamp revisions before the House and Senate in 1977, was involved in the California case in which food-stamp applicants were not required to list federal housing rent subsidies as income because the Secretary of Agriculture had not given proper public notice (*Anderson* v. *Butz*).[101]

In 1977 and 1978 CRLA attorneys testified at hearings before the Department of Interior and congressional committees reviewing proposed enforcement of the Reclamation Act of 1902. They supported enforcement of the 1902 law. A CSA grant of $155,590 in 1977 for reclamation legal and policy research was not renewed in fiscal year 1978 because the unit "did not have the highest likelihood of providing new solutions to the problems of poverty."[102]

In 1979 two issues of major concern to CRLA's clients were agricultural mechanization and misuse of agricultural chemicals. In January, CRLA filed a suit against the University of California, contesting how agricultural research decisions are made as well as whether their end results were intended by Congress in establishing land-grant colleges. The suit was brought on behalf of the California Agrarian Action Project and individual farm workers. It contends that a handful of agribusiness interests largely determine the research priorities of the university. However, university officials have strongly denied these allegations.

The CRLA's pesticides efforts involve representing a coalition of farmworkers, consumers, environmentalists, and others in several states in a concerted attempt to halt the use of the controversial pesticide DBCP. (Competent scientists have refuted criticism against it.) They petitioned the Environmental Protection Agency, seeking to ban DBCP for use nationally. They also have attempted to get a complete ban on 2, 4, 5-T used as a herbicide on rice, in forest defoliation, and other crops.

The CRLA took a key role in the review of the use of all agricultural chemicals used in California—one of the most comprehensive analyses of chemical use ever undertaken by government. The CRLA is part of a labor-consumer-environmental coalition that is trying to keep the findings and proposals of the report intact. A comprehensive plan was to be submitted to the California legislature by late 1979.[103]

In 1979, Ralph S. Abascal, general counsel for California Rural Legal Assistance, was elected chairman of the National Agricultural Research and Extension Users Advisory Board, established under the Food and Agriculture Act of 1977. The board, appointed by the Secretary of Agriculture, will make annual recommendations concerning the USDA's research, extension, and teaching activities to the Secretary of Agriculture, the President, and appropriate congressional committees.[104] The board elects its own chairman.

Abascal received the B.S. degree from San Jose State College, the MBA from the University of California at Berkeley, and a J.D. from Hastings College of Law, University of California, San Francisco. He has served as counsel or cocounsel in over 100 poverty law cases involving farm labor, voting rights, civil rights, environmental quality, student rights, food, health, housing, and income maintenance in state and federal courts. He also served on the board or advisory committees of the Center on Social Welfare Policy and Law in New York; National Health and Environmental Law Program, University of California, Los Angeles; Legal Action Support Project, Bureau of Social Science Research; Children's Foundation; and the American Civil Liberties Union of Northern California.[105]

Information, Coordinating, and Advocacy Groups

Behind the direct lobbying and legislative efforts, as well as the implementation of foundation and federal agency grants to conduct various activities to improve the lives and living conditions of rural people, are several organizations which provide information, serve as a clearinghouse for information, publish reports and newsletters, and generally support the network of citizens and rural community groups across the country.

The Conference on Alternative State and Local Policies has focused on a broad range of state and local policy issues including food and agriculture. It sponsors conferences and prepares publications. It has recently become engaged with public-policy issues arising in agriculture and land use. Reflecting the interest of its membership of state and local officials and activists, it is analyzing these issues and suggesting policies accessible to state and local governments that will promote support for the family farm, preservation of farmland, conservation of energy and natural resources, development of urban and consumer food policies, access to agricultural land for minorities, and support for low-income farmers.

The Center for Community Change also monitors federal policies and programs, helps urban and rural community groups find governmental financial aid, and provides consultant services. It sponsored the Agribusiness Accountability Project in 1970. The publication of *Hard Tomatoes, Hard Times* in 1972 stimulated discussion on the mission and role of the land-grant universities.[106]

When the Agribusiness Accountability Project phased out, Jim Hightower, its director, went to work for Senator Fred Harris, who ran for President in 1976. Later he became editor of the *Texas Observer* and was elected to the Board of Rural America in 1979. Susan Seckler, one of the research staff, worked for a time with other Washington-based groups. In 1977, she became an assistant to Howard Hjort, director of economics, policy analysis, and budget in the U.S. Department of Agriculture. In 1979, she became Deputy to Hjort and coordinated the regional dialogue meetings on farm structure and farm policy. Susan De Marco, project research director, continued as a writer and became a consultant to the Extension Evaluation Project in the USDA in 1978. Al Krebs, another research staff member, moved to San Francisco and continued to operate Agribusiness Accountability publications affiliated with the Center for Rural Studies.

Earthwork, a project of the Center for Rural Studies in San Franciso, is involved in organizing and education on land and food issues. They work with individuals, groups, and coalitions to expand awareness and understanding of social, economic, and political issues related to food and land, and to develop and strengthen cooperatives to organize the production and distribution of food.

Earthwork efforts are aimed at making the food system work for the benefit of farmers, food-industry workers, and consumers. They are involved with direct marketing programs, farm-worker and urban-consumer cooperatives, farmers' markets, and food-buying clubs. They also develop materials and programs related to land, food, and nutrition issues. The National Coalition for Land Reform, associated with the center, is no longer active.

The *Institute for Food and Development Policy* (IFDP) is the creation of two people, Joe Collins and Frances Moore Lappe, who have written about the problems of food production and hunger in developing countries. Through publications and books the IFDP seeks to stimulate discussion of food and hunger issues in developing countries and the economic and political causes of such problems. Their writings strongly criticize many of the established institutions engaged in production and marketing of foodstuffs, but they have few positive alternative policies to propose that would remedy the problems that they describe.

Lappe and Collins strongly criticize U.S. foreign aid and multinational corporations engaged in export crop production in developing countries, suggest that Cuba's government control of agricultural production and exports is an appropriate way to solve hunger and food problems, and advocate land reform in the United States, including a ceiling on the amount of land one person or family could hold.[107]

The National Family Farm Coalition and the National Family Farm Education Project have coordinated efforts to gain support for the Family Farm Development Act, first introduced in 1978 by Congressmen Richard Nolan of Minnesota and George Brown of California. In 1979, efforts were made to rewrite the bill and muster grass-roots support, but with limited success. The date for introduction was delayed until 1980 because the interested groups could not agree on a section dealing with farm price support policy.

The revised bill (H.R. 6295) included tax amendments to promote family farms and limit corporation farming, creation of a family Farm Development Service in the USDA, a family farm preservation program that would involve government purchase of farmland for distribution to small or limited-resource family farmers, farmer direct-marketing programs, research for small farms, farm demonstration and training centers for new farmers, a food price review board to "oversee increases in food prices," and low-income family farmers' legal advocacy program.[108] Part of their strategy was to get the bill introduced and then amend other bills going through Congress with pieces of the Family Farm Development Act.

Catherine Lerza, one of the coalition coordinators, was previously associated with Rural America and was a writer for the Food Day activities of the Center for Science in the Public Interest. Robin Rosenbluth, a native of New York, had previously worked with rural community organizations in North Carolina.

National Catholic Rural Life Conference through its monthly magazine, *Catholic Rural Life*, provides continuing reports, analysis, and presentation of issues of concern to farmers and rural citizens. Articles are staff-written or contributed by others working in policy education, consulting, or implementation of rural community development programs. Its editorial consultant, Roger Blobaum, a graduate of Iowa State University in agricultural communications, operates an agricultural consulting service with offices in Des Moines, Iowa, and Washington, D.C. He has also worked with the National Farmers Organization, National Farmers Union, the Center for Rural Affairs; he serves on the board of Rural America.

World Hunger Year was founded by Harry Chapin and Bill Ayers. Chapin was instrumental in encouraging President Carter to establish the President's Commission on World Hunger in 1977 and was appointed to the commission. They publish *Food Monitor* with editorial consultation and participation from the Institute for Food and Development Policy. It carries articles relating to the concerns and interests of various food, hunger, and rural-oriented advocate groups.

Observations and Conclusions

The citizen, consumer, and specific-interest groups are formed because they have an interest or concern about a particular issue or groups of related issues. The producer and business and industry groups discussed earlier also have specific interests and concerns, but the organization's membership is usually comprised of persons with the same common occupational interest. The "public" interest group's membership or support may come from persons of many occupations.

Membership

Some citizens' and consumer-oriented groups get support from membership dues and business activities. Many are funded primarily by foundation and federal agency grants. Leaders and directors of these groups may be elected by members in some cases, but in some organizations they are appointed by a board of directors or self-appointed as a result of their initiative to establish and organize a specific interest group.

Without membership or with limited membership participation, the policies and positions of these groups are decided by its directors and staff. To what extent they really represent a clientele or constituency is open to question. However, the same can be said for some membership organizations.

Funding and Survival

Funding can become a problem for some groups as grants expire and replacement funds must be found. Part of the organization leader's time must be spent looking for new funding, or else the group will eventually go out of business. The length of life for some of the "public interest" groups is more uncertain than for other organizations because of irregular funding, mobility of the younger staff members, and the realignment of coalitions. Many of these groups have not reached the stage of being an institution like most of the producer, business, industry, and professional organizations.

Networking and Mutual Support

The citizens' and consumers' groups provide more mutual support, publicity for, and promotion of one another's activities than the producer, business, and professional groups. The evidence of such networking activity shows up through newsletters, reports with listing of other organizations and groups for further information, contributions of articles to periodicals and newsletters, persons from one organization serving on the board of another and serving on committees for annual meetings and programs. The networking system is highly developed as a means of gathering strength and support for advancing and advocating certain issues in which these groups have strong interests and concerns. See appendix C.

Grain reserves have become an important issue for groups concerned with food prices, food supplies, and distribution to low-income people at home and overseas. The usual reason for advocating grain reserves, whether held by farmers or by government, is to stabilize prices. The rationale usually given is that stable prices for grains will mean stable prices of food and continued adequate supplies for consumers at home and abroad.

However, if production is to be increased in times of need, higher prices, which will give producers an incentive to expand output, are needed. In times of surplus, a lower price will discourage production by some producers. A central issue remains as to what extent the market, with prices moving up and down, can accomplish desired production compared with government-held or -controlled reserves, which can be held off or released to the market, to influence prices and "stabilize them."

The farmer-held grain reserve system provided in the 1977 Food and Agriculture Act was a compromise between the advocates of completely free markets and complete government control. The system works best when it is not called to function under conditions of extreme shortage or surplus. The market prices in 1978 and 1979 induced only part of the wheat and feed grain producers to participate in the set-aside programs and to use the government-sponsored grain reserve. In these two years, the grain reserve provided a means for some farmers to hold crops off the market when prices were low and provided government a means to encourage farmers to release some reserve stocks onto the market during times of rising demand and prices.

So it seems appropriate to assess the objectives and motives of organizations that advocate grain reserves and stable prices, as well as the probable consequences for consumers, handlers, processors, and producers, and the incentive to continue production in future years.

Federal Funding

A major concern or issue among farm producers and industry groups is to what extent the citizen, consumer, and "public interest" groups, financed in part or largely with federal funds, should be permitted to lobby or carry on legislative and advocacy work that seeks more funding or expansion of their programs.

These "public interest" groups include Community Nutrition Institute, National Consumers League, Consumer Federation of America, Children's Foundation, Food Research and Action Center, National Child Nutrition Project, Migrant Legal Action Program, National Association of Farm Worker Organizations, California Rural Legal Assistance, National Council of Senior Citizens, Legal Services Corporation, Rural America, National Rural Center, and the Center for Rural Affairs. One may raise the question as to what extent such lobbying or legislative activity involves a conflict of interest and whether such activity should be permitted.

Restricting the use of pesticides has created major conflicts between the Environmental Protection Agency, environmental groups, agricultural producers, and the manufacturers and distributors of pesticides. What is really involved is whether new technology should be restricted, as well as the environmental effects if the use of the product is permitted. Farmers may actually benefit from a restriction of new technology if food supplies become limited.

Consumers, unaware of the effects of restricting new technology, would face increased food costs since limits on new technology would result in decreasing food supplies per person as population growth continues.

Restricting exports of pesticides that are not permitted to be used in this country seems to be a fair and considerate policy. However, such restriction, in effect, is requiring the governments of other countries to accept U.S. pesticide policy decisions rather than permitting them to make their own.

The academic and technical qualifications of the persons advocating positions on agricultural, consumer, and environmental issues and representing these groups are difficult to assess. Persons highly trained in one field may not be qualified to thoroughly evaluate various policy choices and the consequences of each. They may be advocating certain proposals dealing with food and agriculture, yet lack the technical knowledge to understand the consequences of the policies they advocate. They may not be trained in economics, yet they may advocate policies that would radically change the present economic system of land holding, production methods, and technology, or the marketing and distribution of food. The policies favored by some groups could lead to a replacement of the free-enterprise capitalist system with a centrally planned, socialist system of agriculture.

Many dedicated and well-meaning persons are associated with groups that want to help the small farmer, low-income persons, and the hungry. But they advocate policies that could weaken or destroy the system which has generated the productive agriculture that has made food surpluses possible to help low-income persons both in this country and overseas.

Many of the complaints and proposals of the public interest groups exhibit a complete lack of understanding of economics and the roles played by land, labor, capital, and management. They are critical of business and in-dustry when they do not understand the contribution of capital investment in plants and factories and the required return for this investment.

Goals and Consequences

The stated goals of these organizations, as presented in the literature and the policies that they advocate, appear to be worthy of support by many citizens. However, what may appear to be worthy of support may need further analysis to determine what the means of reaching these goals would be. Some of the proposed policies involve changes within the present system of private enterprise, private ownership of land, and a market system that establishes prices and allocates production resources and distributes goods and services.

Other policies could lead to major changes in our present system of private land holding, individual, corporate, and cooperative enterprises that provide inputs to farmers and process and distribute food products after they leave the farm. An enlightened and concerned citizen will examine organizations and their goals carefully before joining and providing financial support. United States citizens have a free choice of what groups they join and support, but they will also want to know whether this group really advocates policies which could lead to progressive change or a major revolution. Such caution is also encouraged by William Simon in *A Time for Truth*:

> What then are the real purposes of the various public interest groups? One discovers them readily enough if one identifies, not the fictitious entities for which they pretend to speak, but the actual groups which are their targets and which they seek to control through the power of the state. In practice, the target of the "consumer" movement is *business*, the target of the environmentalists is *business*, and the target of the "minorities," at least where employment is concerned, is *business*. In sum, the Public Interest movement is a lobby, not for the people, but for expanding policy powers of the state over the American producers. There have been few more consistently and vehemently anti-capitalist groups in the history of America.[109]

Notes

1. For a detailed description of public interest groups see Jeffrey M. Berry, *Lobbying for the People, The Political Behavior of Public Interest Groups* (Princeton, N.J.: Princeton University Press, 1977). Reprinted by permission of Princeton University Press.

2. Ibid., p. 27.

3. Ibid., pp. 47-48.

4. "New Lobbying Rules for 580(c)(3) Tax Exempt Organizations," *Economic Development Law Project Report*, Vol. 7, Issue 3, National Economic Development Law Project, Earl Warren Legal Institute, Berkeley, Calif., May/June 1977, p. 1.

5. U.S. Senate Committee on Agriculture, Nutrition, and Forestry hearings, *General Farm and Food Legislation*, March 14, 1977, pp. 885-897.

6. Ibid., Appendix, Book 2, pp. 641-645.

7. R.G.F. Spitze, "The Food and Agriculture Act of 1977: Issues and Decisions," *American Journal of Agricultural Economics* 60, 2 (May 1978): 225-235.

8. "1978 Policy Resolutions," Consumers Federation of America, pp. 21-25.

9. "CFA Celebrates Its 10th Anniversary," Consumer Federation of America, 1978, p. 21.

10. Walterene Swanston, "Washington Pressures: Consumer Federation of America Waging Spirited Battle for Survival," *National Journal*, July 8, 1972, pp. 1126-1136.

11. U.S. Senate Committee on Agriculture, Nutrition, and Forestry hearings, *Nomination of Carol Tucker Foreman*, March 15, 16, 21, 1977, p. 78.

12. Ibid., p. 65.

13. Ibid., p. 78.

14. Swanston, "Washington Pressures," p. 1127.

15. U.S. Senate Agriculture Committee hearings, *Nomination of Carol Tucker Foreman*, p. 67.

16. Ibid., p. 67.

17. Swanston, "Washington Pressures," p. 1127. Board members for 1979-1980 are listed in appendix A.

18. Ibid., p. 1132.

19. Joe Belden, "Toward a National Food Policy," Washington, D.C., Exploratory Project for Economic Alternatives, 1976, pp. iii-vii.

20. U.S. Senate Agriculture Committee hearings, *General Farm and Food Legislation*, pp. 903-909.

21. Ibid., pp. 215-222.

22. Ibid., pp. 887-888.

23. Ibid., Book 2, Appendix, p. 647.

24. U.S. Congress, Joint Economic Committee hearings, *Consumers Opposed to Inflation in the Necessities, There are Alternatives—A Program for Controlling Inflation in the Necessities of Life*, June 29, 1979.

25. U.S. House Committee on Agriculture hearings, *General Farm Bill*, March 3, 1977, pp. 224-225.

26. Ibid., pp. 226-228.

27. U.S. Senate Select Committee on Small Business hearings, *Food Additives*, January 13-14, 1977, p. 454.

28. U.S. Senate Subcommittee on Agricultural Research and General Legislation hearings, *Food Safety and Quality: Nitrites*, September 15, 1978, pp. 103-119.

29. Ibid., pp. 5-28.

30. Ibid., pp. 77-78, 224-225.

31. Ibid., pp. 80-81, 225-228.

32. Thomas B. Smith, "Nitrite, Why the Debate?" Community Nutrition Institute, February 1979.

33. U.S. Senate Subcommittee on Agricultural Research and General Legislation hearings, *Food Safety and Quality: Nitrites*, p. 257.

34. "Valuable Gadfly," *Time*, November 20, 1978, p. 71.

35. "Nader Groups Denied Class Action Standing," *Community Nutrition Institute Newsletter*, April 1979.

36. *National Food Review*, U.S. Department of Agriculture, Winter 1979, p. 9.

37. U.S. Senate Agriculture Committee hearings, *General Farm and Food Legislation*; U.S. House of Representatives hearings, *Food Stamp Program*, March 21, 22, 23, 24, 25, April 5, 1977.

38. U.S. Senate Subcommittee on Nutrition hearings, *Food Stamps*, March 25, 1977, pp. 2-8; U.S. House of Representatives hearings, *Food Stamp Program*, pp. 829-836.

39. U.S. Senate Subcommittee on Nutrition hearings, *Food Stamps*, pp. 50-54; U.S. House of Representatives hearings, *Food Stamp Program*, pp. 637-641.

40. U.S. House of Representatives hearings, *Food Stamp Program*, pp. 222-229.

41. U.S. House of Representatives hearings, *Food Stamp Program*, pp. 188-195, 196-202, 601-606.

42. *National Food Review*, U.S. Department of Agriculture, Winter 1979, p. 9.

43. *News*, U.S. Department of Agriculture, May 22, 1979.

44. "A Crisis of Coupons: An Evaluation of the Food Stamp Program," *Connecticut Law Review* 8, 4 (Summer 1976):660.

45. Judge Skelly Wright, in *Calvert Cliffs' Coordinating Committee, Inc.* v. *Atomic Energy Commission*, 449 F.2d 1109 (D.C. Cir. 1971), reported by Karen Orren, "Standing to Sue: Interest Group Conflicts in the Federal Courts," *American Political Science Review* 70 (1976): 723-741.

46. *Moreno* v. *United States Department of Agriculture*, 345 F. Supp. 310.

47. *Guttierriz* v. *Earl L. Butz*, District Court, District of Columbia 1976, 415 F. Supp. 827.

48. *Anderson* v. *Earl Butz*, U.S. Court of Appeals, Ninth Circuit, 428 F. Supp. 245.

49. *Rodway* v. *United States Department of Agriculture*, 514 F. 2d 809, 822, n. 24 (D.C. Cir. 1975).

50. *The New York Times*, May 19, 1976, p. 57.

51. Ibid., May 29, 1976, p. 9.

52. Ibid., June 23, 1976, p. 24.

53. Cynthia Gorney, "University Is Sued over Development of Sophisticated Harvesting Machines," *Washington Post*, January 18, 1979, p. A-11.

54. The Children's Foundation annual report, 1977-1978.

55. Ibid.

56. "FRAC's Profile of the Federal Food Programs," Food Research and Action Center, Washington, D.C., 1979, p. 1.

57. Ibid., p. 1.

58. *Bermudez* v. *USDA*, 348 F. Supp. 1279 (1972); *Bennett* v. *Butz*, 386 F. Supp. 1059 (1974).

59. *Foundation Grants Index 1977* (New York: Foundation Center, 1978).

60. U.S. House of Representatives hearings, *Food Stamp Program*, pp. 222-231.

61. National Association of Farmworker Organizations, "The American Farmworker, A Report to the Nation," 1976-1977, p. 21.

62. AFBF *Farm Bureau News*, May 28, 1979, p. 108.

63. Appendix to the Budget for the Fiscal Year 1979, Executive Office of the President, p. 878.

64. Community Services Administration, "Grantee Signings and Obligations, Fiscal Year 1978," Report C2826B, December 7, 1978.

65. U.S. Senate Agriculture Committee hearings, *General Farm and Food Legislation*, p. 889.

66. U.S. House of Representative hearings, *Food Stamp Program*, p. 349.

67. Bread for the World annual report, spring 1979.

68. U.S. Senate Agriculture Committee hearings, *General Farm and Food Legislation*, pp. 858-874, 215-228, 543-562.

69. Ibid., Appendix, pp. 336-339.

70. U.S. House of Representatives hearings, *General Farm Bill*, March 3, 1977, pp. 234-237.

71. U.S. House of Representatives hearings, *Federal Insecticide, Fungicide, and Rodenticide Act*, March 7, 8, 9, 1977, pp. 175-176, 26-30.

72. U.S. Senate Agriculture Committee hearings, *Extension of Federal*

Insecticide, Fungicide, and Rodenticide Act, June 8, 9, 1977, pp. 220-225.

73. U.S. House of Representatives hearings, *FIFRA*, pp. 509-515.

74. U.S. Senate Agriculture Committee hearings, *General Farm and Food Legislation*, pp. 240-244.

75. Ibid., Book 2, Appendix, pp. 618-621.

76. Ibid., pp. 614-616.

77. U.S. House of Representatives hearings, *General Farm Bill*, Part 2, March 4, 1977, pp. 379-381.

78. "Environmental Groups Lose Friends in Effort to Control DNA Research," *Science* 202 (December 22, 1978):1265-1266.

79. U.S. House of Representatives Subcommittee on Livestock and Grains hearing, *Humane Methods of Slaughter Act of 1977*, April 25, 1978.

80. Humane Information Services, Inc., *Report to Humanitarians*, no. 39, March 1977, p. 7.

81. U.S. Department of Agriculture *News Summary*, June 29, 1979.

82. "Letter to Humanitarians," Society for Animal Protective Legislation, January 19, 1979.

83. *Report to Humanitarians*, no. 41, September 1977, p. 1; no. 43, March 1978, p. 1.

84. Ibid., no. 39, March 1977, p. 4.

85. *Rural America* 4, 6 (June 1979):20.

86. Rockefeller Brothers Fund Annual Report, 1977, pp. 7-8.

87. Testimony by Carol Coston to the Presidential Commission on World Hunger, January 23, 1979.

88. Center for Rural Affairs, Small Farm Advocacy Project; annual report, 1978; *Small Farm Advocate Newsletter*, Summer 1979.

89. Rusty Davenport, "Farmworker Turned Farmer," *Food Monitor*, no. 3 (March-April 1978):6.

90. William E. Martin, "Economics of Size and the 160-Acre Limitation: Fact and Fancy," *American Journal of Agricultural Economics* 60, 5 (December 1978):923. Reprinted with permission.

91. Ibid., p. 925.

92. Ibid., p. 926.

93. Ann Fredricks, "Agribusiness in the Lettuce Fields," *Food Monitor*, no. 10 (May-June 1979):15.

94. "The RHA Reporter," *Rural America* 12, 11 (February 1979):4-5.

95. Davenport, "Farmworker Turned Farmer," p. 7.

96. National Land for People, *People, Land, Food*, March 1979, p. 22.

97. Stern Fund, Grants Made by Stern Fund, April 1977-June 1978.

98. *American Farm Bureau News* 51, 13 (April 2, 1979):73.

99. U.S. House of Representatives Committee on Appropriations hearings; Labor, Health, Education, and Welfare Subcommittee hearings, April 27, 1979, in print.

100. Legal Services Corporation, annual report, 1978.

101. *Anderson* v. *Butz*, 550 F.2d 459 (1977).

102. U.S. House of Representatives, Appropriations hearings, 1979.

103. "Machines, Bugs, and CRLA," Mimeo distributed by California Rural Legal Assistance at 1979 conference of Rural America.

104. U.S. Department of Agriculture, "Extension Review," January-February 1979.

105. U.S. Department of Agriculture, National Agricultural Research and Extension Users Advisory Board.

106. See Jim Hightower and Susan DeMarco, *Hard Tomatoes, Hard Times* (Cambridge, Mass.: Schenkman Publishing Co., 1973).

107. Frances Moore Lappe and Joseph Collins, *Food First* (Boston: Houghton Mifflin Co., 1977), pp. 208, 251-268, 407.

108. National Family Farm Coalition, "The Family Farm Development Act: An Overview."

109. William E. Simon, *A Time for Truth* (New York: Readers Digest Press, McGraw-Hill Book Co., 1978), p. 193. Reprinted with permission.

6

Public Agency and Professional Organizations: Backstage Support

The nub of the issue then is who are we serving and who is paying the bill?
—Alex McCalla[a]

Employees of public agencies, scientists, and other professionals have established organizations and associations that also have expressed concern with certain food and agricultural issues. In some cases these associations advocate a specific position. In other situations, they may provide information useful in evaluating alternatives among several possible courses of action. In some cases they may suggest what they believe to be more efficient or effective ways to carry out some public program. More detailed information about these groups of organizations is given in appendix A.

The issues and concerns of public agency and professional organizations include farm price supports, food programs, implementation of the Federal Insecticide, Pesticide, and Rodenticide Act (FIFRA), appropriation of research funds, taxation, and education. In contrast to organizations discussed earlier, their concerns more frequently are related to performing their assigned tasks rather than securing direct benefits for members of the group. In a few instances, the organization is registered as a lobbyist; in most cases they are not required to be registered.

Among the organizations mentioned on the following pages, some have their major concerns focused on some aspect of food or agricultural policy. Others have an interest in food or agriculture along with a wide range of other public issues and concerns.

Farm Price Support

The National Association of Agricultural Stabilization and Conservation Service County Office Employees has a major concern in the administration of farm programs. Although they have no specific recommendations for the level of farm support prices, they do believe that farmers need some kind of support based on the cost of production. They do feel that Agricultural Stabilization and Conservation Committees should administer any farm legislation enacted.[1]

---

[a]Alex McCalla, "Public Sector Research and Education and the Agribusiness Complex: Unholy Alliance or Socially Beneficial Partnership?" *American Journal of Agricultural Economics* 55, 5 (December 1973):1000.

Although ASCS employees are not asking for additional functions, they have shown willingness to take on new assignments if asked to do so. They believe that improved records in county offices would facilitate program implementation.

The Agricultural Committee of the National Planning Association, comprised of farmers, farm organizations, university faculty, and businessmen, has encouraged Congress to base crop allotments on a desirable pattern of land use, consider the total crop production pattern, omit land prices from the cost of production in figuring price supports, and build grain reserves with a wider spread between loan and release prices than existed before 1977. It also favored revision of the crop insurance program to give more uniform coverage of all crops on a nationwide basis.[2]

John Schnitker, former undersecretary of Agriculture, called on Congress to increase the level of target prices and loan rates, but to avoid setting them so high that government costs would become excessive or the U.S. position in world markets would be threatened. He also supported the concept of farmer-held grain reserves, but called for a release point 50 percent above the loan level and sale of government-owned stocks at 75 percent above the loan.[3]

Food Programs

Operation of the multibillion-dollar food-stamp program attracts the attention of several public-agency groups. The National Association of Counties, through their Welfare and Social Services Steering Committee, has expressed concerns about the administration of the food-stamp program. In the long run, this organization would favor elimination of food stamps and a shift to an income supplement. They have proposed transfer of the federal responsibility from the USDA to HEW, elimination of the purchase requirement, funding 75 percent of administrative costs from federal funds, applying uniform eligibility between recipients and nonrecipients of public welfare, and simplifying authorization to purchase cards.[4]

The National Conference of State Legislatures has called for placing a maximum income ceiling on eligibility for food stamps, adjusted for cost-of-living differentials in different parts of the country. They also recommended a single standard deduction of at least $125 per month with increases for size of family. They have proposed using the income base of thirty days before date of application for eligibility, the same as used for welfare public assistance programs. They would also favor issue of stamps in emergency situations, such as for migrant farm workers.[5]

The National Welfare Fraud Association, affiliated with the National District Attorneys Association, has expressed major concerns about the need to reform the food-stamp program. They would favor limiting types of food to be purchased with stamps, prohibiting stamps for strikers, making regulations uniform between welfare and food-stamp programs, creating more uniform guidelines for eligibility, limiting eligibility to gross incomes at the poverty line, making college students ineligible or group those living in the same house together to consider eligibility, and setting up work requirements for mothers of children over six years old.[6]

The American Public Welfare National Council of State Administrators has also been concerned with food-stamp-program operations. They have called for positive incentives for a family to become or remain self-supporting. They support the definition of elderly to include those sixty or over, the Office of Management and Budget poverty standards if coupled with reasonable purchase powers and adequate deductions, and recognized food standards that will give adequate nutrition with revisions as food prices go up. They oppose federal penalties for a state that does not carry out the state plan of operation and prefer a state incentive to encourage efficiency of program operation. They do not favor issuing stamps at social security offices.[7]

The American School Food Service has major interests in distribution of foods for school lunches by the USDA. They favor extension of the commodity purchase program, oppose cash payments to schools in lieu of commodities, favor setting state standards for staffing personnel and requiring states to keep up expenditures for food programs. They also feel that schools need nutrition education programs.[8]

Pesticide Regulation

The implementation of the Federal Insecticide, Fungicide, and Rodenticide Act (FIFRA) has created concern in several organizations. The Association of State Departments of Agriculture has called for more cooperation between the Environmental Protection Agency, the Department of Agriculture, and the states. They believe that federal funds should be available to support mandated training programs in the states and that the Delaney amendment needs revision in line with current measurement techniques. They have criticized the EPA for using dual standards when evaluating benefits and risks with pesticides.[9]

The Association of American Pesticide Control Officials has called for revisions of the rebuttable presumption against registration process since it is practically and physically impossible to achieve. They would like to see simplified classification procedures and ways to make continued use of pesticides possible, rather than rejecting and canceling certification. They would also like to see federal funding of state training programs for pesticide applicators.[10]

The Agricultural Research Institute has also expressed concern over the administration of FIFRA. They have called for more flexible regulations and procedures, published guidelines for information needed to support registration of a pesticide, speeded-up review procedures, elimination of the rebuttable presumption against registration, and putting agricultural scientists on the scientific advisory panel that advises the administrator in evaluating benefits from use of pesticides.[11]

The American Registry of Professional Entomologists favors more flexibility in use of pesticides by professional entomologists, state certification of pesticides, training of applicators by professional entomologists, federal funding of applicator training programs, and separate classification of restricted and nonrestricted pesticides.[12]

The Council for Agricultural Science and Technology (CAST) has been concerned with the use of pesticides for minor uses. It would like to see more flexible label requirements and streamlining of registration procedures. If minor uses for pesticides are not permitted, CAST foresees reduced yields of crops and higher food prices to consumers.[13]

The Council for Agricultural Science and Technology has also made a major ef' 't in organizing task forces to study various food, agricultural, and scientific issues. The reports attempt to present the most factual, objective, and thorough analysis possible on a wide range of problems and issues relating to food and agriculture. A concensus among scientists on some issues is not always possible. In 1979, six scientists resigned from a panel studying the problem of using antibiotics in livestock feeds because they felt their views were not presented accurately by the council.[14]

Research and Extension Funds

Since federal appropriations for research provide a key source of research funds for some public institutions, the institutional organizations have a keen interest in federal research policy. Inflation has required continued increases in appropriations. Otherwise, personnel and activities must be cut.

The Hatch Act of 1887 and the Smith Lever Act of 1914 established the principle of joint federal-state cooperation in agricultural research and extension of the research results. In recent years, the National Association of State Universities and Land-Grant Colleges, representing the land-grant universities, has watched with interest and concern the allocation of federal research and extension funds. It has supported designation of the USDA as the lead agency in agricultural research and called for more funding for research and extension, new basic research, nutrition, animal diseases, forest industry, and improved federal-state cooperation. It supports full acceptance of the 1890 land-grant institutions and the Tuskegee Institute as full partners in the community of institutions receiving federal grants for research.[15]

The administration proposals for the 1980 budget called for reduced appropriations for the Extension Service and reduced-formula funding to the states for research. Some observers interpreted these proposals as an effort of the federal government to gain more direct control of extension and research activities. Others saw the move as an effort to get individual states to provide more support for their own research and extension programs. Consequently, in 1979 land-grant institutions, seeing declining support from the executive branch of the federal government, mounted an information campaign to get support from citizens of their individual states and from their own members of Congress.

A special national committee, independent of the Land-Grant University Association, organized by concerned land-grant university leaders and supported by farmers, agricultural and rural groups, ag-related businesses, and concerned nonagricultural groups joined together to alert the public and the Congress of the serious threat.

This Committee for Agricultural Research, Extension, and Teaching (CARET) called for restoration of funds to keep current programs and personnel, restoration of the urban gardening program, farm safety, rural development, and more funding for expanded food and nutrition and forestry extension.[16] E.A. Jaenke and Associates' consulting firm was employed, with funds raised by support groups across the country, to assist in this effort. Final results were considered successful when Congress appropriated $9.5 million more formula funding to the states than the President's budget proposal. Jaenke and Associates were employed again in 1980 to help communicate state extension and research accomplishments.

The American Association of State Colleges and Universities, representing the non-land-grant universities, wants its members to be able to get more federal funds for research programs. Through the increased emphasis on competitive grants programs for research, member institutions may have more opportunities for obtaining research funds than in earlier years.[17]

The American Association of University Agricultural Administrators has expressed concern with grant-awarding procedures and wants its member institutions, mostly non-land-grant institutions, to be able to compete on a fair basis for research funds.[18]

The American Veterinary Medical Association and the Association of American Veterinary Medical Colleges have a major concern with funding of animal disease research. They feel that the USDA gives small support for veterinary research compared with HEW funding for animal and human health.[19] The American Veterinary Medical Association registered as a lobbyist for the purpose of advancement of veterinary medical science. The Association of American Veterinary Medical Colleges has registered as a lobbyist for the purpose of seeking funding for teaching and research.

The internal reorganization of the USDA in 1977 and 1978 created controversy and concern for the cooperative research and extension efforts between the USDA and the state land-grant institutions. The Organization of Professional Employees of the U.S. Department of Agriculture criticized the (1) creation of the Science and Education Administration, because they see adverse effects on Cooperative Research and Extension; (2) creation of an enlarged group of planning and evaluation staff; (3) loss of pilot and special project funds for developing innovative projects on specific problems; and (4) appointment of new administrators who lack understanding of working relationships between the federal government and state land-grant institutions. They see the changes as a threat to the USDA's ability to carry out its long-established role with the land-grant universities and the creation of inefficiencies in government operations.[20]

Other Legislative Issues and Interests

Institutional and professional organizations have a variety of other specific interests and concerns. The University of Hawaii College of Tropical Agriculture has registered as a lobbyist for the purpose of securing congressional appropriations for the college. The National Association of Federal Veterinarians has registered as a lobbyist because of their interests in legislation affecting federal veterinarians, especially as they work as supervisors and managers in federal programs.

The American Society of Farm Managers and Rural Appraisers registered as a lobbyist because of tax legislation and regulations that would affect their clients and the decisions of landowners to seek their services. They have sought clarification of the regulations so that a landowner could qualify for special valuation of farm property in his or her estate if that individual prior to death had engaged the services of a farm management organization to manage or operate his farm. The special valuation for farm property was established in the Tax Reform Act of 1976 to give "family farmers" special tax benefits and enable farms to be operated by the same family from one generation to the next.

The American Dietetic Association has broad interests in legislation involving health, nutrition, and dietetics. They have a registered lobbyist working in Washington to follow legislative developments.

The Westlands Water District in Fresno, California, is a local government body that supervises distribution of water to farmers in the district. It has employed a registered lobbyist since they have specific interests in legislation affecting the San Luis Unit, in this Central Valley project.

The Society of Nutrition Education, testifying before the Senate Subcommittee on Nutrition, called for nutrition education to go along with all food-assistance programs and supports the idea of having nutrition education coordinators in each state.[21]

Research Organizations

Certain research organizations, financed by foundation grants, private contributions, and federal agency grants and contracts, have specific interests in issues and problems relating to food and agriculture. In contrast to lobbying organizations and groups which usually have a specific position on a piece of legislation, the research organizations examine the broader scope of a problem, the alternatives, and the consequences and may or may not advocate a particular position on the issues.

The Brookings Institution, one of the oldest and best known research organizations, conducts independent research and analysis on a wide range of public policy issues, including food and agriculture. Members of the research staff have appeared before congressional committees to provide information and opinions that contribute to legislative decisions. In 1977, a staff member reported on long-term projections of food needs of developing countries.[22]

The American Enterprise Institute for Public Policy Research sponsored a conference on food and agricultural policy in 1977. Participants included members of Congress, government agency officials, university agricultural economists, farm and consumer organization representatives, and former government officials representing members of both political parties. The conference, held before new legislation was to be considered in Congress, covered a broad range of issues and choices that were later addressed in hearings and the Food and Agricultural Act of 1977.

The World Watch Institute engages in studies with broad public interests. Published works such as "The Two Faces of Malnutrition," "The Politics and Responsibility of the North American Breadbasket," and "Cutting Tobacco's Toll" illustrate problems and issues relating to food and agriculture. Lester Brown, founder and director, is an agricultural economist with an international reputation in the field of agricultural development. He worked in the Department of Agriculture during the 1960s and has written and spoken widely on international development and hunger problems.

Resources for the Future examines issues in resources and environment, including food and energy, in both developed and developing countries, with emphasis on the United States. Its published reports are read and studied widely.

The Conservation Foundation was formed to promote the conservation of the earth's life-supporting resources—animal life, forests and other plant life, water sources, and productive soils—and to advance, improve, and encourage knowledge and understanding of such resources. In 1977 the Conservation Foundation began a three-year study of rural land markets in the United States including the new trends in migration from urban to rural areas.

The National Association of Counties Research Foundation launched an Agricultural Lands Project in 1979 to inform people about disappearing U.S. farmland and to help stimulate citizen action designed to come to grips with this pressing national problem.

Conclusions

The organizations and associations of scientists, public officials, employees, institutions, and other professionals perform more varied roles than the farm, business, trade, and citizens' public interest groups. Although they have some of the same concerns about public issues and problems related to food and agriculture, the means by which they make these concerns known to public officials and Congress differ. Some may contact officials and members directly. Others seek support through the constituents they serve and the leaders of other groups who will give them support.

More frequently the public agency and institution-related groups are seeking funds—for research, expanded educational programs, expanded services to some segment of the public—rather than for programs or assistance that would give direct benefits to members or employees.

The laws that regulate and identify the extent of lobbying efforts by these groups are either vague or nonexistent. Consequently only a few of the groups and organizations discussed in this chapter are registered as lobbyists. Many more have an interest in the outcome of government decisions and in some way carry out activities to influence these decisions.

Notes

1. U.S. Senate Committee on Agriculture hearings, *General Farm and Food Legislation*, February 24, 1977, pp. 209-215.

2. Ibid., Book 2, pp. 685-690.

3. U.S. House of Representatives hearings, *General Farm Bill*, March 3, 1977, pp. 198-206.

4. U.S. Senate Committee on Agriculture hearings, *General Farm and Food Legislation*, Book 2, pp. 417-418.

5. U.S. Senate Subcommittee on Nutrition hearings, *Food Stamps*, March 25, 1977, pp. 107-109.

6. U.S. Senate Committee on Agriculture hearings, *General Farm and Food Legislation*, pp. 717-722.

7. Ibid., pp. 629-633; Book 2, pp. 382-387.

8. U.S. Senate Subcommittee on Nutrition hearings, *Child Nutrition Legislation*, May 5-6, 1977, pp. 48-54.

9. U.S. Senate Committee on Agriculture hearings, *General Farm and Food Legislation*, Book 2, pp. 510-513.

10. Ibid., pp. 514-517.

11. Ibid., pp. 834-837.

12. Ibid., pp. 549-565.

13. U.S. House of Representatives hearings, *Federal Insecticide, Fungicide, and Rodenticide Act*, March 7-9, 1977, pp. 438-441.

14. "Six Scientists Quit Panel in Dispute," *The New York Times*, January 23, 1979, p. C2.

15. U.S. Senate Committee on Agriculture hearings, *General Farm and Food Legislation*, Book 2, pp. 340-341.

16. *Congressional Record*, March 26, 1979, pp. E1327-28.

17. U.S. Senate Committee on Agriculture hearings, *General Farm and Food Legislation*, Book 2, pp. 347-350.

18. Ibid., pp. 591-593.

19. Ibid., pp. 599-612.

20. Letter from Organization of Professional Employees of the U.S. Department of Agriculture to Congressman Jamie L. Whitten, June 13, 1979.

21. U.S. Senate Subcommittee on Nutrition hearings, *Child Nutrition Legislation*, May 5-6, 1977, pp. 54-59.

22. U.S. Senate Subcommittee on Foreign Agricultural Policy hearings, *Future of Food Aid*, April 4-5, 1977, pp. 53-57.

7 Political-Action Committees in Food and Agriculture: Money plus Votes

Everyone knows that money often can grease the way for some desired action. But money can also block the way, especially when action by government is needed. —Common Cause

The rapid growth of corporate political-action committees (PACs) is regarded as one of the most significant developments in politics in recent years. These committees are expected to play an expanding role in Presidential, congressional, state, and local election campaigns in 1980 and beyond.

Changes in elections laws in the early 1970s and decisions by the Federal Election Commission made it clear that business firms could establish separate political entities to contribute money to office seekers, just as labor unions had done for many years. The revisions were aimed at limiting the amount of contributions. But they also permitted any organization, including corporations, to raise funds through voluntary donations by executives, employees, or members.

Corporate funds may be used only to cover the expenses of setting up a PAC and the administrative costs of running it. Contributions are limited to $5,000 per candidate for each election, but there is no limit to the number of candidates a fund can support. A candidate who ran in a primary, a runoff election, and a general election could receive up to $15,000 from one political-action committee.[1]

The future role of PACs is linked to what Congress may do about public financing of congressional elections. Public financing legislation is already in effect for Presidential elections. Those who support public financing of congressional races believe the influence of PACs could be limited in this way.

The number of PACs for funding political campaigns about tripled between the 1974 and 1978 national elections. In 1978, some 1,950 PACs provided funding to congressional candidates.[2]

Although PACs are legal and have a right to get their views across, the critics of these committees see them as an influence-buying device. As one editorial writer declared, "The fact is that PACs work. They give companies a very large bang for their bucks."[3]

Although some may have the impression that PACs are formed and operated by large corporations, the organizations connected with political action committees include not only individual corporations, but also business and industry trade associations, labor unions, professional societies, environmental and citizens' groups, and farm and cooperative organizations.

In this chapter we identify and analyze the PACs among those groups with a special interest in some aspect of food and agricultural issues. In some cases, the organization may also have interests outside food and agriculture. Most of the organizations connected with these PACs were identified in chapters 3, 4, or 5.

The Scope of Food and Agriculture Political-Action Committees

Political-action committees may be affiliated with organizations and trade associations or with employees of individual companies who contribute to the fund. A total of eighty-two political-action committees was identified with organizations and associations which have major interests in food and agriculture.[4]

Producers' groups, including cooperatives, represent the largest group, with forty-six organizations and total reported contributions of $1,400,975 in 1977 and 1978. Food and agricultural business and industry groups had thirty-one PACs with total contributions of $744,702. Among the citizen, consumer, labor, and professional groups, five had indicated some interest in food and agriculture issues through testimony and lobbying activity. The contributions of these groups through PACs totaled $135,649. Each of these groups, their total contributions, and the number of contributions to Senate and House candidates in each party are shown in appendix D.

Most of the PAC fund-raising efforts in food and agriculture are relatively small. Among the eighty-two committees, only thirteen made contributions of more than $25,000 to congressional candidates in 1977 and 1978 (table 7-1).

Table 7-1
Food and Agriculture Political-Action Committee Funds
Support to Candidates for Congress, 1977-1978[a]

Total Fund	Producers (Including Cooperatives)	Business and Industry	Citizen, Consumer, Labor, Professional
Under $5,000	21	15	3
$5,000-$24,999	19	9	1
$25,000-$49,999	2	2	—
$50,000-$99,999	—	4	—
$100,000 and over	4	1	1
Total (n)	46	31	5
Total reported contributions	$1,400,975	$744,702	$135,649

Source: Federal Election Commission.

[a]Includes organizations, associations, cooperatives, and labor unions, but excludes individuals and firms.

Among the ten largest PAC funds, four were identified with producers and cooperatives, five with business and industry, and one with organized labor. The amounts and number of candidates supported for House and Senate are shown in table 7-2.

The largest fund was connected with Associated Milk Producers, Inc., which has its headquarters in San Antonio, Texas. The $456,151 contributed by its members was dispersed to 37 candidates for the Senate and 185 candidates for the House of Representatives. Its contributions per candidate were also the largest of any PAC. The sixteen Democratic Senate candidates received an average of $3,250; the twenty-one Republican Senate candidates received an average of $3,081. In the House races, 129 Democrats averaged $1,971 and 56 Republican candidates averaged $1,480. It made thirty-four contributions of $4,000 or more.

The second largest fund was Dairymen, Inc., with total contributions of $266,300 including nine state funds (table 7-2). Their funds were disbursed to 149 House and Senate candidates. Nineteen candidates received $4,000 or more. The third largest fund was connected with the Chicago Mercantile Exchange. Its $230,225 went to 153 candidates. Eleven received $4,000 or more. The fourth largest fund of $228,900, assembled by Mid-America Dairymen, Inc., was distributed to 197 House and Senate candidates. Twelve candidates received $4,000 or more.

The fifth largest fund of $217,900 was brought together by the National Rural Electric Cooperative Associations and included seven state funds. The Action Committees for Rural Electrification supported 253 House and Senate candidates, more than any other food- and agriculture-related PAC. Seven candidates received $4,000 or more.

The next five largest PACs related to food and agriculture were connected with the Amalgamated Meat Cutters and Butcher Workmen, the Chicago Board of Trade, Tobacco Institute, American Sugar Cane League of the U.S.A., and the American Textile Manufacturers Association. (See table 7-2 and appendix E.)

Although associations and organizations are the more frequent sponsors of political-action committees, employees of individual companies with major food and agricultural interests also set up their own PACs. Some examples of these committees and amounts contributed to congressional candidates are shown in table 7-3. Food and agriculturally related companies that reported PACs to the Federal Elections Commission in 1977-1978 included A&P; Anheiser Busch; Borden; J.G. Boswell Co.; Cargill, Inc.; Central Soya, Inc.; Coca Cola Co.; Del Monte Corporation; Dr. Pepper; Dow Chemical; Eli Lilly; Food Fair Stores; Gerber Products; W.R. Grace & Co.; Hardee's Food Systems; Heublein, Inc.; International Multi-Foods; Kellogg Co.; Kraft Inc.; Krause Milling; Kroger; Land-O-Lakes; McDonald's; Merrill Lynch & Co.; Monsanto; Nabisco Inc.; Peter Paul Inc.;

Table 7-2
Ten Largest Political-Action Committee Funds Related to Food and Agriculture

Fund and Organization	1977-1978 Contribution to Candidates for Congress ($)	Candidates Receiving Funds
Committee for Thorough Agricultural Political Education; Associated Milk Producers, Inc.	456,151	222
Trust for Special Political Agricultural Community Education;		
Dairymen, Inc.	$181,600	
Louisiana Committee, Dairymen, Inc.	18,750	
Kentucky Committee, Dairymen, Inc.	18,000	
Georgia Committee, Dairymen, Inc.	15,950	
Mississippi Committee, Dairymen, Inc.	11,500	
Tennessee Committee, Dairymen, Inc.	10,000	
Virginia Committee, Dairymen, Inc.	6,000	
North Carolina Committee, Dairymen, Inc.	4,500	
Total	266,300	149
Commodity Futures Political Fund; Chicago Mercantile Exchange	230,225	153
Agricultural and Dairy Educational Political Trust; Mid-America Dairymen, Inc.	228,900	197
Action Committee for Rural Electrification (ACRE);		
National Rural Electric Cooperative Association	$192,450	
Louisiana ACRE	5,900	
Mississippi ACRE	5,700	
Missouri ACRE	4,670	
Iowa ACRE	4,500	
Kansas ACRE	2,875	
Ohio ACRE	950	
Colorado ACRE	855	
Total	217,900	253
AMCOPE; Amalgamated Meat Cutters and Butcher Workmen	111,500	214
Auction Markets PAC; Chicago Board of Trade	96,400	86
Tobacco People's Public Affairs Committee; Tobacco Institute, Inc.	75,975	228
American Sugar Cane League Political Action Committee; American Sugar Cane League of U.S.A.	72,495	179
American Textile Industry Good Government Committee; American Textile Manufacturers Association	55,750	118

Source: Federal Election Commission.

Table 7-3

Selected Individual Agribusiness Company Political-Action Committee Funds, 1977-1978[a]

Fund and Company	Total Amount Contributed ($)
Florida Agricultural Education Committee; United States Sugar Corporation	49,918
Cargill Political Action Committee; Cargill, Inc.	38,100
J.G. Boswell Co. Employees PAC; J.G. Boswell Co. (California)	34,890
Del Monte Voluntary Nonpartisan Good Government Committee; Del Monte Corporation	16,350
Central Soya Political Action Committee; Central Soya, Inc.	11,375
Staley PAC; A.E. Staley Manufacturing Company	4,950

Source: Federal Election Commission.

[a]Many other firms handling agricultural and food products have employee political action committees. These are mentioned in the text.

Pfizer Inc.; Pillsbury Co.; Producers Cotton Oil Co.; Quaker Oats; R.J. Reynolds Industries; Ralston Purina Co., Schipps Dairy, Inc.; A.O. Smith; A.E. Staley Manufacturing Co., Southland Corporation; Stouffer Corporation; United States Sugar Corporation; Wilson Foods; and Winn Dixie Stores.

Political-action committees which were registered with the Federal Elections Commission but reported no contributions to congressional candidates in 1977-1978 included those connected with Archer-Daniels-Midland Co.; California Farm Bureau; Dairy Farmers, Inc. of New York; Indiana Rural Electric Cooperative; Missouri Farm Bureau Northeast Agricultural Committee; Missouri Farm Bureau South East Farmers Action Committee; Missouri Farm Bureau South West Farmers Action Committee; Ohio Farm Bureau; Sun Maid Growers of California; Tuna Research Foundation; and United Farm Workers of America (AFL-CIO).

In addition, PACs of uncertain or unidentified organizational connections also operate on a small scale. A Futures Industry Good Government Committee, organized by individual brokers at the Chicago Board of Trade, contributed $2,000 to five congressional candidates in 1978. A Committee Organized for the Trading of Cotton and a Food Operators Political-Action Trust were registered, but no contributions were identified.

Observations on Political-Action-Committee Contributions

Although some of the food and agriculturally connected PACs appear substantial, they are not the largest. In 1978, the political-action committees connected with the American Medical Association contributed $1,644,795 to congressional candidates; the National Association of Realtors, $1,122,378; the National Automobile Dealers Association, $975,675; the United Auto Workers, $964,465; and the AFL-CIO, $920,841.[5]

The number of large contributions made in 1977-1978 seems closely related to the total size of the PAC fund. The number of contributions of $4,000 or more were Associated Milk Producers, Inc., thirty-four; Dairymen, Inc., nineteen (including six by state committees); Mid-America Dairymen, Inc., twelve; Chicago Mercantile Exchange, eleven; and National Rural Electric Cooperative Association, seven.

The chairman of the House Agriculture Committee receives favored treatment from food and agriculturally related PACs. Chairman Thomas Foley (Washington) received forty-three contributions totaling $35,750, more than any other House Agriculture Committee member. Ranking minority member William Wampler received twenty-seven contributions totaling $21,402—the highest of any Republican on the committee.

Agriculture subcommittee chairmen also received more contributions than ranking minority members. Seven of the ten House agriculture subcommittee chairmen received more than $10,000 in contributions from food and agriculturally related PACs. Wampler was the only subcommittee ranking minority member who received more than $10,000 in contributions from the food and agriculture PACs. He was also ranking minority member of the House Agriculture Committee (table 7-4).

The food and agriculture PACs disperse their large contributions widely. In Senate races, twenty-two candidates received one contribution or more of $4,000. Rudolph Boschwitz of Minnesota received five $4,000 or larger contributions; William Roy of Kansas received four (defeated by Nancy Kassebaum); Charles Percy, Illinois, received three; Patrick Leahy (a 1980 candidate), Vermont, received three; and the others received one or two.

In the House races, thirty-five candidates received one or more contributions of $4,000 or more. Receiving three were Thomas Huckaby, Louisiana; Ed Jones, Tennessee; Richard Nolan, Minnesota; Ike Skelton, Missouri; and Michael Sullivan, Minnesota. The others received one or two $4,000 or larger contributions.

The big three dairy cooperatives—Associated Milk Producers, Inc., Dairymen, Inc., and Mid-America Dairymen, Inc.—contribute to Agriculture Committee members as well as others. However, each contributed to nine of the twelve members on the Dairy and Poultry Subcommittee of the House Agriculture Committee. Agriculture Chairman Tom

Table 7-4

Food and Agriculturally Related PAC Contributions to House Agriculture Committee and Subcommittee Chairmen and Ranking Minority Members, 1977-1978

	Number of Contributions	Total Contributed ($)	Average Contribution ($)
Chairman: Thomas Foley	43	35,750	831
Subcommittee Chairmen and Committee Assignment:			
Baldus, Alvin Dairy and Poultry	14	14,200	1,014
Bowen, David Cotton	21	16,660	793
Garza, E. de la Investigations and Oversight	16	5,750	359
Jones, Ed Conservation, Credit	30	31,675	1,056
Jones, Walter Tobacco	6	4,700	783
Mathis, Dawson Oilseeds and Rice	17	17,850	1,050
Nolan, Richard Family Farms	15	20,300	1,450
Richmond, Fred Domestic Marketing	15	11,800	787
Rose, Charles Livestock and Grains	25	12,100	484
Weaver, James Forests	9	3,600	400
Ranking Minority Members			
Findley, Paul Oilseeds and Rice	9	4,600	511
Grassley, Charles Family Farms	8	6,600	825
Heckler, Margaret Cotton	12	5,600	467
Jeffords, James Dairy and Poultry	8	2,388	299
Johnson, James Forests	2	900	450
Kelly, Richard Tobacco	14	5,850	418
Madigan, Edward Conservation and Credit	7	2,500	357
Sebelius, Keith Livestock and Grains	11	6,850	623
Symms, Steven Domestic Marketing	17	6,250	368
Wampler, William Investigation and Oversight	27	21,402	793

Source: Federal Election Commission.

Foley received $6,500; John Jenrette, Jr., South Carolina, (Appropriations) received $11,500; and Michael Sullivan, Minnesota, (defeated) received $11,000.

Alvin Baldus (Wisconsin), who heads the dairy and poultry subcommittee, received $11,300 from the three. James Jeffords (Vermont), the ranking minority member, received $500. Ed Jones (Tennessee), a dairy farmer on the Agriculture Committee, received $18,000. Thomas Huckaby, (Louisiana), another Agriculture Committee member, received $20,000 from AMPI, Dairymen, Inc., and the Louisiana Dairymen Inc. PAC. Richard Nolan (Minnesota) received $14,000. Fred Richmond from Brooklyn, New York, who heads the Subcommittee on Domestic Marketing which has jurisdiction over federal food programs, received $7,500. Arlan Strangeland (Minnesota), who occupies the seat once filled by Secretary of Agriculture Bob Bergland but is not on the Agriculture Committee, received $13,500 from Associated Milk Producers and Mid-America Dairymen. Ike Skelton (Missouri) received $14,500, and Tom Colemen (Missouri), $11,000.

In the Senate, the big three dairy cooperatives contributed $13,700 to Rudolph Boschwitz of Minnesota, $15,000 to Patrick Leahy of Vermont, $18,000 to William Roy of Kansas, $13,750 to Howard Baker of Tennessee, and $12,000 to Dick Clark of Iowa (who lost to Roger Jepsen).

Party Preferences of Political-Action-Committee Support

The political-action committees connected with food and agricultural organizations support candidates from both major parties, but not in equal numbers or in amounts of money. The forty-six producer and cooperative groups contributed to 1,319 candidates, of which 66 percent were Democrats and 34 percent Republicans. The business and industry PACs contributed to 1,596 candidates, of which 57 percent were Democrats and 43 percent were Republicans. The citizen, labor, consumer, and professional groups contributed to 259 candidates, of which 90 percent were Democrats (table 7-5)

Table 7-5
Party Affiliations of Candidates Supported by Food and Agricultural Political-Action Committees

Type of Sponsor	Democratic (Number)	Republican (Number)	Democratic (Percent)	Republican (Percent)
Producers and cooperatives	910	469	66	34
Business and industry	906	690	57	43
Citizen, labor, consumers, professional	234	25	90	10

Source: Federal Election Commission.

Among the producer groups, twenty-five PACs supported more Democrats while eleven PACs supported more Republicans. About ten PACs supported about the same numbers of candidates from each party.

Among the business groups twenty-one PACs supported more Democrats while nine contributed to more Republicans and one supported about the same number from each party. The citizen, labor, consumer, and professional PACs supported more Democrats than Republicans (table 7-6).

Among the citizens' and labor groups, the Consumers Federation of America supported Democrats 92 percent of the time; the Amalgamated Meat Cutters and Butcher Workers, 94 percent. The Cotton Warehouse Association supported candidates with 86 percent affiliation with the Democratic Party. The National Rural Electric Cooperatives supported candidates from the Democratic Party 71 percent of the time. Among the big three dairy cooperatives, the candidates supported by Dairymen, Inc., were 77 percent, by Mid America Dairymen 73 percent, and by Associated Milk Producers 65 percent Democratic.

The strongest support for Republicans came from American Meat Institute, which supported 81 percent Republican candidates; the National Canners (Food Processors) Association, 70 percent; and the National Confectioners, 64 percent. The American Feed Manufacturers Association contributions went to 56 percent Republican candidates, the Chicago Mercantile Exchange to 55 percent, and the National Cattlemen's Association to 55 percent.

Average contributions to Democratic candidates were usually larger if that organization was supporting a majority of candidates from that party. However, if the organization was supporting a majority of Republicans, the average contribution to Republican candidates was not always higher than the Democrats that organization supported. (See appendix D.)

Some PACs supported both candidates in a race, but in most cases they supported only one. When two candidates in the same race received con-

Table 7-6
Party Preferences of Food and Agricultural Political-Action Committees

Sponsor	Democrats (Number)	Republicans (Number)	Equal Support[a] (Number)
Producers and cooperatives	25	11	10
Business and industry	21	9	1
Citizens, labor, consumers, professional	5	—	—

Source: Federal Election Commission.

[a]Based on the party affiliation of a majority of candidates supported. Committees were considered to support equal numbers from each party if the difference was not more than one candidate of one party over another.

tribution's from the same organization, one candidate usually received more than the other.

Criteria for Support

Each PAC and its connected organization have some interest in specific issues as well as a concern for the welfare of their organization, members, and the industry they represent. The dairy cooperatives generally do not contribute to candidates unless they receive a request from that candidate. One group makes contributions only if the candidates meet with the governing commitee of that PAC.

The amount a candidate receives will depend on how close the race is, whether it is in a big spending area, the actual or potential leadership of the candidate, and his financial need. The voting records of the candidate are also considered.[6]

Conclusions

Formulation and operation of political-action committees are actually another part of the political process by which individuals, organizations, and groups attempt to influence the direction of decisions on public and legislative issues. The major difference is that PACs attempt to influence the choice of a candidate for Congress. Lobbying efforts are usually directed toward influencing a vote on a specific piece of legislation or federal agency regulatory decision.

PACs operated by organizations and groups with interests in food and agriculture are not the largest, but have a wide range of size and number of candidates supported.

To what extent the support given to candidates in election campaigns affects their votes on legislation at a later time remains open to question. Support for individual candidates is based on their understanding and interest in food and agricultural problems. Most PACs probably accept the fact that the candidates they support will not always vote as they would like.

Future legislation that would deal with public financing of congressional elections could have a major impact on all political action committees, including those with interests in food and agriculture.

Notes

1. "Business Dollars—A New Political Force," *U.S. News and World Report*, April 30, 1979, p. 52.

2. Common Cause, "Special Interests at Center Stage," *In Common*, Spring 1979, pp. 3-5.

3. "Let's Buy Congress Back," *The New York Times*, editorial, June 7, 1979.

4. All data and identified organizations in this chapter are based on reports to the Federal Election Commission.

5. *In Common*, Spring 1979, pp. 5-6, 31. Common Cause reported that in terms of gross receipts, the largest PACs in 1977-1978 were: Citizens for the Republic (A Ronald Reagan organization), $3,114,514; National Conservation Political Action Committee, $2,989,923; Committee for the Survival of a Free Congress, $2,010,260; Realtors Political Action Committee, $1,853,774; American Medical Association, PAC, $1,656,265. The largest labor union PAC was AFL-CIO COPE Political Contributions Committee, $1,443,385. The largest farm cooperative PAC was Committee for Thorough Agricultural Political Education (TAPE), Associated Milk Producers, $917,493.

6. "The Dairy Coops: A Leader of the PAC's," *National Journal*, October 23, 1976, p. 1516.

8 Assessing the Strategies and Tactics of Food and Agricultural Lobbyists

I am impressed to the extent to which vested interests and going institutions seem to have the power to generate ideas congruent with themselves.
—Jacob Viner

Organizations and groups interested in food and agricultural issues spend substantial sums of money to testify, write letters, make phone calls, visit congressional offices, write and publish newsletters and publications, contribute to election campaigns, and conduct meetings to develop resolutions. Not all groups use the same methods or have the same degree of success in making their views known.

Just how effectively do those with food and agricultural concerns communicate their points of view? In this chapter we summarize the observations and comments from staff and legislative assistants of members of the House and Senate Agriculture Committees.

Effective and Ineffective Methods

Lobbying is a professional job. Some persons in this business know how to perform more effectively than others. The successful lobbyist will know the system of representation and work within that system.

Testimony

Quality of testimony is important. A witness's credibility does not necessarily depend on the organization he or she represents. A good witness must be concise and give figures to back up the points presented.

A witness does not have to be part of a big organization. Individuals presenting short statements with accurate figures to back them up are respected and have had some impact with committee members.

Emotions are less effective than facts. Congress pays more attention to analysis of the issues and the suggested consequences and impacts of various proposed legislation. Reliability of facts and statements is very important. Over time, a group gets pegged as to their reliability. If a group continually twists the data, the staff will know and committee members will be so informed.

Some groups get identified as presenting objective and responsible information. Some groups must always be checked out.

Effective lobbyists understand the adversary role. If they know the member of Congress does not agree with them, they should accept this and try to develop a professional relationship, explain their point of view, and realize that not everyone will agree with them. Just because there is disagreement on an issue does not mean the member or staff does not like a lobbyist personnally.

The most effective groups to testify are reasonable in their presentations, understand the nature of politics, and follow the group ideal. This means that they will tell the committee what they want and what they really must have. They must be ready to accept less than all they want, but a serious group may often achieve something by stating their minimum requirements.

Some of the less successful group witnesses are not well prepared, have not done a thorough research job, and give subjective, impassioned pleas. Some are hostile and do not consider the needs of others who have a stake in the issue. Sloppy testimony, shown by poor preparation and changes in their position after testifying, gains no support for the views presented.

An effective lobbyist tries to understand the audience he or she is addressing. It is possible to assume that the committee members know more about the subject than they really do. A major task in testifying is to educate the committee members so they understand the problem and the proposed way to solve it.

Too many groups say something is wrong and want their representatives in Congress to do something. But they have no ideas to propose. If they are dissatisfied, they should have alternative proposals.

Good testimony is written to persuade committee members that a given point of view is correct or worthy of consideration. Too often, testimony really does not persuade, but appears to be written more for public relations with the group's members back home.

Respected witnesses appear before the committee in an organized manner and communicate with a low-key style. They try to be objective, have good solid facts, and not be hopelessly biased, even though they may present one side of an issue. Members of Congress and their staffs become astute evaluators of witnesses and their testimony. One staff member commented, "Groups totally committed to one side of any issue are leaving something out."

Office Calls

Direct office visits to members of Congress and their staff can be effective, but advance preparation is needed. An effective lobbyist will find out the member's committee assignments and his or her seniority rank on the committee. It will be helpful to determine the member's philosophy on the issues. Some groups or individuals make a mistake by trying to lobby only through the staff aides. The staff may not really know how the member will vote.

More effective contacts are made by some groups who try to determine in advance where a member stands on the issue—for, against, or undecided. Then the group can develop its strategy for an office visit based on the member's position.

What if the member is known to oppose a group's point of view? Representatives of the group should still talk to their representative or senator and make their views known. Groups will be more effective when they document and substantiate the reasons for their position.

Members of Congress are busy people. Short, well-planned visits, by recognizing the constraints on time, can be just as effective as long, drawn-out visits. Breakfast, lunch, or dinners are appropriate settings to present points of view and concerns, but a visit in the office on the same trip to present the same ideas is unnecessary and a waste of time. Lunches or dinners should be started at the scheduled time, even if not all invited guests have arrived.

Education is an important function of an effective lobbyist. Both the member and his staff often need information on the issues. Such information and viewpoints should be presented in a rational manner. Facts and figures, balance sheets, and other evidence can be convincing. "Gut feelings don't count," advised one congressional staff member.

The issue is often the key to how groups can work effectively. Setting up continuing contacts with staff rather than waiting until mark-up time in committee will be more effective in keeping the member informed. Many members depend heavily on their staff for advice.

Some members of Congress like to talk to people when they visit their home district. They feel that they get a better picture of how things really are. One veteran Senate staff member counsels that the best way to reach a member is through residents back home. Many members do not pay much attention to contacts from outside their home state. But since they get advice on both sides of an issue, just making a contact does not mean that they will always vote favorably for all who contact them.

Letters and Phone Calls

Letters and phone calls from the home state or district are important. Local interest is the primary basis for decisions by many House members. In writing, it is important to be concise, state clearly your desire or position, give brief facts, and then attach longer pieces of information if desired.

Genuine mail is effective, but not contrived mail. Individual, original letters in the writer's own words are much preferred over form letters prepared by someone else. Contrived mail is described as that kind when the computer writes the letter on one end and writes the answer on the other.

State and local representatives of organizations usually are welcomed in congressional offices. Representing a group carries more weight than individuals making a visit. But all visitors should remember the time limits of members and staff.

Organizations with Washington offices serve an important function in keeping in touch with congressional offices through direct contact, sending newsletters and publications, and keeping their own members across the country informed about legislative developments.

The most effective lobbyists are viewed as quiet, reasonable, responsible, and having faith in members of Congress. Effective groups also try to avoid putting a member sympathetic to their view in a difficult position by asking for a commitment on a bill too early. The member may be able to gain more in negotiations if he is not committed to a set position.

Farm Producer Groups

Farm producer groups are viewed as a diverse set of organizations with a wide range of ability to carry out lobbying professionally. Some have real knowhow. Some farmers can be better witnesses than the paid employees of an organization with a Washington office.

Generally farm groups make favorable impressions in their lobbying efforts. But if they want to win friends with the staff and influence the members of Congress, they must avoid needless repetition with successive calls, not make pests of themselves, and recognize the time pressures in each office. "Just camping out is not going to work," emphasized one staff member.

Producers are often seen as part of the old-line lobbying groups with strong membership support, a Washington office, a strong state network, and local organizations—all of which transfer into votes.

The general farm organizations, however, observed along with other food and agricultural groups, are viewed as having less influence than in earlier years. Farm Bureau has been traditionally conservative, the Farmers Union has been a rubber stamp for high price supports, and the Grange holds on to the middle of the road. The National Farmers Organization (NFO) has joined the farm coalition and appears to display a more moderate image than in earlier years.

The American Farm Bureau Federation, largest of any producer organization, is viewed as weaker in recent years. The Washington staff seem to be making fewer contacts with staff members in congressional offices. State officers are known and respected. The state groups come in to visit and listen to their senators and congressmen, but they seem to be missing the opportunity to discuss the issues. The groups have a good time, but they do not seem to be really communicating their concerns when they meet with members of Congress.

The National Grange membership thoroughly debates and develops its resolutions, but it does not have members in every state. The Washington staff make few contacts.

The National Farmers Union passes general resolutions at the national convention and presents their wishes to committees and members of Congress, but research and information to support them are usually non specific. Farmers Union seems to target their efforts to Democratic senators. They are viewed as more partisan, may not be very effective, but seem to have more influence in the Great Plains.

The general farm organizations are respected for their efforts to look beyond the farm and present their views on social and other issues. However, the commodity groups focus on their special interests.

Farm commodity groups are viewed as having increased influence, although they may have many divergent interests. They seem to zero in on an issue and are usually better informed. Some see the strength and influence shifting from general farm organizations to commodity groups because of their ability to be specific and research the issues. They also seem to have maintained a nonpartisan image.

The large commodity groups, such as the wheat growers, may have more strength with their national membership, but they may not always be consistent in their policies.

The dairymen, who received a minimum of 80 percent of parity support under the 1977 Food and Agriculture Act, are viewed as "pretty notorious" in their campaign contributions. One Senate staff member observes that people do not vote against a candidate for accepting such contributions. You cannot document that anybody sold out, he commented, but milk interests have done better than other commodity groups in keeping price supports pegged to 75 or 80 percent of parity.

The American Agricultural Movement (AAM) participants received a sympathetic hearing in many congressional offices in 1978 and 1979. But in mid-1979 they were still viewed as a leaderless group with too many viewpoints. They failed to focus on a few issues and lacked policy resolutions, consistent statements, and central leadership, and, as one staff member observed, were "without portfolio." Their belligerent, insulting approach produced negative reactions. They did not understand the legislative process and consequently made enemies on Capitol Hill. They had no point to fall back to in negotiations on issues. Their fanaticism was viewed as unrealistic and their 90 to 100 percent of parity goal as ineffective. "They just plain irritated a lot of people with their brash behavior and ceaseless repetition," related one staff member. Perhaps the futility of the AAM effort is best illustrated by the picture of the farm strike billboard, half hidden by the wheat growing up in front of it the following summer.

Among cooperative groups, the National Rural Electric Cooperative Association is considered very credible, trusted, gives both sides of the issues, and understands tradeoffs in legislative negotiations. It prepares its visiting board members and local officials with a one-and-one-half-day seminar orientation, briefing them on the issues before they visit Capitol Hill. Then they visit the members of Congress from their home state and district.

Farm groups who claim to be nonpartisan must be careful not to deviate from that position. Members of Congress are sensitive to news coverage and photographs appearing in the organization publications, especially during the campaign periods, and resent coverage which appears to favor their opponent.

Farm women's groups are seen as less knowledgeable on the issues than other groups, more naive, and very emotional. Their testimony and discussions have shown a lack of understanding of how many farm programs and government regulations work. Yet they do get sympathy and good treatment from committee members when they testify.

The farm organizations have direct connections with residents in the congressional district. Local district contact is significant and represents one of the major strengths of these groups.

Business and Industry Groups

Business and industry groups are usually better organized than farm and citizens' groups. They come in, state their case, tell what they want, carry a wealth of information, describe the effect on the economy of their proposals, and come in and go out quickly, being very considerate of the member's time. Congressional staff members especially appreciate the efforts of these groups to get acquainted with them.

Industry groups often are able to bring in a concensus and can unite on an issue, while other groups are move divided.

Many of these groups have offices in Washington, establish regular contacts with committee members, send information continuously, and are always ready to respond to inquiries. Industry response to questions is appreciated and considered very helpful. With members of Congress and their staff expected to be expert on everything, the staff is spread thin.

Money alone does not account for the success and respect of business and industry representatives. Their work is seen as well documented and well planned. Their staffs work within the system. They are respected because they use analysis rather than emotion. However, one staff member was concerned that at times even business groups could leave out facts to support their views and instead just proclaim their philosophical opposition to government involvement that would compete with private business.

Appearances at hearings are seen as effective ways to communicate. Many industry groups have a reputation for giving thorough, well-reasoned statements. As a result, changes in federal grain inspection were made at the export points, and none were made at the state level.

However, some business interests are viewed with suspicion. Some members of the sugar lobby, in jockeying to get foreign import quotas for their clients under the Sugar Act prior to 1974, included some very deceiving persons or, as one staff member viewed it, "outright crooks."

Citizens' and Consumers' Special-Interest Groups

The citizens' and consumers' special-interest groups are effectively orgaized and are concerned with regulations as well as legislation. Some view their work as well prepared and homework well done. Witnesses are carefully selected. Others view these groups as confusing the issue or as fadists who do shoddy research. Yet they are also recognized as providing a balance to the broad spectrum of views on an issue. They are respected as representing a special interest of some people. Their efforts may be more effective with the House or Senate as a whole than with particular members of the agriculture committees.

Membership strength may be the major weakness of some special-interest groups. They have been described as long on research, providing a lot of studies, but short on back-home representation. They are viewed as Washington-based with no extensive network in the home districts. They have a mailing list, but that is not viewed as being a card-carrying member of a major farm organization. As one staff member phrased the situation, "They don't represent buyers back home." Another assessed the situation this way: "There are 27 environmental groups in our state; the same 100 people belong to all of them." Many of these groups have no means of identifying their membership.

Environmental and conservation groups with different objectives are viewed from different perspectives.

In the Western states with large areas of public lands and national forests, the issues focus on whether to carefully use the land for agriculture, mining, and forestry to provide a living for the lcoal residents. The people who live there do not want to "lock it up." Out-of-state environmental interests are looked at unfavorably because they do not have to depend on use of those resources for a living. Although cattle grazing is permitted in wilderness areas, the only way to go in to look after them is with a horse.

So environmental groups who want to avoid disrupting the environment often face opposition from those who want to use the natural resources and may be labeled "proenergy." Both groups will have effective arguments, and committee members must take personal experience into account.

Members of Congress who represent states with substantial public land areas are concerned that many other members do not understand the issues and concerns of local residents in the public land areas, since so many members do not have public lands in their states or districts.

The Sierra Club and Friends of the Earth are viewed as organizations that would like to conserve everything. They can generate mail on any issue of interest.

The National Association of Conservation Districts and the Wildlife Management Institute (WMI) have an interest in proper land use and are viewed as moderates. The WMI receives support from the gun manufacturers and professional wildlife people and also gets some use of the resources of state game and fish departments. They have more influence than their membership would indicate.

As a result of the sharp division in views among environmental and conservation groups, one close observer feels that some of the worst legislation written deals with use of public lands. Open debate and compromise yield little agreement, so the major interest groups get around the table to hammer out agreeable legislation. Wording is vague, and full meaning may not be understood.

Setting aside wilderness areas is a political issue. The extreme groups would like to double the acreage set aside in wilderness. The National Audubon Society is seen as more moderate in its views. The National Wildlife Federation is moving to a more conservationist stance. Friends of the Earth and the Izaak Walton League are believed to be having financial problems in maintaining their legislative activity.

The conservation and environmental interests have been effective in getting legislation passed. The National Wilderness Act, Federal Insecticide, Fungicide, and Rodenticide Act, and creation of the Environmental Protection Agency are credited to their efforts. However, the crunch between resources and economics has come, so that future efforts may be less successful.

The environmental groups' positions may have a regressive economic impact which would hurt lower-income people most. As one staff member summed it up, "They are sincere but the consequences of their proposals may lead us to do evil in the name of good."

Citizens' groups are sometimes viewed as undependable. They do not show up at hearings to present their views. Dairy and sugar programs seem to draw the most interest. Sometimes they come in with their script written and are not ready to listen to other points of view. Others describe them as very rigid and too basic in their arguments. They would be more effective if they knew the background of the staff to whom they are talking. On sugar program issues, they are concerned about consumer sugar prices and make positive arguments. But they may lack some of the facts in the complete picture. Organized labor is viewed as having "political clout" and could pass or defeat a sugar bill with the minimum-wage provisions in it that they want.

Some of these groups appear hostile and do not consider what some rural-oriented members of Congress see as legitimate needs of producers. When a witness representing one organization testifies but is employed by another organization, the relationship between the organizations may be confusing. In some cases, it is not clear what groups of people they represent. If a group receives government grants or contracts for certain work, that may also affect how their testimony is received. In predominately rural districts, these groups may have little activity and are relatively unknown.

Groups representing churches, or church-related in their objectives, are viewed as expanding their efforts and having an important potential for effective lobbying. Bread for the World is noted for getting attention from members and their staffs. Lay church groups can develop informed public sentiment, which is what counts. Church groups, in supporting food shipments under the Public Law 480 subsidized export programs, have been quite effective. On the other hand, one staff member observes that they have been especially effective in getting inocuous things done and have accomplished little or nothing in getting actual dollars because they did not follow through on appropriations. It is easy to get a study authorized since there is not much cost.

Rural-oriented citizens' groups include persons with concerns for rural communities, low-income people, rural housing, small farmers, and other associated problems in rural areas. Rural America is looked on as the "poverty lobby." The National Rural Center is viewed as having capable leadership, but no constituency. The National Family Farm Coalition is viewed sympathetically, but it includes few (if any) real farmers, and they need farm support to succeed.

Special-interest groups related to diet and health are viewed as having an organized constituency, but being more limited than some other agricultural and food groups. They were not strong enough to prevent the Senate Select Committee on Nutrition from being merged with the Senate Agriculture Committee in 1977.

The classic hunger groups identified with food issues are the Center for Science in the Public Interest, Children's Foundation, Community Nutrition Institute, and the Food Research and Action Center (FRAC). They are actively making contacts with government officials, but are viewed as having little or no organization membership as such. Yet through newsletters they can generate letters to members of Congress.

Hunger is conceived as having a constituency and a sense of legitimacy; FRAC, although a public interest law firm, is viewed with credibility, performing a sincere representation of poor people. Sometimes, however, the food and hunger groups do not separate the issues on nutrition for the total population from issues related to expanding food-assistance programs for low-income people.

The citizens' and consumers' special-interest groups, including those with concerns for environment, welfare and food assistance, world hunger, and organized labor, are faulted for failing to put their positions in a context with the total economy. Sometimes they exaggerate their position. They are generally latter-day entrants into the food and agricultural lobbying scene. To the farm-oriented member of Congress, they are viewed almost as a foreign intruder. As one rural district staff member commented, "They don't communicate what we want to hear."

Many consumer and liberal groups are basically Democratic. They look to the majority party members and forget the Republicans. But if Democrats are split, then they contact both sides. Minority staff members believe they should consult with both sides. Sometimes Republicans will oppose a group just because they were not consulted.

Although citizens' groups have been fairly effective in getting favorable public sentiment and support from Congress, some see the "golden era" about to end. Program costs may be getting too high for further congressional support.

Some citizen and consumer group participants have been described as zealots. They call attention to issues and present a point of view. But sometimes their facts are not straight, and they are impractical. They have too simplified answers and very little flexibility. Farm groups are viewed as often more willing to compromise.

Fragmented and diverse interests are a problem with special interest and citizens' groups. How homogeneous is the consumer interest? Can one group represent all consumers? As with any large group, internal differences must sometimes be resolved.

Coalitions

Coalitions have been formed to strengthen legislative effort on specific food and agricultural issues in recent years. These include a farm coalition, consumer coalition, an ad hoc committee of rice consumers, and a sugar users' group. Opinion varies about how effective coalitions can be, but they can claim some successes.

The end of the food-stamp purchase requirement written into the 1977 Food and Agriculture Act is credited to a coalition effort of consumer, church, and labor groups. However, it also received bipartisan support through joint sponsorship by Senators McGovern and Dole.

Producers put together a coalition that wrote the sugar provisions in the 1977 Food and Agricultural Act.

A coalition of consumer, professional, hunger, labor, and farm commodity groups united to keep school food programs under the USDA instead of moving them to a newly proposed Department of Education in 1978. Although the Department of Education Bill was not acted on until 1979, the coalition efforts still took credit for success.[1]

The farm coalition was first formed in 1970 and testified again in 1973 and 1977. In 1977, fewer organizations joined in the effort. Although they met and agreed on coalition testimony, the existence of a coalition did not change actions by individual members. They really did not have a united front, and after the coalition testified, many of the member organizations also testified separately.

The National Family Farm Coalition is viewed as including some strange bedfellows. It appears to be made up mostly of groups supporting organic farming and less energy use or appropriate technology, farm workers, sharecroppers, and consumers who want low food prices.

The Farm Water Alliance, formed to oppose the 160-acre limitation in federal water projects, is also comprised of unusual groups that would not normally be expected to support a single issue.

A coalition of consumer groups, led by Congress Watch and Community Nutrition Institute and with the sympathetic support of the Consumer Federation of America, is credited with the defeat of the 1978 Farm Bill in the House after approval by the Senate. The bill probably would have increased government costs and consumer food prices. Farm groups were divided on the bill, but were able to push it through the Senate. However, when diligent workers from their Washington offices moved onto Capitol Hill and informed members of Congress and their staffs about the probable consequences, the result was an overwhelming defeat for the American Agricultural Movement which spearheaded the efforts that the National Farmers Union and National Farmers Organization supported. The American Farm Bureau Federation did not actively oppose the bill, but was pleased with its defeat.

Just what are the conditions under which coalitions will be effective, and when will they fail?

A coalition most effectively bands together for a single issue or bill and usually disbands after a decision is made. Usually they do not have a long or continuous life, but may come together again later. Coalitions can save time for the committee, but they should be able to document whom they represent and persuasively demonstrate that the leadership of the groups is behind the coalition. The support of the groups they represent is what really counts.

Coalitions are viewed as carrying more weight since they speak for a larger membership. The nature of their activity depends on the bill or the issue. Formation of a coalition involves an evolution of thinking that moves opinions toward the center of the range of issues. It is often easier for commodity groups to join a coalition than general farm organizations. Coalitions can be potentially effective and very important on major bills. Since the committee needs a concensus, the coalition can assist in reaching it by bringing together some groups in advance of committee debate. They are most effective with members of the committee if someone from the district or that state can make direct contact to substantiate the coalition's views. Committees also look at the makeup of the coalition.

It is generally agreed that a coalition can accomplish more as a united group. They can reach understanding on a common issue and seek a broader range of people to support it. But much of its effectiveness will depend on the issue and what they want. Coalitions formed by groups that have been divided on past issues may be viewed with suspicion.

General Conclusions

Many new groups and interests are moving in to influence food and agricultural policies. Even a small minority of active people can be a new factor in the consideration of a bill. However, the key to success in dealing with Congress is the ability to mobilize people. The focal point is in the congressional district. As one veteran staff member observes, "There are a lot of weighty intellects around Capitol Hill, but they don't add up to votes in the home district."

Earlier observers looking at lobby groups concluded that congressmen see interest groups as having a helpful and legitimate role in the legislative process, and they appear to have no quarrel with groups as long as the groups do not step out of that role. The point which all groups must remember is that "if it is the privilege of the interest groups to propose, it is the unquestioned prerogative of Congress to dispose."[2]

Notes

1. The members of the coalition included:

Amalgamated Meat Cutters and Butcher Workmen (AFL-CIO)

American Academy of Pediatrics

American Home Economics Association

American School Food Service Association

Children's Foundation

Community Nutrition Institute

Congress Watch

Consumer Federation of America

Council for Responsible Nutrition

Food Research and Action Center

National Broiler Council

National Cattlemen's Association

National Milk Producers Federation

National Turkey Federation

Peanut Growers of Alabama and Georgia

Poultry and Egg Institute

United Egg Producers

2. Andrew M. Scott and Margaret A. Hung, *Congress and Lobbies, Image and Reality* (Chapel Hill: University of North Carolina Press, 1965), pp. 58-59.

The Future Role for Food and Agricultural Lobbyists

What is past is prologue. —Shakespeare

There is no doubt that public interest activists believe that they know what is best. This is a sin, however, of which all lobbyists and interest groups are guilty. —Jeffrey M. Berry[a]

The organizations and groups attempting to influence the future direction of federal-government policies and programs have a wide range of membership, operating funds, programs, activities, and degree of effectiveness. Whether through testimony, letters, research reports, news articles, or direct contact with government officials, each is practicing the art of influence and persuasion.

Farm Producer and Rural-Oriented Groups

In chapter 1 the general farm organizations were identified as part of the agricultural establishment. Members of these groups do, with input from the various staff personnel, provide the outline for organizational lobbying. It is expected that the priorities for these organizations will continue to be influenced strongly by members, even though priority-issue decisions will often be decided by the staff.[1]

The broad range of issues that the general farm organizations address make it difficult for them to pinpoint specific issues as well as the commodity organizations have been able to do. The commodity and special interests such as tobacco, dairy, rice, peanuts, wool, sugar, and cotton tend to fragment the food and agricultural policy-making process. Some view commodity organizations as more effective politically than general farm organizations because they can zero in on legislation, are more sophisticated and better organized, and have better access to power than many other special-interest groups.[2]

Nevertheless, the farm organizations, which carry on open discussion and debate at state and national meetings, prepare resolutions that probably more accurately represent a consensus of membership opinion than any other group with concerns over food and agricultural issues.

---

[a]Jeffrey M. Berry, *Lobbying for the People, The Political Behavior of Public Interest Groups* (Princeton, N.J.: Princeton University Press, 1977), p. 292.

New producer groups organized primarily for legislative and lobbying efforts face an uncertain future. The American Agricultural Movement, which emerged from the financial strains faced by farmers in the winter of 1978, staged its tractorcades to Washington and made persistent contacts with congressmen and government officials; yet by early 1980, it had not become established as an institution like the other major farm organizations. The results of formal organization efforts in 1979 remain uncertain as its leaders want to establish an organization with national leadership but with individual state organization autonomy somewhat different from other national farm organizations. Their efforts to promote alcohol fuel production from farm products may attract and hold members' interest.

The major farm organizations will continue to provide business services to their members and also carry on legislative activity on state and national issues. As in recent years, the general farm organizations' legislative efforts will be competing for attention in varying degrees with farm commodity and cooperative groups who will focus in on fewer and more specific issues. Consumer groups will also voice their concerns. This situation in no way diminishes the support from their membership; it means only that there are many groups who will continue to speak out on food and agricultural issues. The general farm organizations, although older and more firmly established, will have to compete for time and attention at public hearings, in the offices of members of Congress, and before federal agencies, in making their views known.

Another challenge to the established agricultural organizations comes from the small farmers, hired farm workers, minority groups in rural areas, rural nonfarm people, and environmental groups. These groups maintain that farm policies of the past have done little for them. They have challenged the farm policy agendamakers and have succeeded in getting their issues on the agenda.[3] Federal programs and agencies and private foundations are giving these groups financial support and visibility.

As Paarlberg sees the situation, "The better informed, the more astute and the politically sophisticated groups are writing up the requests for federal grants under these various programs and are getting them. The bureaucracy is digging in, supporting the programs in which it has an interest. Political power is congealing around these new programs.[4]

How extensive the activities of these groups will continue to be depends on how well federal grants continue to provide the major part of their financial operating base. In 1979, Rural America was threatened with substantial loss of support for its rural housing activities funded by the Department of Labor. A national trend toward less government and an administration fighting to hold the line against inflation will mean continued review of all federal programs.

However, funding from several federal sources and assistance through public-interest law firms, private foundations, and other private contributions will help some of these groups survive despite the loss of some financial support.

Farm women's groups add a new dimension to the food and agricultural legislative scene. Their future will depend on the calibre of their leadership and the persistence of their efforts to establish themselves as a new voice from a segment of the farm population that has not previously been active outside the traditional farm organizations. The national movement to provide more nearly equal economical, social, and political status for women should lend support to continued activities by farmwives.

With rising costs of energy and threatened shortages of petroleum, more active participation by the alternative agricultural movement may emerge in the 1980s. Alternative agriculturalists believe that conventional agriculture is destructive of both human and natural resources and is therefore destined to destroy itself as well as the larger population.

The alternative agriculturalists are deeply committed to the reorientation of agricultural practices and techniques. The participants in this group include a variety of beliefs, practices, and goals. Some have been identified as organic and ecofarmers.[5] The alternative farmers are not well organized, and few (if any) lobbies directly and specifically represent their ideological goals. But an elaborate networking system of publications, newsletters, and contact groups will likely see some of their ideas being proposed in the policy-making processes of the 1980s.

Business and Industry Groups

As long as private, independent business firms continue to provide products and services to the food and agricultural industry, there will be trade associations and groups providing various business and information services to these firms. The extent of lobbying varies with associations, and such variation will continue to exist.

Many business and industry groups are highly respected by members of Congress because they can provide helpful information for legislative decisions. They work at the job continually of keeping congressional staff and government officials informed of new developments.

Although often criticized by the press and consumer, citizen, and environmental groups, private industry and the free-enterprise system provide the goods and services that the U.S. public depends on. The efforts to regulate and control these activities will result in group reactions by various business and trade groups to make their concerns and interests known to the federal-policy decisionmakers.

Citizens' and Consumers' Groups

Lobbying in a general sense is the act of representation where an interest group becomes an intermediary between citizens and government. Most of the producer, business and industry, professional, institutional, and organized labor groups were organized for several purposes. Lobbying and legislative activity is usually only one.

Many of the citizen, consumer, or public-interest groups, on the other hand, were established with lobbying and educational activity as their major purpose, and they may not have an established and financially secure organization behind them. Financial stress will threaten or curtail activities of some public interest groups in future years while others will thrive from membership and support.

One example is the National Consumers Congress which had strong interests in dairy policy until its 1977 merger with the National Consumers League. The project leader cited difficulties in maintaining press, staff, and membership interest on an extremely technical issue, lack of vital foundation support, and competing priorities pressing on limited resources as reasons for the suspension.[6]

Citizen and consumer groups, however, have emerged as a major force influencing food and agricultural policy decisions in the 1970s. Continued input can be expected in the 1980s as a result of (1) the fact that more than half of the USDA budget is devoted to food and nutrition programs; (2) consumer and rural community welfare-oriented leadership in the Department of Agriculture, as illustrated by the appointment of Carol Foreman as assistant Secretary of Agriculture for food and nutrition programs, Alex Mercure as assistant secretary for rural development and community affairs, and M. Rupert Cutler as assistant secretary for conservation, research, and education; (3) the administration of legislation such as the Federal Insecticide, Pesticide, and Rodenticide Act outside of the USDA which in the past has been more producer-oriented than other agencies are likely to be in the future; (4) the funding and growth of rural poverty, housing, farm worker assistance, and community development programs by the Departments of Health, Education, and Welfare, and Labor;[7] (5) activities by the antitrust division of the Justice Department and congressional discussion to bring farmer cooperatives under the jurisdiction of the antitrust laws; and (6) a growing interest among some citizens' groups concerning issues dealing with domestic and world hunger problems, environmental concerns, and the welfare of the poor.

Close observers of citizens' and consumers' groups with food, agricultural, and rural community-oriented interests see these groups communicating to a large segment of the nonfarm population through churches and labor groups that the traditional farm producer groups do not reach.

The increased interest and activity by churches and church-related groups in food and agricultural issues stems largely from the drought, famines, and reduced grain supplies that occurred in Central Africa and other parts of the world in the early 1970s. The positions and testimony presented in Washington by church-oriented groups may or may not represent a majority of their members.

Berry reported that almost all the church representatives interviewed acknowledged that the Washington office took much more liberal positions than the parishioners would mandate if they had the opportunity.[8] However, church-supported lobbies are the least likely to be staff-dominated, and movement into new policy areas is likely to be debated in the light of church doctrine.[9] The future role of church-related and oriented groups will depend on how well the leadership can rally local community membership support across the country to issues being considered by federal policymakers.

Some leaders of organized labor have participated in legislative activity dealing with food and agricultural issues. They have also helped organize the Consumer Federation of American and are represented on the board. They have given major support to the National Council of Senior Citizens. No serious conflicts seemed to have arisen over wages and rising consumer prices. The philosophy seems to be that workers and retired workers are also consumers, and unions have a role to play representing their members as consumers as well as working for their economic benefits through higher wages.

Causes and Coalitions

The groups and organizations concerned with food and agricultural issues have used law, confrontation, information, and constituency influence and pressures to achieve their goals. Usually a group will use more than one of these strategies, but seldom will they be able to utilize all four. Such strategies can be expected to be used to a varying extent by the different groups.

With the many groups and issues facing national policymakers, the continued use of coalitions seems likely. These coalitions will be most active during the periods when specific legislation is under active consideration. The coalitions will not eliminate conflict of views on many of the crucial food and agricultural issues. They are more likely to bring together similar viewpoints of the past, such as consumers and users of specific products, producers who use and businessmen who supply important equipment and supplies employed in production, and consumer and organized labor interests that are concerned with prices and supplies of food.

Producer-consumer group coalitions will be difficult to form because of the conflicting interests of consumers who want abundant supplies of food at stable prices and producers who want higher incomes and relief from rising costs in the face of shrinking profits. Coalitions between some segments of the processing industry with consumers are possible. However, the antiagribusiness sentiment among many citizen and consumer groups is more likely to encourage joint efforts between producer and business groups who find more common grounds for cooperative efforts.

The fact remains that legislative efforts will require dealing with a Congress that is, in a sense, made up of 535 small businesses. The proprietor of each business is responsible to a segment of the U.S. public for his or her continued tenure in office.

Conflict and Conformity

The degree of conflict or agreement on policy decisions will affect the effectiveness of interest groups attempting to influence public policy. Citizen and consumer groups have faced conflict concerning policy decisions. Friends of the Earth was established by David Brower when his leadership and policies in the Sierra Club were questioned. Consumers Union and Consumer Federation of America have suffered from significant internal disputes.[10]

The farm producer groups also have had internal differences. Oren Lee Staley, one of the founders and president of National Farmers Organization, resigned in January 1979 "to unify the membership for an all-out effort to achieve NFO goals."[11]

The American Farm Bureau Federation elected Allan Grant as president in 1975 even though its incumbent president, William Kuhfuss, was a candidate for reelection. The differences within the organization were not centered on basic philosophy and policies, but rather of regional preferences for national leadership, a desire for change, and the type of administrative structure that the national organization should have. The election of Robert Delano in 1980 brings the Southeast into top leadership.

While any organization can be expected to have members with different points of view, the strength of any membership group attempting to influence policy decisions will depend on how broadly it represents a segment of the population and how well it can communicate concerns and positions that represent a large majority of its membership.

Those organizations without membership will face a continuing problem convincing members of Congress, as well as some other government officials, that they speak for a constituency that really supports their lobbying efforts.

Consensus and Consequences

Lobbyists and advocacy group participants are influenced and motivated by their formal education and training, the community environment under which they grew up, and the values, policies, and philosophies of the organizations which they represent. The actors and the supporting staff behind the scenes in food and agriculture policy making vary from extremely conservative to liberal in political, economic, and social philosophy.

Some would maintain the status quo because they have benefitted and are satisfied under the present system and with policies of the past. Others would favor complete overhaul in the organization and structure of food production and distribution, in the ownership and control of land, and in the distribution of incomes to farmers, landowners, workers, and business firms engaged in food and agricultural production.

For every policy decision there is a consequence to all groups or segments of the population. In a democratic system where all the population is represented, the final policy decisions usually are a compromise between the extreme points of view. The consequence is usually gradual change within the present system rather than abrupt change or disruptions.

The goals of different groups lead to different consequences. For some participants, the major goal is economic efficiency, where the policies proposed will lead to the greatest quantities produced at the lowest costs. For some producer groups the goal is a price that provides a cost of production and a reasonable profit. Some activists advocate goals to bring about social justice through land reform and redistribution, setting up of rules as to who can own land, and special credit programs for young people and minorities who want to become established as farm operators. Those concerned with hunger problems of the poor at home and abroad would seek to expand food assistance programs through the domestic food-stamp program and international food aid financed through federal funds.

The most important responsibility for citizens who join or contribute to an organization concerned with food and agricultural issues is that they fully understand what policies this organization supports and what the consequences of such policies are likely to be for producers, consumers, and the U.S. economic, political, and social systems.

Lobbyists and others who make their views known to Congress and other government decisionmakers are participating in the process of reaching policy decisions—a vital part of the U.S. system of representative government. Participation by so many groups and organizations, trying to influence 535 members of Congress and hundreds of administrative officials, may appear costly and confusing. But decisions by a few, with no opportuni. or citizens to participate, is one alternative that most of us in the United States are not yet ready to accept.

Notes

1. William P. Browne and Charles W. Wiggins, "Resolutions and Priorities: Lobbying by the General Farm Organizations," *Policy Studies Journal* 6, 4 (Summer 1978):497. Reprinted with permission.

2. Charles M. Hardin, "Agricultural Price Policy: The Political Role of Bureaucracy," *Policy Studies Journal* 6, 4 (Summer 1978):471.

3. Don Paarlberg, "A New Agenda for Agriculture," *Policy Studies Journal* 6, 4 (Summer 1978):505.

4. Ibid., p. 506.

5. Garth Youngberg, "The Alternative Agricultural Movement," *Policy Studies Journal* 6, 4 (Summer 1978):524. Reprinted with permission.

6. James L. Guth, "Consumer Organizations and Federal Dairy Policy," *Policy Studies Journal* 6, 4 (Summer 1978):502.

7. A separate Department of Education was created by Congress in 1979. The remaining health and welfare functions were to become the Department of Health and Human Services.

8. Berry, *Lobbying for the People*, p. 194.

9. Ibid., p. 198.

10. Ibid., p. 208.

11. *NFO Reporter* 24, 1 (January-February 1979).

Appendix A
Directory of
Organizations and
Firms with Legislative
Interests in Food
and Agriculture

To be included in this appendix, an organization or firm testified before congressional committees, registered as a lobbyist with the Clerk of the House of Representatives, was represented by a registered lobbyist, participated in hearings on rules or regulations held by a federal agency, maintained a Washington office for contact with government officials and communication with its members, or engaged in research and information activity designed to influence federal policy decisions. More complete information is included about those groups engaged both in public testimony and in lobbying and legislative activities. The registered lobbyists listed were employed by or represented the organization some time during 1977, 1978, or 1979. A classification by type of group is indicated by the number following the name. The code number following each organization or firm classifies it into these categories:

1. General farm organizations
2. Producer commodity organizations
3. Producer cooperatives
4. Farm wives
5. Other producer advocates
6. Business and industry
7. Citizens or consumers
8. Conservation or environmental
9. Organized labor
10. Public employees or public institutions
11. Professional, research, or information
12. Indian tribes

When funding is listed, the amounts and sources may be only part of what that organization has received.

ABBOTTS DAIRIES DIVISION, FAIRMOUNT FOODS   (6)
333 W. Loop North
Houston, Texas   77025

Registered Lobbyist: Marshall, Bratter, Greene, Allison, & Tucker
1140 Connecticut Avenue NW
Washington, DC 20036

AD HOC COMMITTEE OF INDUSTRIAL RICE USERS   (6)

Washington Representative
and Registered Lobbyist: Thomas H. Boggs, Jr.
                                Patton, Boggs, & Blow
                                2550 M Street NW
                                Washington, DC   20037
                                202/233-4040

The Ad Hoc Committee of Industrial Rice Users is a group of industrial rice users including millers, processors, distributors, and exporters of rice and rice products. Testimony was given before House and Senate Agricultural Committees in February 1977.

Membership: Adolph Coors Co.; Anheuser-Busch, Inc.; Baker-Beechnut Corp.; Campbell Soup Co.; Connell Rice & Sugar Co., Inc.; Food Corp. International; General Foods Corp.; General Mills, Inc.; Gerber Products Co.; Kellogg Co.; Ralston Purina Co.; Riviana Foods, Inc.; Uncle Ben's, Inc.; United States Brewers Association, Inc.

AD HOC COMMITTEE OF RICE CONSUMERS   (7)

Washington Representative: Wayne Horiuchi
                             1730 Rhode Island Ave.
                             Washington, DC

The Ad Hoc Committee of Rice Consumers is a coalition of consumers concerned about the production and price of rice. They testified before the House and Senate Agriculture Committees in 1977 when renewal of the Rice Production Act was being considered.

Membership: Chinatown Planning Council; Chinese American Restaurant Association of Greater New York; The Harlem Consumer Education Council and National Black Consumers; Japanese American Citizens League; League of United Latin American Citizens; The New York Consumer Assembly; Organization of Chinese Americans; World Hunger Year.

AGRI-BUSINESSMEN, INC.   (6)
141 W. Jackson Boulevard, Suite 1245
Chicago, Illinois   60604

Founded: 1977

Washington Representative: Robert W. Blanchette
                             Alston, Miller, & Gaines
                             1800 M Street NW, Suite 1000
                             Washington, DC   20036   202/223-1300

Agri-Businessmen, Inc. is a group of commodity futures traders, hedgers, speculators, and brokerage firms who have an interest in how government regulates commodity futures trading.

Registered Lobbyists: Robert W. Blanchette
                        Martin, Ryan, Haley, & Associates
                        1511 K Street NW
                        Washington, DC   20005

AGRICO CHEMICAL CO.   (6)
Bank of Oklahoma Tower
1 Williams Center
Tulsa, Oklahoma   74103

Registered Lobbyist: Charls E. Walker Associates, Inc.
                       1730 Pennsylvania Avenue NW
                       Washington, DC   20006

AGRICULTURAL PUBLISHERS ASSOCIATION, INC.   (6)
P.O. Box 2351
Falls Church, Virginia   22042

Registered Lobbyist: Frank R. Cawley

AGRICULTURAL RESEARCH INSTITUTE   (10)
2100 Pennsylvania Avenue NW
Washington, DC   20036   202/659-2517

Executive Director: Paul Truitt

The Agricultural Research Institute is a nonprofit organization of research managers of state and federal agencies, experiment stations, colleges, university and industrial firms, trade organizations engaged in research, education, development, and extension in agriculture.

Membership: 140

Publications: Annual proceedings, quarterly newsletter, others available upon request.

AGRICULTURAL TRADE COUNCIL   (6)

Founded: 1976

Chief Executive Officer: Peter J.T. Nelson

The Agricultural Trade Council was a nonprofit trade association representing export interests of agricultural growers, producers, agricultural equipment, and other manufacturers. It was active in 1977, but has since closed its Washington office.

Membership: Louis Dreyfus Corp., Stamford, Conn.; American Breeders Service, Deforest, Wis.; The All American Nut Co., Carritos, Calif.; Angel Farmers, Butte City, Calif.; Gateway International Co., Washington, D.C.; Livestock Marketing Association, Kansas City, Mo.; The Port Authority, Port of Portland, Portland, Ore.; The Seattle First National Bank, Seattle, Wash.

AGRICULTURE COUNCIL OF AMERICA   (11)
1625 Eye Street NW, Suite 708
Washington, DC   20006   202/466-3100

President: Allen Paul

AGRI. INTERNATIONAL, Inc.   (6), (3)
Washington, DC

Registered Lobbyist: Leighton, Conklin, & Lemov
                        2033 M Street NW
                        Washington, DC   20036

AK CHIN INDIAN COMMUNITY   (12)
Route 1, Box 12
Maricopa, Arizona   85239

Registered Lobbyist: Rebecca D. Shapiro & Associates
                        111 C Street SE
                        Washington, DC   20003

AMALGAMATED MEAT CUTTERS AND BUTCHER WORKERS OF AMERICA, AFL-CIO   (9)
2800 N. Sheridan Road
Chicago, Illinois   60657   312/248-8700

Founded: 1897

Washington Office: 100 Indiana Avenue NW, Room 502
                     Washington, DC   20001   202/347-1203

Legislative Representative and Registered Lobbyist: Arnold Mayer

The Amalgamated Meat Cutters and Butcher Workers of America is comprised of 500 local unions whose members work in meat, retail, poultry, egg, canning, leather, fish processing, sugar refining, and fur industries.

Membership: 500,000 local members

Funding: Membership dues

AMERICAN AGRICULTURAL MOVEMENT (5)
Box 57, Springfield, Colorado 81073 303/523-6223

National Chairman: Marvin Meeks
Plainview, Texas 79072

Washington Office: 308 Second Street SE
Washington, DC 20003 202/544-5750

Founded: Movement started in 1977; formal national organization proceedings underway in 1979.

The American Agricultural Movement has drawn together farm operators faced with financial stress who seek higher prices and incomes through parity prices and more control of farm policy decisions by farmers.

Membership: Thirty state organizations expected to affiliate with national organization.

AMERICAN AGRI-WOMEN (4)
Evelyn Cooper (Mrs. Russell), Secretary
4555 15 Mile Road NW
Kent City, Michigan 49330 616/998-9527

Founded: 1974

National President: Joan Adams (Mrs. Don)
Box 424
Buffalo, Oklahoma 74834 405/735-2000

The AAW is a communications link-up for twenty-one affiliated farm and ranch women's organizations in thirty-four states.

Membership: 29,000 family members (1979)

AMERICAN ASSOCIATION OF MEAT PROCESSORS (6)
224 East High Street
Elizabethtown, Pennsylvania 17022

AMERICAN ASSOCIATION OF NURSERYMEN (2)
230 Southern Building
Washington, DC 20005 202/737-4060

Founded: 1875

Washington Representative
and Registered Lobbyist: Leo J. Donahue

This is a national trade association of firms selling, installing, and producing nursery stock, fruit trees, vines, small fruits, trees, and shrubs with $3 billion annual sales.

Membership: 2,700

Publication: *Update* (bimonthly), membership directory (annual).

AMERICAN ASSOCIATION OF STATE COLLEGES AND
UNIVERSITIES   (10)
1 Dupont Circle
Washington, DC   20036   202/293-7070

Founded: 1961

Executive Director: Allan Ostar

The American Association of State Colleges and Universities represents the
state universities not part of the land-grant system.

Membership: 323 institutions in fifty states, fifty departments and schools
of agriculture.

Publications: Memo to the President, proceedings of annual meeting,
"Cooperative Arrangement between Public and Private Colleges," others
available.

AMERICAN ASSOCIATION OF UNIVERSITY AGRICULTURAL
ADMINISTRATORS   (10)

President: James Dalton, Dean
             College of Agriculture, University of Wisconsin
             River Falls, Wisconsin   54022

The American Association of University Agricultural Administrators
represents state-supported, non-land-grant universities which offer degrees
in agriculture or renewable natural resources.

Membership: Fifty universities with 29,365 students and 1,387 graduate
students (1976-1977).

AMERICAN ASSOCIATION OF UNIVESITY WOMEN   (7)
2401 Virginia Avenue NW
Washington, DC   20037

Registered Lobbyist: Ellen S. Griffee

AMERICAN BAKERS ASSOCIATION   (6)
2020 K Street, Suite 850
Washington, DC   20006   202/296-5800

Founded: 1894

President: Robert J. Wager

The American Bakers Association is the trade association of the wholesale baking industry with a wide range of concerns about legislative and regulatory issues dealing with the food industry, energy, and wage-price standards.

Membership: 350

Registered Lobbyists: Donald Gerrish; Acacia G. Hunt; Marcus W. Sisk, Jr.; Robert J. Wager; Van Ness, Feldman, & Sutcliffe; J. Bruce Burkland.

AMERICAN BANKERS ASSOCIATION, AGRICULTURAL BANKERS DIVISION   (6)
1120 Connecticut Avenue NW
Washington, DC   20036   202/467-4000

Founded: 1875

Executive Officer: Willis Alexander

The American Bankers Association is the national trade association of commercial banks. They claim 92 percent of the nation's 14,000 full-service banks as members.

Membership: 12,880 (estimated 1977)

Registered Lobbyists: Katherine O'Flaherty Thompson, Willis W. Alexander, Gerald M. Lowrie.

Publications: *Capital* (weekly), list available on request.

AMERICAN BEEKEEPING FEDERATION, INC.   (2)
13634 NW 39th Avenue
Gainesville, Florida   32601   904/375-0012

Founded: 1940

President: G.C. Walker, Jr.
                   Rogers, Texas

Executive Secretary: Frank Robinson

This national association of beekeepers from all states and segments of the industry includes dealers in beekeepers' supplies and honey packers.

Membership: 1,800 estimated (1979)

Publication: *American Beekeeping Federation News Letter*

AMERICAN CORN MILLERS FEDERATION   (6)
1030 15th Street NW
Washington, DC   20005   202/296-5488

President: Fred H. Mewhinney

AMERICAN COTTON SHIPPERS ASSOCIATION   (6)
318 Cotton Exchange Building, P.O. Box 3366
Memphis, Tennessee   38103   901/525-2272

Founded: 1924

Washington Office: 1707 L Street NW, Suite 460
                                  Washington, DC   20036   202/296-7116

Vice-President and General Counsel: Neal P. Gillen

The American Cotton Shippers Association is a group of U.S. cotton merchants. Its members handle 80 percent of the domestic cotton crop and 90
percent of the export market.

Membership: 500 member firms. Federated Associations: Arkansas-
Missouri Cotton Trade Association; Atlantic Cotton Association; Southern
Cotton Association; Texas Cotton Association; Western Cotton Shippers
Association.

Registered Lobbyist: Neal P. Gillen

AMERICAN COUNCIL ON SCIENCE AND HEALTH   (11)
1995 Broadway
New York, New York   10023   212/362-7044

Founded: 1978

Executive Director: Elizabeth M. Whelan

The American Council on Science and Health is a nonprofit association
promoting scientifically balanced evaluations of chemicals and human
health.

Funding: Subscriptions to publications, donations, foundation grants.

Publications: List available upon request.

AMERICAN COUNCIL OF VOLUNTARY AGENCIES FOR FOREIGN
SERVICE   (7)
200 Park Avenue South
New York, New York   10003   212/777-8210

Executive Director: Leon O. Marion

This confederation of forty-four U.S. voluntary agencies represents major
religious and nationality groups who have overseas operation capabilities to
distribute food commodities.

Founded: 1944

Membership: American Council for Judaism Philanthropic Fund, Inc.;
American Council for Nationalities Service; American Friends Service
Committee, Inc.; American Foundation for Overseas Blind; American
Fund for Czechoslovak Refugees, Inc.; American Mizachi Women; Ameri-
can National Committee to Aid Homeless Armenians (ANCAHA); Ameri-
can ORT Federation, Inc.; Assemblies of God, Foreign Service Committee;
Baptist World Alliance; CARE, Inc. (Cooperative for American Relief
Everywhere); Catholic Relief Services, U.S. Catholic Conference; Christian
Reformed World Relief Committee; Church World Service; CODEL, Inc.
(Cooperation in Development); Community Development Foundation,
Inc.; Foster Parents Plan, Inc.; Foundation for the Peoples of the South
Pacific, Inc.; Hadassah, The Women's Zionist Organization of America,
Inc.; Heifer Project International; HIAS; Holt International Children's
Service, Inc.; Interchurch Medical Assistance, Inc.; International Rescue
Committee, Inc.; Lutheran Immigration and Refugee Service; Lutheran
World Relief, Inc.; MAP, Inc. (Medical Assistance Programs); Mennonite
Central Committee, Inc.; Migration and Refugee Service, U.S. Catholic
Conference; Near East Foundation; PACT, Inc. (Private Agencies Col-
laborating Together); Project Concern, Inc.; The Salvation Army; Save the
Children Federation, Inc.; Seventh-Day Adventist World Service, Inc.;
Tolstoy Foundation, Inc.; Travelers Aid-International Social Service of
America; United Israel Appeal, Inc.; United Lithuanian Relief Fund of
America, Inc.; United Ukranian American Relief Committee, Inc.; World
University Service; Young Men's Christian Association, International Divi-
sion; Young Women's Christian Association of the U.S.A., National
Board, World Relations.

AMERICAN CYANAMID CO.   (6)
1625 I Street NW, Suite 401
Washington, DC   20006

Registered Lobbyist: Donald W. Dalrymple

AMERICAN DIETETIC ASSOCIATION   (11)
430 N. Michigan Avenue
Chicago, Illinois   60611   312/822-0330

Founded: 1917

Executive Director: Clara Zempel

The American Dietetic Association is the national association of professional dieticians.

Membership: 34,715 (1978)

Washington Representatives
and Registered Lobbyists: Betty Blouin, Issabelle Hallahan.

Publication: *Journal of the American Dietetic Association*

AMERICAN ENTERPRISE INSTITUTE FOR PUBLIC POLICY RE—
SEARCH   (11)
1150 17th Street NW
Washington, DC   20036   202/296-5616,   862-5800

Founded: 1943

President: William J. Baroody, Jr.

The American Enterprise Institute for Public Policy Research is a private,
nonpartisan organization engaged in research and education on a broad
range of public issues including economics, law, government, and foreign
policy.

Funding: Contributions and foundation grants.

Publications: List available upon request.

AMERICAN FALLS RESERVOIR DISTRICT   (10)
1132 Locust Street
Twin Falls, Idaho 83301

Registered Lobbyist: Jim Casey
                        1010 16th Street NW, Suite 700
                        Washington, DC   20036

AMERICAN FARM BUREAU FEDERATION   (1)
225 Touhy Avenue
Park Ridge, Illinois 60068   312/339-5700

Founded: 1919

Washington Office: 425 13th Street NW
                     Washington, DC   20004   202/637-0500

President: Robert B. Delano

Director, National Affairs, Washington Office: Vernie R. Glasson

Farm Bureau is a free, independent, nongovernmental, voluntary organization of farm and ranch families united for the purpose of analyzing their
problems and formulating action to achieve education improvement,
economic opportunity, and social advancement and, thereby, to promote
the national well-being. It operates through national, state, and county offices. It is nonpartisan, nonsectarian, and nonsecret in character.

Membership: 3,198,631 (1979) in forty-nine states and Puerto Rico.

Funding: Membership and payments from members for direct services or through affiliated companies and cooperatives. Total revenue was $5,759,388 in 1978.

Registered Lobbyists: John Datt, C.H. Fields, Vernie Glasson, Allan Grant, Thomas A. Hammer, Bruce Hawley, Kirk Miller, Grace Ellen Rice, Michael Stientjes, W. Glenn Tossey, Edward R. Yawn.

Publication: *Farm Bureau News*

AMERICAN FEED MANUFACTURERS ASSOCIATION   (6)
1701 N. Fort Myer Drive
Arlington, Virginia   22209   703/524-0810

Founded: 1909

President: Oakley M. Ray

The American Feed Manufacturers Association is the national association of feed manufacturers. Membership includes firms which manufacture formula feed and related firms which provide ingredients, services, equipment, and supplies to manufacturers.

Membership: 850

Registered Lobbyists: Collier, Shannon, Rill, Edwards, & Scott

Publications: *Feedgram* (newsletter)

AMERICAN FISHERIES DEFENSE COMMITTEE   (6)
10th Floor, 2101 L Street
Washington, DC 20037

Registered Lobbyist: Michael Guimond

AMERICAN FROZEN FOOD INSTITUTE   (6)
919 18th Street NW
Washington, DC 20006

Registered Lobbyists: Michael F. Brown, Victoria R. Calvery, Thomas B. House, Robert Leibner.

AMERICAN HONEY PRODUCERS ASSOCIATION   (2)
P.O. Box 368
Minco, Oklahoma   73059   405/352-4126

Founded: 1969

Executive Secretary and Registered Lobbyist: Glenn Gibson

This is a national association of beekeepers from forty-three states.

Membership: 600

AMERICAN HORSE COUNCIL   (2)
Suite 400, 1700 K Street NW
Washington, DC   20006   202/296-4031

Founded: 1969

General Counsel: George Smathers

Washington Representative
and Registered Lobbyist: Thomas A. Davis, Davis & McLeod;
                                Smathers, Symington, & Herlong.

This is a federation of 100 organizations with membership of 2.5 million
horsemen and -women whose purpose is to promote and protect the U.S.
equine industry.

Publication: *AHC Newsletter*

AMERICAN HUMANE SOCIETY   (7)
P.O. Box 1266
Denver, Colorado   80201   303/750-5599

Founded: 1877

The American Humane Association is a federation of state and local
humane organizations.

Membership: 25,000

Washington Representative
and Registered Lobbyist: Jo V. Morgan, Jr.
                                1060 17 Street NW
                                Washington, DC   20036

Publication: *American Humane Magazine*

AMERICAN KITCHEN FOODS, INC.   (6)
99 Powerhouse Road
Roslyn, New York   11577

Registered Lobbyist: Birch, Horton, Bittner, & Monroe
                        4400 Jenifer Street NW, Suite 300
                        Washington, DC   20015

AMERICAN MEAT INSTITUTE   (6)
P.O. Box 3556
Washington, DC   20007   703/841-2400

Founded: 1906

President: C. Manly Molpus

The American Meat Institute is the trade association of the meat packing industry with members in fifty states. General members are meat packers with federal or state inspection. Associate members are firms providing equipment, supplies, or services to the industry.

Membership: 1,000 firms including 300 meat packers.

Registered Lobbyists: Richard Lyng, A. Dewey Bond, Michael E. Brunner, C. Manly Molpus.

Publications: *Meat Facts* (annual), annual financial review of the meat packing industry, *Newsletter* (weekly).

AMERICAN PUBLIC WELFARE ASSOCIATION (10)
1125 15th Street NW
Washington, DC   20005   202/293-7550

Established: 1930

Executive Director: Edward T. Weaver

The American Public Welfare Association is a national professional association of workers in the field of public welfare. The National Council of State Administrators is a constituent group of the American Public Welfare Association.

Membership: The National Council of State Administrators includes representatives from each of the fifty states and U.S. territories.

Publications: *Public Welfare Journal* (quarterly), *Washington Report* (monthly).

AMERICAN REGISTRY OF PROFESSIONAL
ENTOMOLOGISTS   (11)
4603 Calvert Road
College Park, Maryland   20740   301/864-1336

Founded: 1971

Manager: Bill Wimer

The American Registry of Professional Entomologists is the organization that certifies, through an examining board, individuals who meet their standards for a professional entomologist.

Membership: 1,249

Publications: *ARPE News*, Registry Notes.

AMERICAN RICE, INC.   (3)
P.O. Box 2587
Houston, Texas   77001   713/869-8241

Founded: 1969

Executive Vice-President: Ralph S. Newman

American Rice, Inc., is a marketing and processing cooperative representing about 15 percent of the total U.S. production of rice.

Membership: 2,500

Washington Representative
and Registered Lobbyist: Graham Purcell
                              Doub, Purcell, Muntzing, & Hansen
                              1775 Pennsylvania Ave. NW
                              Washington, DC   20006

Publication: *Directions*

AMERICAN SCHOOL FOOD SERVICE   (10)
4101 E. Iliff Avenue
Denver, Colorado   80222   303/757-8555

Founded: 1946

Executive Director: Lyle Stenfors

The American School Food Service is an organization of mostly public employees directly involved in preparing and serving meals to children.

Membership: 65,000

Publication: *School Food Service Journal*

AMERICAN SEED TRADE ASSOCIATION   (6)
Suite 964, Executive Building
1030 15th Street NW
Washington, DC   20005   202/223-4080

Founded: 1883

Executive Vice-President: Harold D. Loden

The American Seed Trade Association is the national trade association for persons, firms, and corporations engaged in seed production and marketing; associations of seedsmen; and firms providing products and services to the seed industry.

Membership: 747 (1978)

Registered Lobbyists: Harold D. Loden, Robert J. Falasca, Wayne Underwood

Publication: Annual yearbook and proceedings.

AMERICAN SOCIETY OF FARM MANAGERS AND RURAL APPRAISERS   (11)
360 S. Monroe Street, P.O. Box 6857
Denver, Colorado   80206   303/388-4858

Founded: 1929

Executive Vice-President: Carl Norberg

The American Society of Farm Managers and Rural Appraisers is the national professional organization of professional farm managers and rural appraisers.

Membership: 3,625 (June 1979)

Registered Lobbyists: Jack Arthur Kirby
1516 Country Line Road
Rosemont, Pennsylvania   19010

Thomas R. Hendershot
Obermayer, Rebmann, Maxwell, & Hipple
2001 I Street NW
Washington, DC 20006

AMERICAN SOYBEAN ASSOCIATION   (2)
777 Craig Road
St. Louis, Missouri   63141   314/432-1600

Founded: 1920

Washington Representative: Dr. William King
1101 Connecticut Avenue NW
Washington, DC   20036   202/872-1585

The American Soybean Association is an organization of soybean producers with twenty-four affiliated state associations. Market check-off programs are carried out in nineteen states, with 350,000 farmers contributing funds for market development and research programs.

Membership: 20,000

Publications: *Soybean Update* (weekly), *Soybean Digest* (monthly), *Soybean Bluebook* (annually), *Soy World* (monthly).

AMERICAN SUGARBEET GROWERS ASSOCIATION   (2)

Founded: 1940 (incorporated 1975)

Washington Office: Richard W. Blake, Executive Vice-President
                           and Registered Lobbyist
                     Suite 900, 1776 K Street NW
                     Washington, DC   20006   202/833-2398

The American Sugarbeet Growers Association is an organization of sugar beet growers in twelve states with sixteen affiliated associations.

Publication: *Sugargram* (biweekly)

AMERICAN SUGAR CANE LEAGUE OF THE U.S.A., Inc.   (6)
416 Whitney Building
New Orleans, Louisiana   70130

Founded: 1922

Washington Office: 918 16th Street NW
                     Washington, DC   20006   202/785-4070

President: P.J. De Gravelles, Jr.

The American Sugar Cane League of the U.S.A., Inc., is a nonprofit association organized to protect and preserve the welfare of the Louisiana sugar cane producers and processors of sugar cane.

Membership: Includes all the Louisiana sugar cane processors who operate twenty-eight factories and about 97 percent of the more than 4,000 sugar cane growers and landlords.

Registered Lobbyists: Don Wallace Associates, Inc.
                        1707 L Street NW
                        Washington, DC   20036

Publication: *Sugar Bulletin*

AMERICAN TEXTILE MANUFACTURER'S INSTITUTE, INC.   (6)
1101 Connecticut Avenue NW, Suite 300
Washington, DC   20036   202/862-0554

Founded: 1949

Executive Vice-President: W.R. Schockley

The American Textile Manufacturer's Institute, Inc., is a trade association representing 85 percent of the domestic capacity for spinning, weaving, knitting, and finishing cotton, wool, silk, and synthetic fibers.

Membership: 200 regular members; 250 associate members.

Registered Lobbyists: Douglas W. Bulcao, Jack A. Crowder, Ronald L. Floor, Carol A. Kelly, W. Ray Schockley.

Publications: *Textile Hi-Lites* (quarterly)

AMERICAN VETERINARY MEDICAL ASSOCIATION   (11)
930 N. Meacham Road
Schaumburg, Illinois   60196   312/885-8070

Founded: 1863

Washington Office: Suite 828, 1522 K Street NW
Washington, DC   20005   202/659-2040

The American Veterinary Medical Association is the association of professional veterinarians whose purpose is to advance the science and art of medicine, including its relationship to public health and agriculture.

Membership: 30,000

Washington Representatives
and Registered Lobbyists: Winston M. Decker, John W. Thomas.

Publications: *Journal of the American Veterinary Medical Association* (twice monthly), *American Journal of Veterinary Research* (monthly).

AMEX COMMODITIES EXCHANGE, INC.   (6)
86 Trinity Place
New York, New York 10006

Registered Lobbyist: Cadwalder, Wickersham, & Taft
11 Dupont Circle NW, Suite 450
Washington, DC   20036

AMFAC, INC. (sugar)   (6)
San Francisco, California

Registered Lobbyist: Raymond K. Pope
Washington, DC

AMFAC NURSERIES, INC. (6)
1710 Gilbreth Road, Suite 220
Burlingame, California   94010

Registered Lobbyist: Jim Casey
                       1010 16th Street NW, Suite 700
                       Washington, DC   20036

ANIMAL HEALTH INSTITUTE (6)
1717 K Street NW
Washington, DC   20006

Registered Lobbyist: Frederick A. Kessinger
                       9001 Seven Locks Road
                       Bethesda, Maryland   20034

ANIMAL PROTECTION INSTITUTE OF AMERICA (7)
613 Pennsylvania Avenue SE
Washington, DC   20003   202/543-7450

Director: Jane Risk, Eastern Region

The Animal Protection Institute is a nonprofit, humane education
organization with nationwide membership. They have a major interest in
the humane slaughter of animals.

Membership: 100,000

ARAPAHOE TRIBE OF INDIANS (12)
Fort Washakie, Wyoming

Registered Lobbyist: Wilkinson, Cragun, & Barker
                       1735 New York Ave.
                       Washington, DC   20006

ARCHER-DANIELS-MIDLAND CO. (6)
Decatur, Illinois   62525

Washington Address: 475 L'Enfant Plaza SW, Suite 4400
                      Washington, DC   20024

Registered Lobbyists: Robert A. Best, Joseph E. Karth

ASSOCIATED ELECTRIC COOPERATIVE, INC. (3)
Springfield, Missouri   65801

Registered Lobbyist: Northcutt, Ely Law Offices
                       Watergate 600
                       Washington, DC   20037

ASSOCIATED MILK PRODUCERS, INC.   (3)
P.O. Box 32287
San Antonio, Texas   78284   512/341-8651

Founded: 1969

Executive Vice-President and General Manager: Ira E. Rutherford

Associated Milk Producers is a regional dairy cooperative serving dairy farmers through the Central states from Texas to Minnesota and Wisconsin.

Membership: 32,619 dairy farm families operating 27,410 farms.

Government Relations: Works through National Milk Producers Federation.

Net Sales Revenues: $1,739,037,000 (1978)

ASSOCIATION OF AMERICAN PESTICIDE CONTROL
OFFICIALS (AAPCO)   (10)
Dept. of Bio-Chemistry, Purdue University
W. Lafayette, Indiana   47907   317/749-2391

Founded: 1947

The Association of American Pesticide Control Officials is comprised of regulatory officials of agricultural, environmental, and health departments and universities responsible for regulating production, labeling, distribution, sale, and use of pesticides.

Membership: 50 to 60

Publication: *Pesticide Compendium*

ASSOCIATION OF AMERICAN VETERINARY MEDICAL
COLLEGES   (10)
1522 K Street NW, Suite 828
Washington, DC   20005   202/659-2040

Founded: 1954

The Association of American Veterinary Medical Colleges is an organization that expresses the need of education to government and other groups and creates an educational opportunity for faculty.

Membership: Twenty-four colleges, twelve departments of veterinary science, and 640 individuals.

Washington Representative
and Registered Lobbyist: John W. Thomas

Publication: *Journal of Veterinary Education*

ASSOCIATION OF FAMILY FARMERS   (5)
1130 17th Street NW
Washington, DC   20036

Registered Lobbyist: Williams & Jensen
                         1130 17th Street NW
                         Washington, DC   20036

AVCO CORP.   (6)
750 Third Avenue
New York, New York   10017

Registered Lobbyists: John B. Kelly

                         Clifford, Glass, McIlwain, & Finney
                         815 Connecticut Avenue NW
                         Washington, DC   20006

BIG PRAIRIE FARMS, INC. (c/o J.J. White)   (5)
100 State Street
Beardstown, Illinois 62618

Registered Lobbyist: Francis O. McDermott
                         1750 K Street NW, Suite 1110
                         Washington, DC 20006

BISCUIT AND CRACKER MANUFACTURERS' ASSOCIATION
OF AMERICA   (6)
1660 L Street NW, Suite 714
Washington, DC   20036   202/223-3127

Executive Vice-President: Joseph M. Creed

BIXBY RANCH CO.   (5)
523 West Sixth Street
Los Angeles, California 90014

Washington Address: 2550 M Street NW, Suite 800
                         Washington, DC   20037

Registered Lobbyists: Patton, Boggs, & Blow

                         Shaw, Pittman, Potts, and Trowbridge
                         1800 M Street NW
                         Washington, DC   20036

BOARD OF TRADE CLEARING CORPORATION   (6)
141 W. Jackson Boulevard
Chicago, Illinois 60604   312/341-1160

Founded: 1925

President: Walter W. Brinkman

Washington Representative: John H. Brebia, Counsel; Timothy J.
Kincaid; Robert W. Blanchette
Alston, Miller, & Gaines
1800 M Street, Suite 1000
Washington, DC   20036   202/223-1300

The Board of Trade Clearing Corporation is an independent organization at the Chicago Board of Trade that matches trades and guarantees each trade. Members are individuals, partnerships, and corporations that are members and users of the board. Requirements for membership are strict, specific, and continuing. The organization performs technical and administrative tasks and does not control activities of the market.

Membership: 100

Registered Lobbyists: Margaret H. Barton, Robert W. Blanchette, John
Henry Brebia, G. Conley Ingram, Timothy J. Kincaid ,
Robert C. Lower, Michael Wasserman.

BOARD OF TRADE OF KANSAS CITY, MO., INC.   (6)
4800 Main
Kansas City, Missouri   64112   816/753-7363

Founded: 1865

Executive Vice-President: W.N. Vernon, III

The Board of Trade of Kansas City includes millers, processors, farmer-owned cooperatives, grain merchants, country and terminal elevator operators, exporters, cash and futures brokers, futures commission merchants, and others who are engaged in hedging, marketing, and transporting grain from producers to processors and users.

Membership: 214 (1978)

Washington Representative
and Registered Lobbyist: Doub, Purcell, Muntzing, & Hansen
1775 Pennsylvania Avenue NW
Washington, DC   20006
202/467-6460

J.G. BOSWELL CO.   (5)
333 South Hope Street
Los Angeles, California   90017

Registered Lobbyist: H. Wesley McAden
                        1707 L Street NW
                        Washington, DC   20036

BREAD FOR THE WORLD   (7)
207 E. 16th St.
New York, New York   10003   212/260-7000

Executive Director: Arthur Simon

Founded: 1973

Washington Office: 110 Maryland Avenue NE
                     Washington, DC   20002   202/544-8363

Bread for the World is a Christian citizens' movement whose major concerns are food needs for low-income people overseas as well as in the United States.

Membership: 25,317 (June 1979)

Funding: Membership and contributions, sale of materials; $25,000 grant from Lilly Endowment in 1976 for staff development and program support. Total income in 1978 was $562,536.

BROOKINGS INSTITUTION   (11)
1775 Massachusetts Avenue NW
Washington, DC   20036   202/797-6000

Founded: 1927

Director: Stanley A. Nicholson

The Brookings Institution is a nonprofit research organization engaged in studies of public issues and problems dealing with economics, government, foreign policy, and the social sciences.

Funding: Foundations; National Science Foundation, $844,623 in 1980 fiscal year; federal Agency grants and contracts.

Publications: List available.

BROWN AND WILLIAMSON INDUSTRIES, INC.   (6)
2000 Citizen's Plaza
Louisville, Kentucky   40232

Registered Lobbyist: Cook & Henderson
                        1735 K Street NW
                        Washington, DC   20006

BURGER KING CORP.   (6)
P.O. Box 520783 General Mail Facility
Miami, Florida 33152

Registered Lobbyist: Ronald L. Platt

BURLEY AND DARK LEAF TOBACCO EXPORT ASSOCIATION   (6)
1100 17th Street NW, Suite 306
Washington, DC   20036

Registered Lobbyist: Frank B. Snodgrass

H.E. BUTT GROCERY CO.   (6)
Corpus Christi, Texas   78400

Registered Lobbyist: Miller & Chevalier
                       Suite 800, 1700 Pennsylvania Avenue
                       Washington, DC   20006   202/393-5600

CALIFORNIA CANNERS & GROWERS   (6)
3100 Ferry Building
San Francisco, California 94106

Registered Lobbyists: Henry Schacht; Wyman, Bautzer, Rothman, &
                        Kuchel

CALIFORNIA CANNING PEACH ASSOCIATION   (6)
1101 Connecticut Avenue NW, Suite 800
Washington, DC   20036   202/457-0120

Registered Lobbyists: Thomas A. Hammer, Nancy L. Smith; Nelson &
                        Harding.

CALIFORNIA & HAWAII SUGAR CO.   (6)
1 California Street
San Francisco, California   94106

Registered Lobbyist: E.A. Jaenke & Associates, Inc.
                       1735 I Street NW
                       Washington, DC   20006

CALIFORNIA OLIVE ASSOCIATION   (2)
1101 Connecticut Avenue NW, Suite 800
Washington, DC   20036   202/437-0120

Registered Lobbyists: Thomas A. Hammer, Nancy L. Smith; Nelson &
                        Harding

CALIFORNIA PLANTING COTTON SEED DISTRIBUTORS   (6)
P.O. Box 1281
Bakersfield, California   93302

Washington Address: 1707 L Street NW, Suite 650
                      Washington, DC   20036

Registered Lobbyist: H. Wesley McAden

CALIFORNIA RAISIN ADVISORY BOARD   (6)
1101 Connecticut Avenue NW, Suite 800
Washington, DC   20036   202/457-0120

Registered Lobbyists: Thomas A. Hammer, Nancy L. Smith; Nelson &
                        Harding

CALIFORNIA RURAL LEGAL ASSISTANCE   (7)
1900 K Street, Suite 203
Sacramento, California   95814   916/446-3155

115 Sansome St. Suite 900
San Francisco, California   94104   415/421-3405

Founded: 1966

Director: Alberto Saldamando

General Counsel: Ralph S. Abascal (Sacramento)

Food Law Center: Robert M. Teets, Jr.

The California Rural Legal Assistance is a public interest law firm funded
solely to serve rural people. It has thirteen offices in rural California.

Staff: 65 lawyers, 130 support staff.

Funding: Legal Services Corporation: $2,266,000, 1976; $2,584,564,
1977; $3,085,761, 1978. Community Services Administration: $183,218,
1978 (food and nutrition); $155,590, 1977 (reclamation law).

CALIFORNIA WESTSIDE FARMERS   (5)
1101 Connecticut Avenue NW, Suite 800
Washington, DC   20036

Registered Lobbyist: James H. Lake, Nelson & Harding.

CALORIE CONTROL COUNCIL   (6)
64 Perimeter Center East
Atlanta, Georgia   30346   404/393-1340

Founded: 1966

President: Robert H. Kellen

The Calorie Control Council is an association of manufacturers and suppliers of dietary foods and beverages. It seeks to provide an effective channel of communication among its members, the public, and government officials to ensure that scientific, medical, and other pertinent research and information are developed and made available to all interested parties.

Membership: 60

Registered Lobbyists: H. Redford Bishop, Richard E. Cristol, Larry C. Davenport, David F. Dunning, Robert C. Gelardi, Robert H. Kellen Co., Nelson B. Moore, Jr., Frank Slover.

CAMPBELL SOUP CO.   (6)
Campbell Place
Camden, New Jersey   08101

Registered Lobbyists: Covington & Burling
888 16th Street NW
Washington, DC   20006

Raymond S. Page, Jr.
Mill Creek Terrace
Gladwyne, Pennsylvania   19035

CANNED AND COOKED MEAT IMPORTER'S ASSOCIATION   (6)
888 17th Street NW, Suite 700
Washington, DC   20006   202/466-2930

Executive Secretary: George C. Pendleton

Registered Lobbyist: Pendleton & McLaughlin

CARE, INC. (Cooperative for American Relief Everywhere)   (7)
660 First Avenue
New York, New York   10016   212/686-3110

Executive Director: Frank Goffie

Deputy Director: Fred W. Devine

Founded: 1945

A voluntary, nonprofit, nonpolitical, nonsectarian, nongovernment agency, CARE, Inc. was founded by twenty-two major organizations to help people in developing countries in their struggle against hunger, ill health, and low productivity. It converts contributions of Canadians and people in the United States into various forms of relief and development assistance with help of national and local governments in host countries.

Washington Representative
and Registered Lobbyist: Leva, Hawes, Symington, Martin,
                                  & Oppenheimer
                              815 Connecticut Avenue NW
                              Washington, DC   20006

CARGILL, INC.   (6)
P.O. Box 9300
Minneapolis, Minnesota   55440

Washington Address: 1050 17th Street, 12th Floor
                      Washington, DC   20036

Registered Lobbyists: Delaney & Patrick
                        1801 K Street NW, No. 1104
                        Washington, DC   20006

                        Robert R. Fahs

CATERPILLAR TRACTOR CO.   (6)
100 NE Adams Street
Peoria, Illinois 61629

Washington Address: 1850 K Street NW, Suite 925
                      Washington, DC   20006

Registered lobbyists: Rita L. Castle, Timothy L. Elder, Henry W.
                        Holling, H. Richard Kahler, Michael C. Maibach,
                        Donald R. Neimi.

CATFISH FARMERS OF AMERICA   (2)
P.O. Box 2551
Little Rock, Arkansas   72203   501/376-1921

President: S.L. Reed

Executive Secretary: Porter Briggs

Catfish Farmers of America is a trade association of catfish farmers and also represents U.S. trout farmers.

Membership: 200

Publication: *Update*

CAYMAN TURTLE FARM, LTD.   (5)
P.O. Box 645
Grand Cayman Island
Cayman Islands
British West Indies

Registered Lobbyists: Shaw, Pittman, Potts, & Trowbridge
                        1800 M Street NW
                        Washington, DC   20036

CENEX (FARMERS UNION CENTRAL EXCHANGE, INC.)   (3)
Box G
St. Paul, Minnesota   55165

Registered Lobbyist: E.A. Jaenke & Associates
                       1735 I Street NW
                       Washington, DC   20006

CENTER FOR COMMUNITY CHANGE (RURAL COALITION)   (7)
1000 Wisconsin Avenue NW
Washington, DC   20007   202/338-4804

Director: Pablo Eisenberg

Founded: 1969

The Center for Community Change monitors federal policies and programs affecting rural communities, farm workers, and small farmers. It provides information and technical assistance to rural community-based groups, has helped initiate a rural coalition, a network of groups which will advocate increased attention, funds, and programs for rural communities and rural poor.

Funding: Foundation grants: $65,000 Lilly Endowment, 1977, for general support; $25,000 for welfare reform study, 1976; Field Foundation for work with National Farm Workers Service Center, 1976, $10,000; Ford Foundation, staff training of community organization workers, $9,600, 1977; New York Foundation, national revenue-sharing project, $10,000, 1977; Rockefellers Brothers Fund, $280,000, for program assistance to community and economic development organizations, 1977.

CENTER FOR RURAL AFFAIRS   (7)
Post Office Box 405
Walthill, Nebraska   68067   402/846-5428

Codirectors: Don Ralston, Marty Strange

Founded: 1973

The Center for Rural Affairs is a nonprofit, unaffiliated, tax-exempt corporation chartered in Nebraska to promote rural development within the state of Nebraska and throughout the United States by providing information and opportunities for discussion, conducting research, and publishing reports.

Funding: Contributions, foundation grants, and federal contracts; Campaign for Human Development, U.S. Catholic Conference; Shalon Foundation, $11,000 to develop small farm advocacy project, 1978; expenditures during year ending August 31, 1978: $272,325.

Publications: Newsletter, *Small Farm Advocate*

CENTER FOR RURAL STUDIES—EARTHWORK   (7)
3410 19th Street
San Francisco, California   94110   415/626-1266

Director: Eleanor McCallie

The Center for Rural Studies is a clearinghouse for information on farm and land-related issues and organizations working in related areas of interest.

Founded: 1972

Funding: Sale of publications, books, and films, including Agribusiness Accountability publications. Grant of $25,000 from Stern Fund and $15,000 from Field Foundation "for general support of organization concerned with basic land reform in rural areas where incidence of poverty is highest."

Publications: List available upon request.

CENTER FOR SCIENCE IN THE PUBLIC INTEREST   (7)
1757 S Street NW
Washington, DC   20009   202/332-4250

Executive Director: Michael F. Jacobson

The Center for Science in the Public Interest is a nonprofit, tax-exempt, consumer activist organization which investigates and publicizes food and nutrition, consumer, and environmental problems.

Founded: 1971

Funding: Sales of reports and publications, private donations, and foundation grants: $5,000, Shalan Foundation, 1976 Food Day; $20,000, Arca Foundation, 1976, for cooperative effort on food and nutrition issues.

Publications: *Nutrition Action* (monthly); catalog of other publications available on request.

CENTRAL BANK FOR COOPERATIVES AND ASSOCIATED
DISTRICT BANKS   (3)
P.O. Box 17389
Denver, Colorado 80217

Registered Lobbyist: Hamel, Park, McCabe, & Saunders
                       1776 F Street NW, Suite 400
                       Washington, DC   20006

CENTRAL STATES RESOURCE CENTER (Formerly Coalition on
American Rivers)   (8)
P.O. Box 2667, Station A
Champaign, Illinois   61820   217/384-5831

Executive Director: John Marlin

Founded: 1972

The Central States Resource Center is a registered lobby working to maintain the economic and environmental integrity of the Midwest, including
preservation of rivers, floodplains, and productive farmland.

Funding: Donations and grants from interested groups, including industries and the Council for Sound Waterways.

Registered Lobbyists: John Marlin, Barbara Klosterman, and April
                        Richards.

CF INDUSTRIES, INC. AND ENERGY COOPERATIVE, INC.   (3)
Salem Lake Drive
Long Grove, Illinois   60047

Washington Address: 1025 Connecticut NW, Suite 402
                      Washington, DC   20036

Registered Lobbyists: Bill Brier, Rosemary L. O'Brien.

CHAMBER OF COMMERCE OF THE UNITED STATES   (6)
1615 H Street NW
Washington, DC   20062   202/659-6000

Founded: 1912

President: Richard L. Lesher

Director of Food and Agriculture: E. Clinton Stokes

The Chamber of Commerce of the United States is the national organization representing the nation's businessmen on major national issues.

Membership: 74,000 (including 70,100 business and professional firms), 2,700 state and local chambers of commerce, and 1,200 professional trade associations.

Registered Lobbyists: Linda M. Anzalone, Betty Jane Clark, Harold P. Coxson, Jr., Ted A. Heydinger, Jeffrey H. Joseph, Gary D. Knight, Richard L. Lesher, John S. McLees, Harold R. Mayberry, Mark Schultz, G. John Tysse.

CHEESE IMPORTERS ASSOCIATION   (6)
480 Park Avenue
New York, New York   10022

Registered Lobbyists: Berry, Epstein, Sandstrom, & Blatchford
1700 Pennsylvania Avenue NW
Washington, DC   20006

CHEYENNE RIVER SIOUX TRIBE   (12)
P.O. Box 590
Eagle Butt, South Dakota   57625

Registered Lobbyist: Rebecca D. Shapiro & Associates
111 C Street SE
Washington, DC   20003

CHICAGO BOARD OF TRADE   (6)
141 W. Jackson Boulevard
Chicago, Illinois   60604

Founded: 1848

President: Robert Wilmouth

The Chicago Board of Trade is the nation's largest futures market for agricultural commodities. Members are merchants, processors, and brokers who engage in futures trading.

Membership: 1402

Washington Representatives
and Registered Lobbyists: Douglas P. Bennett, Thomas A. Davis, Michael R. McLeod
Davis & McLeod
499 South Capitol Street SW, Suite 407
Washington, DC   20003   202/785-3170

CHICAGO MERCANTILE EXCHANGE (Formerly Butter & Egg Board) (6)
444 W. Jackson Boulevard
Chicago, Illinois 60606   312/648-1000

Founded: 1898

President: Clayton Yeutter

Washington Office: C. Dayle Henington
                    Vice-President, Government Relations
                    1101 Connecticut Avenue
                    Washington, DC 20036   202/223-6673

The Chicago Mercantile Exchange is the world's second largest commodity exchange dealing in cattle, hogs, frozen pork bellies, lumber, eggs, yellow sorghum, hams, boneless beef, turkeys, russet Burbank potatoes, gold and currencies, and financial instruments.

Membership: 1,300 (including International Monetary Market and Associate Market).

Registered Lobbyists: Doub, Purcell, Muntzing, & Hansen; C. Dayle Henington; James H. Lake.

Publication: Annual report

CHILDREN'S FOUNDATION   (7)
1521 16th Street NW
Washington, DC 20036   202/387-6119

Regional Offices: Atlanta, Georgia; Santa Fe, New Mexico; Pierre, South Dakota

President: Barbara Bode

Founded: 1969

The Children's Foundation is a nonprofit organization established to give impoverished children and their families a voice in the nationwide effort to eliminate hunger in the United States. As advocates for a very particular special interest, the Children's Foundation connects the Capitol with communities, translating needs into national policy, and serves as a vehicle for community organizations that seek to reform and expand the federal food-assistance programs.

Funding: Supporters include the American Legion Child Welfare Foundation; ARCA Foundation; Avon Products Foundation, Mary Reynolds Babcock Foundation; Community Services Adminstration; Field Foundation;

Ford Foundation; Herman Goldman Foundation; Joint Foundations Support; Levi-Strauss Foundation; National Foundation; March of Dimes; The New World Foundation; New York Foundation; Presbyterian Church in the United States; Fredrick W. Richmond Foundation; Riverside Church of New York City; Rockefeller Brothers Fund; Rockefeller Foundation; Helena Rubinstein Foundation; Shalan Foundation; Southern Education Foundation; United Church of Christ.

Newsletter: *Feed Kids . . . It's the Law* (monthly); *WIC Bulletin; Rise and Shine* (school breakfast newsletter); *Child Care Food Project Bulletin; Summer Food Bulletin*

CHIPPEWA-CREE TRIBE   (12)
Rocky Boy Reservation
Box Elder, Montana   59521

Registered Lobbyist: Patton, Boggs, & Blow
                       2550 M Street NW
                       Washington, DC   20037

CHURCH WORLD SERVICE   (7)
475 Riverside Drive
New York, New York   10027   212/870-2257

Executive Director: Paul McCleary

Founded: 1946

The Church World Service is the overseas relief and development agency of the National Council of Churches. It is the primary foreign service organization for thirty Protestant and orthodox denominations and has a close working relationship with the World Council of Churches and its constituent agencies. It provides crises relief aid and also conducts agricultural training, irrigation, conservation, land reclamation, livestock, and poultry projects in developing countries and works in a wide variety of rural community development projects.

Publication: *CWS Update, DOM Notes*, Church World Service annual report

CHOCOLATE MANUFACTURERS ASSOCIATION OF AMERICA   (6)
7700 West Park Drive, Suite 514
McLean, Virginia   22102   703/790-5011

Founded: 1923

President: Richard T. O'Connell

The Chocolate Manufacturers Association of America is a national trade association of companies engaged in manufacturing and processing chocolate products. Its activities include research to improve manufacturing procedures and techniques, public relations programs featuring chocolate, and government relations affecting chocolate manufacturing operations.

Membership: 14 (Ambrosia Chocolate Co.; Blommer Chocolate Co.; E.J. Bach & Sons; Cocoline Chocolate Co., Inc.; Ghirardelli Chocolate Co.; Guittard Chocolate Co.; L.S. Heath and Sons, Inc.; Hershey Foods Corporation; Hooton Chocolate Co.; M&M/Mars, Inc.; The Nestle Co., Inc.; Peter-Paul Cadbury, Inc.; Van Leer Chocolate Corp.; World Finest Chocolate, Inc.)

Publications: *Chocolate Short Takes, Chocoletter*

CIBA-GEIGY CORP.   (6)
556 Morris Avenue
Summit, New Jersey   07901

Registered Lobbyist: J.L. Disque

CIGAR ASSOCIATION OF AMERICA, INC.   (6)
1120 19th Street NW
Washington, DC   20036

Registered Lobbyist: Michael J. Kowalsky

CITIZENS AGAINST SUGAR HIKES (C.A.S.H.)   (7)
1012 14th Street NW, Suite 901
Washington, DC   20005

Registered as Lobbyist: 1979

CLAYTON BROKERAGE CO. OF ST. LOUIS, INC.   (6)
Clayton, Missouri   63105

Registered Lobbyist: Doub, Purcell, Muntzing, & Hansen
                      1775 Pennsylvania Avenue NW
                      Washington, DC   20006

COALITION OF CONSUMER ORGANIZATIONS   (7)
Founded: 1977

The Coalition of Consumer Organizations was formed in 1977 to present joint testimony on national food and farm policy issues before the Senate and House agriculture committees.

Membership: Consumer Federation of America, Public Citizens Congress Watch, Community Nutrition Institute, Center for Science in the Public Interest, National Consumers Congress, and Consumer Affairs Committee of Americans for Democratic Action.

Registered Lobbyists: Registered with individual organizations.

COCA-COLA BOTTLERS' ASSOCIATION   (6)
166 16th Street NW
Atlanta, Georgia   30318

Registered Lobbyists: John S. Know, Jr.

Sutherland, Asbill, & Brennan
1666 K Street NW
Washington, DC   20006
and 3100 First National Bank Tower
Atlanta, Georgia   30303

COCA-COLA CO.   (6)
P.O. Box 1734
Atlanta, Georgia   30301

Registered Lobbyists: Coca-Cola Bottlers' Association
166 16th Street NW
Atlanta, Georgia   30301

Ovid R. Davis; Earl T. Leonard, Jr.

McClure & Trotter
1100 Connecticut Avenue NW, Suite 600
Washington, DC   20036

Williams & Connolly
1000 Hill Building
Washington, DC   20006

COFFEE, SUGAR & COCOA, INC.   (6)
4 World Trade Center
New York, New York   10048   212/938-2800

Founded: 1979 (Merger of New York Coffee and Sugar Exchange with New York Cocoa Exchange)

President: Bennett J. Corn

The New York Coffee and Sugar Exchange, founded in 1882, and the New York Cocoa Exchange, founded in 1925, were the designated contract markets for coffee, sugar, and cocoa. Members include persons and firms engaged in the coffee, sugar, and cocoa business; futures commission merchants; and floor brokers.

Membership: 344

Washington Representative
and Registered Lobbyist: Clifford and Warnke
                              815 Connecticut Avenue NW
                              Washington, DC   20006

Other Registered Lobbyists: Barrett, Smith, Schapiro, Simon, and Armstrong; Bennett Corn; Joseph L. Fraites; James J. Garry; John W. Schobel, Jr.; Alan J. Goldenberg.

COOK INDUSTRIES, INC.   (6)
1707 L Street NW, Suite 650
Washington, DC   20036

Registered Lobbyist: H. Wesley McAden

COOPERATIVE LEAGUE OF THE USA   (3)
Suite 1100, 1828 L Street NW
Washington, DC   20036   202/872-0550

Founded: 1916

President: Glenn M. Anderson

The Cooperative League is a national confederation of cooperatives with membership representing all types of customer-owned businesses. Its purpose is to aid member organizations in their government relationships and to defend cooperatives against unjust or discriminatory treatment.

Membership: Membership organizations in fifty states totals 20 million families or 50 million individuals.

Registered Lobbyists: E.A. Jaenke & Associates, Shelby E. Southard.

Publication: *In League*

COMMITTEE TO ASSURE THE AVAILABILITY OF CASEIN   (6)
1700 Pennsylvania Avenue NW
Washington, DC   20006

Registered Lobbyist: Max N. Berry
                       Berry, Epstein, Sandstrom, & Blatchford
                       1700 Pennsylvania Avenue NW
                       Washington, DC   20006

COMMITTEE FOR HUMANE
LEGISLATION, INC.   (7)
2101 L Street NW
Washington, DC   20037
202/452-1430

FRIENDS OF ANIMALS, INC.
11 W 60th Street
New York, New York   10023
212/247-8120

Executive Director: Alice Herrington

Washington Director: Jowanda Shelton

Founded: 1967

The Committee for Humane Legislation is the lobbying arm which represents Friends of Animals, a national, nonprofit, tax-exempt organization
concerned with the humane treatment of animals and opposed to the killing
of wildlife.

Membership: 100,000

Funding: Membership fees and contributions; 1977 contribution income:
$214,000; expenditures: $210,600.

Registered Lobbyists: Jowanda Shelton, Bernard Fensterwald, Jr.

COMMITTEE IN SUPPORT OF EXISTING U.S. TARIFF POLICY
WITH RESPECT TO HONEY   (6)

Registered Lobbyist: Daniels, Houlihan, & Palmenter
                         1819 H Street NW
                         Washington, DC   20006

COMMON CAUSE   (7)
2030 M Street NW
Washington, DC   20036   202/833-1200

Founded: 1970

President: David Cohen

Common Cause is a citizen's lobby with a wide range of concerns including
food and agriculture. It was founded by John W. Gardner, Secretary of
Health, Education, and Welfare under President Lyndon Johnson.

Membership: 220,000 (1979)

Publication: *Front Lines* (six times a year)

Registered Lobbyists: Richard W. Clark, David Cohen, Thomas Cohen,
                        Michael Cole, Carol Coston, Margaret Fitzgerald-
                        Bare, John W. Gardner, Kirk L. Gray, Kenneth J.

Guide, Randy Huwa, Kathryn Kavanagh-Baran
Patricia Keefer, Susan Paris Lewis, Alan McBride,
Sally McCormick, Robert Rodriguez, Theodore P.
Stein, Susan Tannenbaumm, Nan Waterman, Fred
Wertheimer, Alvert Winchester, Nathaniel
Williams.

COMMUNICATING FOR AGRICULTURE, INC. (5)

Registered Lobbyist: Milton E. Smedsrud
Law Office Building
Fergus Falls, Minnesota 56537

COMMUNITY NUTRITION INSTITUTE (7)
1146 19th Street Room 300 NW
Washington, DC 20036   202/833-1730

Founded: 1970

Executive Director: Rod Leonard

Director, Consumer Division: Ellen Haas

The Community Nutrition Institute is a nonprofit food and nutrition advocacy organization with an overall goal to facilitate the access of all people in the United States to an adequate, safe, nutritious, and affordable diet. It is recognized as a leader in the development of a national food and nutrition policy that serves consumer interests at the community level.

Funding: Community Services Administration, food and nutrition program; $509,683 from October 1978 through December 1979. Consumer Education Program, HEW; contracts with individual states to train people to administer the food-stamp program in state and community offices; USDA Science and Education Administration competitive grant award with Marketing Science Institute, Cambridge, Massachusetts, $175,000 in 1979; sales of publication and newsletter; conference fees.

Registered Lobbyists: Ellen Haas, Rodney Leonard.

Publication: *CNI Weekly Report*; list of other publications available on request.

Staff: 26 employees (1979)

CONFEDERATED SALISH AND KOOTENAI TRIBES OF THE FLAT-HEAD RESERVATION (12)
Montana

Registered Lobbyist: Wilkinson, Cragun, & Barker
                        1735 New York Avenue NW
                        Washington, DC   20006

CONFEDERATED TRIBES OF THE COLVILLE INDIAN
RESERVATION   (12)
P.O. Box 150
Nespelem, Washington

Registered Lobbyist: Zionty, Pirtle, Morisset, Ernstoff, & Chestnut
                        208 Pioneer Building, 600 First Avenue
                        Seattle, Washington   98104

CONFERENCE ON ALTERNATIVE STATE AND LOCAL POLICIES
(Institute for Policy Studies)   (11)
2000 Florida Avenue
Washington, DC   20009   202/387-6030

Founded: 1975

Executive Director: Lee Webb

Agriculture Project Coordinator: Cynthia Guyer

The Conference on Alternative State and Local Policies is a nonprofit
organization which serves as an information clearinghouse on issues dealing
with energy, housing, women in the economy, pension rights, and agriculture. Its purpose is to act as a networking agent of other public interest
organizations in areas of similar interests.

Funding: Sale of publications; churches; foundations, $25,000 from Stern
Fund, 1977-1978.

Publication: *Ways and Means* (bimonthly), list of others available on
request.

CONGRESS WATCH (Public Citizen)   (7)
133 C Street SE
Washington, DC   20003   202/546-4936

Director: Mark Green

Coordinator, Food Issues: Frances Zwenig

Founded: 1974

Congress Watch, affiliated with Public Citizen, Inc., works as a consumer
advocacy and oversight group dealing with consumer product safety, food
and agriculture, and a wide range of public issues coming before Congress.

Employees: 14 with 7 full-time advocates.

Funding: Operated with a budget of $197,154 in 1977 from contributions to Public Citizen, Inc., founded by Ralph Nader.

Registered Lobbyists: Nancy Drabble, Andrew A. Feinstein, Mark J. Green, David Moulton, Martin Rogel, Mitch Rofsky, Frances Zwenig, Gene Karpinski, Robert F. Furniss, Howard Symons, Carol Brickey.

Publication: *Public Citizen*

THE CONSERVATION FOUNDATION (11)
1717 Massachusetts Avenue NW
Washington, DC 20036   202/797-4300

Founded: 1948

President: William K. Reilly

The Conservation Foundation is engaged in research and analysis on a wide variety of public issues with major emphasis on land use, economics and the environment, coastal resources management, pollution control, and toxic substances and energy.

Funding: Total support and revenues, 1978, $2,090,223; private foundations, $848,000 (about 40 percent); government agencies, $830,000 (about 40 percent); remainder from individuals, sales of publications, and miscellaneous.

Publications: List available upon request.

CONSERVATIVE CAUCUS (7)
7777 Leesburg Pike
Falls Church, Virginia 22043   703/893-1550

National Director: Howard Phillips

Founded: 1974

The Conservative Caucus is a national citizens' organization of concerned voters in all 435 congressional districts which promote conservative causes.

Membership: 210,000

Publication: *Grass Roots* (members' report)

Registered Lobbyist: Donald T. Ubban

CONSOLIDATED FOODS CORP. (6)
1305 South LaSalle Street
Chicago, Illinois 60603

Registered Lobbyist: Williams & Jensen
                        1130 17th Street NW
                        Washington, DC   20036

CONSUMER ACTION NOW, INC.   (8)
355 Lexington Avenue
New York, New York   10017   212/682-8915

Founded: 1970

Consumer Action Now, Inc., is a registered lobby with concerns dealing with energy, solar energy use, and environmental problems.

Funding: Donations and gifts; $7,650 grant from San Mateo Foundation, 1977, for initial operating expenses.

Registered Lobbyists: Ann Harrison Clark, Susannah C. Lawrence, Joan
                        Porte, Lola Redford, Barbara Gross.

CONSUMER FEDERATION OF AMERICA   (7)
1012 14th Street NW
Washington, DC   20005   202/737-3732

Executive Director: Kathleen F. O'Reilly

Founded: 1968

The Consumer Federation of America is a federation of consumer organizations comprised of Consumers Union, publisher of *Consumer Reports*, seventeen cooperative and credit union leagues, fifty state and local consumer organizations, sixty-six rural electric cooperatives, twenty-seven national and regional organizations (including the National Board of the YMCA and the National Education Association), and sixteen national labor organizations. It operates with a forty-member board of directors representing the member organizations.

Membership: 220 organizations representing an estimated 30 million consumers in the United States.

Board of Directors, 1979:   Peter Jacobson, Alliance for Consumer Protection; Arnold Mayer, Amalgamated Meat Cutters and Butcher Workmen; Charles Wheatley, American Public Gas Association; Alex Radin, American Public Power Association; Glenn Nishimura, Arkansas Consumer Research; Dan McCurray, Chicago Consumer Council; Steve Brobeck, Cleveland Consumer Action; Al Luzi, Concerned Consumer League; Marc Caplan, Connecticut Citizen Action Group; Allan Classen, Consumer Center; Betsy Wood, Consumers Cooperative of Berkeley, Inc.; Jim Royal, Consumer Education and Protection Association; Mary Solow, Consumer

Federation of California, Los Angeles, and Orange County; Alfred A. Riley, Consumer Research Advisory Council, Inc.; Warren Barren, Consumers Union; Mark Silbergeld, Consumers Union; Shelby Southard, Cooperative League of U.S.A.; Sharon Stack, Credit Union National Association; Ann Brown, D.C. Consumers Affairs Committee, Americans for Democratic Action; Leroy Schecher, Grand Electric Co-op, Inc.; Stan Yarkin, Greenbelt Consumer Services; Jacob Claymen, Industrial Union Department, AFL-CIO; Robert Kalaski, International Association of Machinists; Evelyn Dubrow, International Ladies Garment Workers Union; Sheila Sidles, Iowa Consumers League; Ellen Haas, Maryland Citizens Consumer Council; Joe Tuchinsky, Michigan Citizens Lobby; Sara Newman, National Consumers League; William Hutton, National Council of Senior Citizens; Reuben Johnson, National Farmers Union; Cushing Dolabeare, National Low-Income Housing Coalition; Bill Matson, Pennsylvania League for Consumer Protection; William Olwell, Retail Clerks, International; Helen Nelson, Toward Utility Rate Normalization; Hildred Drew, United Auto Workers; Betty Schimling, Washington Committee on Consumer Interests.

Funding: Membership dues and contributions, sale of publications; grants and contracts for research: Office of Consumer Education, HEW, $100,000, 1976; USDA, $23,000 for net-weight study, 1978.

Registered Lobbyists: Gerald Hogan, Peter Ginsberg (resigned 1979), Kathleen O'Reilly, Linda Hudak, Kathleen Dillon Sheeley, Michael Podhorzer.

Publication: *Consumer Federation of America News*

CONSUMERS OPPOSED TO INFLATION IN THE NECESSITIES
(COIN)   (7)
2000 P Street NW, Suite 415
Washington, DC   20036   202/659-0800

Founded: 1978

Executive Director: Roger Hickey

Chairman, Food Task Force: Ellen Haas

Consumers Opposed to Inflation in the Necessities is a group of sixty-nine organizations representing consumers, senior citizens, labor, environmentalists, women, minorities, religious groups, and others, working together to fight rising prices of food, housing, medical care, and energy.

Steering Committee Organizations: Public Citizen, Consumer Federation of America, National Council of Senior Citizens, Exploratory Project for

Economic Alternatives, Environmental Action, International Association
of Machinists, International Union of Operating Engineers, National Consumers League, Community Nutrition Institute.

Publication: *There Are Alternatives*

CONSUMERS FOR WORLD TRADE   (7)
1346 Connecticut Avenue NW
Washington, DC   20035   202/785-4835

Founded: 1977

President: Doreen L. Brown

Consumers for World Trade is a group of citizens and consumers working
for enlightened trade policies that will provide stable prices, free consumer
choice, free and fair world trade, and a strong productive and international-
ly competitive U.S. economy.

Membership: 600

Board Members: Joan R. Braden, Doreen L. Brown, Thomas B. Curtis
(member of Congress, 1951 to 1969), Isaiah Frank, Hendrik S. Houthakker
(member of President's Council of Economic Advisers, 1969 to 1971), D.
Gale Johnson, Peter F. Krogh, William Matson Roth, Seymour J. Rubin,
Charles P. Taft, Philip H. Trezise (assistant Secretary of State, 1969 to
1971), Roy Wilkins.

Registered Lobbyist: Organization is registered.

Publication: *CWT Newsletter*

CONTI-COMMODITY SERVICES, INC.   (6)
141 West Jackson Boulevard
Chicago, Illinois   60604

Registered Lobbyist: Lawrence H. Hunt, Jr.
                         Sidney & Austin
                         First National Plaza
                         Chicago, Illinois   60603

CONTINENTAL GRAIN CO.   (6)
277 Park Avenue
New York, New York   10017

Registered Lobbyist: DeLaney & Patrick
                         1801 K Street NW, Suite 1104
                         Washington, DC   20006

CORN REFINERS ASSOCIATION, INC.   (6)
1001 Connecticut Avenue
Washington, DC   20036   202/331-1634

Founded: 1913

President: Robert C. Liebenow

The Corn Refiners Association is the trade association of wet-corn millers in the United States.

Membership: ADM Corn Sweetners (Division of Archer-Daniels-Midland Co.); American Maize Products Company; Amstar Corporation; Anheuser-Busch, Inc.; Cargill, Inc.; Clinton Corn Processing Co.; CPC International, Inc.; Hubinger Company; National Starch and Chemical Corporation; A.E. Staley Manufacturing Company.

Publication: *Corn Annual*

COTTON WAREHOUSE ASSOCIATION OF AMERICA   (6)
1707 L Street NW, Suite 540
Washington, DC   20035   202/223-4838

Founded: 1969

The Cotton Warehouse Association of America is in an association of warehousemen in all major cotton states handling a significant portion of the U.S. cotton crop.

Membership: 146 firms, 269 plants, 61 associate members.

Registered Lobbyist: Don Wallace Associates

Publication: Bimonthly report

COUNCIL FOR AGRICULTURAL SCIENCE AND TECHNOLOGY (CAST)   (11)
250 Memorial Union, Iowa State University
Ames, Iowa   50011   515/294-2036

Founded: 1972

Executive Vice-President: Charles A. Black

The Council for Agricultural Science and Technology is a consortium of twenty-six agricultural scientific societies and associations and individual scientists for the purpose of presenting scientific information on various public problems and issues.

Membership: American College of Veterinary Toxicologists, American Dairy Science Association, American Forage and Grassland Council,

American Meat Science Association, American Meteorological Society, American Phytopathological Society, American Society for Horticultural Science, American Society of Agricultural Engineers, American Society of Agronomy, American Society of Animal Science, Aquatic Plant Management Society, Association of Official Seed Analysts, Crop Science Society of America, Council of Soil Testing and Plant Analysis, Entomological Society of America, Institute of Food Technologists, North Central Weed Control Conference, Northeastern Weed Science Society, Poultry Science Association, Rural Sociological Society, Society for Range Management, Society of Nematologists, Soil Science Society of America, Southern Weed Science Society, Weed Science of America, Western Society of Weed Science.

Funding: Memberships and contributions, $254,908 (year ending September 30, 1978).

Publications: List available upon request.

CROP QUALITY CONTROL   (6)
307 Fourth Avenue South, P.O. Box 15047
Minneapolis, Minnesota   55415

Registered Lobbyist: Vance V. Goodfellow

DAIRY AND FOOD INDUSTRIES SUPPLY ASSOCIATION, INC.   (6)
5530 Wisconsin Avenue NW
Washington, DC   20015   202/652-4420

Public Relations Director: Wesley Dibbern

DAIRYMAN, INC.   (3)
200 West Broadway
Louisville, Kentucky   40202

Registered Lobbyists: Barnett, Algia, & Carey
                        1627 K Street NW, Suite 900
                        Washington, DC   20006

DAIRY RESEARCH, INC.   (6)
3100 North Nelson Street
Arlington, Virginia   22207   703/527-1744

Consultant: Harold E. Meister

DEERE AND CO.   (6)
John Deere Road
Moline, Illinois   61265

Registered Lobbyists: Robert L. Anderson, Wade P. Clarke, Jr.

DEKALB AG RESEARCH   (6)
Sycamore Road
DeKalb, Illinois   60115

Registered Lobbyists: Margaret R. Murray
1339 Wisconsin Avenue NW
Washington, DC   20007

Michael A. Nemeroff
Sidney & Austin
1730 Pennsylvania Avenue NW
Washington, DC   20006

O'Conner & Hannan
1747 Pennsylvania Avenue NW, Suite 600
Washington, DC   20006

DELMARVA POULTRY INDUSTRY, INC.   (6)
R.D. No. 2, Box 47
Georgetown, Delaware   19947

Registered Lobbyist: Covington & Burling
888 16th Street NW
Washington, DC   20006

DEL MONTE CORP.   (6)
1 Market Plaza
San Francisco, California   94119

Washington Address: 1825 K Street NW
Washington, DC   20006

Registered Lobbyist: Alan Caldwell

DELTA & PINE LAND CO. OF MISSISSIPPI   (5)
Scot, Mississippi   38772

Washington Address: 1707 L Street NW, Suite 540
Washington, DC   20035

Registered Lobbyist: Don Wallace Associates

DOW CHEMICAL CO.   (6)
Midland, Michigan   48640

Washington Address: 1800 M Street NW, Suite 700 South
Washington, DC   20036

Registered Lobbyists: R.S. Chamberlin, Thomas E. Jones, Lynette B. Lenard, Charles T. Marck, J.J. Panella, Richard M. Patterson.

DR. PEPPER CO. (6)
P.O. Box 225086
Dallas, Texas 75265

Registered Lobbyist: William F. Massmann

E.I. DU PONT DE NEMOURS & CO. (6)
1007 Market Street
Wilmington, Delaware 19898

Washington Address: 1701 Pennsylvania Avenue NW, Suite 210
Washington, DC 20006

Registered Lobbyists: H. Stewart Van Scoyoc
1701 Pennsylvania Avenue NW, Suite 210
Washington, DC 20006

Charls E. Walker Associates, Inc.
1730 Pennsylvania Avenue NW
Washington, DC 20006

John J. Klocko, III

E. Rogers Pleasants

ELI LILLY AND CO. (6)
307 East McCarty Street
Indianapolis, Indiana 46206

Washington Address: 1030 15th Street NW
Washington, DC 20005

Registered Lobbyists: Groom and Nordberg
1775 Pennsylvania Avenue NW, Suite 450
Washington, DC 20006

Stephen A. Stitle

ENVIRONMENTAL DEFENSE FUND (8)
475 Park Avenue
New York, New York 10016 212/686-4191

Executive Director: Janet Welsh Brown

Pesticides Coordinator: Maureen Hinkle

Washington Office: 1525 18th Street NW
                     Washington, DC   20036
                     202/833-1484

Regional Offices: Berkeley, California   94704; Denver, Colorado   80203

The Environmental Defense Fund is a national environmental organization with membership of scientists, lawyers, economists, and others interested in finding scientifically sound solutions to environmental problems.

Membership: 46,000 (1979)

Funding: Membership dues and contributions, $922,267, 1978; income from endowments; $127,500 from Ford Foundation, 1977, to assist community and citizen groups and to monitor government policies and programs; $30,000, Bingham Foundation, to study cancer causes, 1976; $70,000, Rockefeller Brothers Fund, 1977, for toxic-chemical programs to reduce involuntary human exposure to chemical carcinogens in food, air, and water; $15,000, Shalan Foundation, 1978, for study of integrated pest management. Total revenue in 1978 was $1,743,489.

Registered Lobbyists: Charlene Doughterty, Anita Johnson.

THE ENVIRONMENTAL FUND   (8)
1302 18th Street NW
Washington, DC   20036   202/293-2548

Founded: 1973

President: Justin Blackwelder

The Environmental Fund is a nonprofit corporation formed to make the public aware that if population growth continues indefinitely, the environment cannot be saved.

Publication: *The Other Side*

ENVIRONMENTAL POLICY CENTER   (8)
317 Pennsylvania Avenue SE
Washington, DC   20003   202/547-6500

Executive Vice-President: Louise C. Dunlap

Founded: 1972

The Environmental Policy Center is a nonpartisan lobby and research organization working on energy, water resources, and environmental issues on behalf of local, regional, environmental, agricultural, and community organizations.

Funding: Private contributions, foundation grants.

Registered Lobbyists: David Berick, Brent Blackwelder, Peter Carlson,
Lynn Coddington, Garry Deloss, John C. Doyle,
Louise C. Dunlap, Janet Hieber, Marc Messing,
John McCormack, Cary Ridder, Hope E. Robert-
son, Sydney M. Wolf.

Publication: *Lobby Report* (monthly)

EVAPORATED MILK ASSOCIATION   (6)
15 West Montgomery Avenue
Rockville, Maryland   20850   301/424-2150

Executive Vice-President: J.C. Flake

EXPLORATORY PROJECT FOR ECONOMIC ALTERNATIVES   (7)
2000 P Street NW
Washington, DC   20036   202/833-3208

Codirector: Jeff Faux, Gardiner, Maine

Founded: 1976

The Exploratory Project for Economic Alternatives is a study group
organized "to help determine how we Americans might reorganize our
economic system around new principles of democracy, cooperation, efficient and conserving use of resources."

Funding: Grant of $125,000 from Arca Foundation in 1976, $150,000 in
1977, $75,000 in 1978; $10,000 from Shalan Foundation, 1977; sale of
publications; church group contributions.

Publication: *Toward a National Food Policy* (1976)

FARM BUREAU MUTUAL INSURANCE CO.   (6)
KFB Insurance Co.
Manhattan, Kansas   66502

Registered Lobbyist: Sutherland, Asbill, & Brennan
1666 K Street NW
Washington, DC   20006

FARM WATER ALLIANCE   (5)
955 L'Enfant Plaza SW
Washington, DC   20024

Registered Lobbyist: Gordon E. Nelson

FARMLAND INDUSTRIES (3)
P.O. Box 7305
Kansas City, Missouri   64116

Washington Representative
and Registered Lobbyist: E.A. Jaenke & Associates
                                1735 I Street NW
                                Washington, DC   20006

THE FERTILIZER INSTITUTE (6)
1015 18th Street NW
Washington, DC   20036   202/466-2700

Founded: 1970 with merger of National Plant Food Institute and The
Fertilizer Association.

President: Edward M. Wheeler

The Fertilizer Institute is the national trade association of the fertilizer industry. Members are engaged in the manufacturing and distribution of fertilizer products.

Membership: 350 industry members, 41 affiliated U.S. associations, and 6 affiliates in Canada and France.

Registered Lobbyists: David T. Crow, Gary D. Myers, and Edwin
                        Wheeler.

Publication: Member letter (monthly)

FIRST COLONY FARMS (5)
Route 1, Box 130
Creswell, North Carolina   27928

Registered Lobbyist: Ragan & Mason
                       900 17th Street NW
                       The Farragut Building
                       Washington, DC   20006

FISHERIES DEVELOPMENT CORPORATION (6)
17 Battery Place
New York, New York   10004

Registered Lobbyist: Preston, Thorgrimson, Ellis, Holman & Fletcher
                       919 18th Street NW, Suite 300
                       Washington, DC   20006

FLAVOR AND EXTRACT MANUFACTURERS ASSOCIATION OF
THE U.S.   (6)
900 14th Street NW
Washington, DC   20006

Registered Lobbyist: Desautels Associates, Inc.
                        1725 K Street NW, Suite 811
                        Washington, DC   20006

FLORIDA FRUIT AND VEGETABLE ASSOCIATION   (6)
4401 East Colonial Drive
Orlando, Florida   32814

Registered Lobbyist: Barnett, Alagia, & Carey
                        1627 K Street NW
                        Washington, DC   20006

FLORIDA RESTAURANT ASSOCIATION   (6)
1077 Northeast 125th Street
North Miami, Florida   33161

Registered Lobbyist: Jerome Robinson

FLORIDA SUGAR CANE LEAGUE, INC.   (6)
P.O. Box 1148
Clewiston, Florida   33440

Registered Lobbyists: Thomas A. Davis, Michael R. McLeod
                        Davis & McLeod
                        499 South Capital Street SW, No. 407
                        Washington, DC   20003
                        Horace Godfrey

FMC CORPORATION   (6)
1627 K Street NW, Suite 500
Washington, DC   20006

Registered Lobbyist: James L. Burridge

FOOD AND BEVERAGE TRADES DEPARTMENT, AFL-CIO   (9)
815 16th Street NW
Washington, DC   20006   202/347-2640

Registered as Lobbyist: March 1977

FOOD DISTRIBUTORS TASK FORCE; NATIONAL WHOLESALE GROCERS ASSOCIATION (6)
51 Madison Avenue
New York, New York 10010

Registered Lobbyist: Cook & Henderson
1735 K Street NW, Second Floor
Washington, DC 20006

FOOD MARKETING INSTITUTE (6)
1750 K Street NW
Washington, DC 20006 202/452-8444

Founded: 1977 with the merger of the National Association of Food Chains and the Supermarket Institute.

President: Robert O. Aders

The Food Marketing Institute is the national trade association of firms engaged in retail and wholesale distribution of food and grocery products.

Membership: 950 to 1,000 (1979)

Registered Lobbyists: Robert Bradford; Karen Brown; Collier, Shannon, Rill, Edwards, & Scott; Dennis DeVaney; Vicki Erickson; John W. Farquhar; William S. Kies; P. Anne McGhee; Hardy L. Nathan; James T. Rogers; Harold Sullivan.

Publication: *FMI Washington Report* (weekly)

FOOD POLICY CENTER (7)
538 Seventh Street SE
Washington, DC 20003 202/547-7070

Director: Martin Rogol

Founded: 1977

The Food Policy Center conducts research and lobbies on hunger, food, and farm-related issues, both domestic and international. It has been involved with the President's Commission on World Hunger, studying the consequences of various policy proposals.

Funding: Grant from Harry Chapin, well-known singer, food activist, and one of the commissioners on the President's World Hunger Commission.

Registered Lobbyist: Martin H. Rogol

FOOD PROCESSING MACHINERY AND SUPPLIES
ASSOCIATION   (6)
1828 L Street NW, Suite 700
Washington, DC   20036   202/833-5770

President: Dewey W. Clower

FOOD PROTEIN COUNCIL   (6)
1800 M Street NW
Washington, DC   20036   202/467-6610

Director of Public Affairs: Jack Duvall

FOOD RESEARCH AND ACTION CENTER, INC.   (7)
2011 I Street NW, Suite 700
Washington, DC   20006   202/452-8250

Director: Roger Schwartz

Founded: 1970

The Food Research and Action Center (FRAC) is a private, nonprofit,
public interest law firm and advocacy center representing the poor people
and poor people's organizations around the country with regard to federal
food programs.

Funding: $644,615 in grants in 1978-1979 from the Community Services
Administration, Food and Nutrition Program (HEW); the Campaign for
Human Development of the U.S. Catholic Conference; Arca Foundation,
$25,000 (1976); New York Foundation, $10,000 (1973); and Rockefeller
Brothers Fund, $40,000 (1973).

Staff: 21 full-time (1979)

Registered Lobbyists: Edward Conney, Jeff Kirsch, Lynn Parker, Ron
                        Pollack, Paula Roberts, Michael Sandifer, Roger
                        Schwartz, Frances Zwenig.

Publications: List of available publications and prices available upon
request.

FOOD SERVICE & LODGING INSTITUTE   (6)
1666 K Street NW
Washington, DC   20006

Registered Lobbyist: William G. Giery

FOOD SERVICE ORGANIZATION OF DISTRIBUTORS (F.O.O.D.)   (6)
1800 M Street NW
Washington, DC   20036   202/452-8100

Director of Government Relations: William F. Sullivan

FORDHOOK FARMS   (5)
Doylestown, Pennsylvania   18901

Registered Lobbyist: David Burpee

FOREST FARMERS ASSOCIATION   (2)
P.O. Box 95385
Atlanta, Georgia   30347

Registered Lobbyist: J. Walter Myers, Jr.

FRIENDS COMMITTEE ON NATIONAL LEGISLATION   (7)
245 Second Street NE
Washington, DC   20002   202/547-4343

Executive Secretary: Edward Snyder

Founded: 1943

The Friends Committee on National Legislation is a Quaker-sponsored lobby for humanitarian concerns.

Registered Lobbyists: Edward F. Snyder, Frances E. Neely, Don Reeves.

Publication: *FCNL Washington Newsletter* (eleven times a year)

FRIENDS OF THE EARTH   (8)
620 C Street SE   124 Spear Street
Washington, DC   20003   San Francisco, California   94105
202/543-4312   415/495-4770

President: David R. Brower

Founded: 1969 when Brower left the Sierra Club.

Friends of the Earth is a registered environmental lobby group with 29,000 members in the United States and affiliated groups in fourteen foreign countries.

Funding: Membership, grants, contributions; $6,000 grant from Rockefeller Family Fund for internship program in Alaska relating to environmental implications of resource exploration, use, and development, 1977; $5,000 from Shalan Foundation to Friends of the Earth Foundation, 1978.

Registered Lobbyists: Elizabeth R. Kaplan, Jeffrey W. Knight, Pamela Lippa, David Masselli, Pamela Rich Minier, David E. Ortman, Rafe Pomerance, Marc Reis, Cathy Smith, Jerome R. Waldie, Anne Wickham.

Publication: *Not Man Apart* (bimonthly)

THE FUND FOR ANIMALS, INC.   (7)
140 W. 57th Street
New York, New York   10019   212/246-2096

Washington Representative
and Executive Vice-President: Lewis Regenstein
                                1765 P Street NW
                                Washington, DC   20036
                                202/234-4002

The Fund for Animals is a national, nonprofit, conservation and animal protection organization whose purpose is to preserve wildlife, save endangered species, and promote humane treatment for all animals.

Membership: 60,000

Registered Lobbyist: Milton M. Kaufman

Publication: Newsletter

FUTURES INDUSTRY ASSOCIATION   (6)
1919 Pennsylvania Avenue NW
Washington, DC   20006   202/466-5460

Founded: 1955

President: John W. Clagett

The Futures Industries Association is an association of firms in the commodity business whose main purpose is to raise the ethical and financial standards of the futures trading industry and to assist the industry and government to give greater protection to the public, individuals, and firms that use or are affected by the futures market. The association prepares and disseminates educational materials and statistical data.

Membership: 100

Publication: *FIA Newsletter* (monthly), quarterly report

E&J GALLO WINERY   (6)
P.O. Box 1130
Modesto, California   95353

Registered Lobbyists: Akin, Gump, Hauer, & Feld
1100 Madison Office Building
1155 15th Street NW
Washington, DC   20005

GENERAL FOODS   (6)
1707 L Street NW
Washington, DC   20036

Registered Lobbyist: Beth Peacock

GENERAL MILLS, INC.   (6)
P.O. Box 1113
Minneapolis, Minnesota   55440

Washington Address: 1629 K Street NW, Suite 300
Washington, DC   20006

Registered Lobbyists: Robert Bird

Gilbert B. Lessenco
Wilner & Scheiner
2021 L Street NW
Washington, DC   20036

Linda F. Mills

Patton, Boggs, & Blow
1200 17th Street NW
Washington, DC   20036

GERBER PRODUCTS, CO.   (6)
445 State Street
Fremont, Missouri   49412

Registered Lobbyists: Robert B. Heiney
Box 569, Lake of the Woods
Locust Grove, Virginia   22508

Frank R. Wolf
1901 North Moore Street, Suite 804
Arlington, Virginia   22209

GLOBAL SEAFOODS, INC.   (6)
1 Canal Plaza
Portland, Maine   04111

Registered Lobbyist: Birch, Horton, Bittner, & Monroe
                        4400 Jenifer Street NW, Suite 300
                        Washington, DC   20015

GRAIN PRODUCTS INTERNATIONAL   (6)
Forman, North Dakota   58032

Washington Representative
and Registered Lobbyist: Martin, Ryan, Haley, and Associates
                                1511 K Street NW
                                Washington, DC   20005

GRAIN SORGHUM PRODUCERS ASSOCIATION   (2)
Lubbock, Texas   79400   806/763-4425

Founded: 1956

Executive Director: Elbert Harp

The Grain Sorghum Producers Association represents grain sorghum producers spread throughout the sorghum production areas of the United
States. It is a member of the U.S. Feed Grains Council.

Members: 4,000 (1979)

GREAT ATLANTIC AND PACIFIC TEA CO., INC.   (6)
2 Paragon Drive
Montvale, New Jersey   07654

Washington Address: 1800 M Street NW, Suite 645
                      Washington, DC   20036

Registered Lobbyist: Thomas K. Zaucha

GREAT WESTERN SUGAR CO.   (6)
P.O. Box 5308
Denver, Colorado   80217

Registered Lobbyists: Berry, Epstein, Sandstrom, & Blatchford
                        1700 Pennsylvania Avenue NW
                        Washington, DC   20006

                        Clarence Davan

                        Art Stewart

GREEN GIANT CO.   (6)
Hazeltine Gates
Chaska, Minnesota   55318

Registered Lobbyist: Mahlon C. Schneider

GROCERY MANUFACTURERS OF AMERICA   (6)
1010 Wisconsin Avenue NW
Washington, DC   20007   202/337-9400

President: George W. Koch

The Grocery Manufacturers of America is a trade association of the
leading manufacturers and processors of food and nonfood products sold
in retail grocery outlets through the United States. The membership
believes that the interests of the consuming public are best served through
the maintenance and strengthening of a competitive marketplace, char-
acterized by maximum freedom of choice by consumers, appropriate
regulation for assurance of consumer health and safety, and fair returns
for responsible manufacturers.

Membership: 140

Registered Lobbyists: Michael Butler; Andrews, Kurth, Campbell, &
                        Jones; Bryce L. Harlow; Robert C. Hunt;
                        Kirkland, Ellis, & Rowe; George W. Koch;
                        Leighton & Conklin; Everett MacIntyre (Room 710,
                        1900 L Street NW, Washington, DC 20036);
                        Leonard W. Mall; Scott L. Mall; James C. May;
                        Mays, Valentine, Davenport, & Moore; Matthew
                        D. O'Hara; Pierson, Ball, & Dowd; Steven J.
                        Rukavina; Robert Taft, Jr., Taft, Stettinius, &
                        Hollister, Cincinnati; Frank J. Kulhanek.

HAWAIIAN SUGAR PLANTERS' ASSOCIATION   (2)
Aiea, Hawaii   96701

Washington Address: 723 Investment Building
                      1511 K Street
                      Washington, DC   20005   202/628-6372

Vice-President: Roger H. Sullivan

Registered Lobbyists: Williams & Jensen
                        1130 17th Street
                        Washington, DC   20035

                        O'Malveney & Meyers
                        1800 M Street NW
                        Washington, DC   20036

HEALTH RESEARCH GROUP (PUBLIC CITIZEN)   (7)
2000 P Street NW, Suite 708
Washington, DC   20036   202/872-0320

Director: Sidney Wolfe, M.D.

Founded: 1971

The Health Research Group is affiliated with Public Citizen, Inc., a consumer research and advocacy organization. The Health Research Group watches the activities of the Food and Drug Administration, health-care delivery, and occupational health.

Employees: 10 (one M.D., four lawyers, one chemist, one economist, three support staff)

Funding: Voluntary donations to Public Citizen, Inc., founded by Ralph Nader; operated on a budget of $155,796 in 1977.

Registered Lobbyists: Sidney M. Wolfe, Theodore D. Bogue, Robert B. Leflar, Robert B. Stulberg, Deborah M. Schechter, Benjamin Gordon, Daniel Sigelman.

Publications: List available on request.

HEINOLD COMMODITIES, INC.   (6)
222 South Riverside Plaza
Chicago, Illinois   60606

Registered Lobbyists: Lawrence H. Hunt, Jr.
Sidney & Austin
First National Plaza
Chicago, Illinois   60603

Margaret R. Murray
1339 Wisconsin Avenue NW
Washington, DC   20007

H.J. HEINZ CO.   (6)
P.O. Box 57
Pittsburgh, Pennsylvania   15230

Registered Lobbyist: Timmons & Co., Inc.
1776 F Street NW
Washington, DC   20006

HEUBLEIN, INC.   (6)
Farmington, Connecticut   06032

Registered Lobbyist: Herman Wolf

HOLSTEIN FRIESIAN ASSOCIA-
TION OF AMERICA   (2)
1 South Main Street
Brattleboro, Vermont   05301
802/254-4551

HOLSTEIN FREISIAN
SERVICES, INC.
Suite 2500, 1500 Main Street
Springfield, Massachusetts   01115

Founded: 1885

Executive Chairman: Robert H. Rumler

Washington Representative
and Registered Lobbyist: Dickstein, Shapiro, & Morin
                              2101 L Street NW
                              Washington, DC   20037

The Holstein Friesian Association of America is the national organization
of breeders of Holstein dairy cattle. Holstein Friesian Services, Inc.,
handles exports of Holstein breeding animals.

Membership: 37,322 (1977)

Funding: Registration and transfer fees, production testing, classification
and international marketing services for members.

Publication: *Holstein Friesian World*

HUMANE INFORMATION SERVICES, INC.   (7)
4495 Ninth Avenue North
St. Petersburg, Florida   33713   813/821-6396

Executive Secretary: Emily F. Gleockler

Founded: Incorporated 1965.

Membership and Subscribers: 19,000 (1977)

Humane Information Services, Inc., is a nonprofit, tax-exempt national
humane society for the prevention of animal suffering.

Funding: Contributions, bequests, endowment income.

Publication: *Report to Humanitarians* (quarterly)

HUMANE SOCIETY OF THE UNITED STATES   (7)
2001 L Street NW
Washington, DC   20036   202/452-1100

President: John Hoyt

Founded: 1954

The Humane Society of the United States is a national, nonprofit, tax-exempt organization dedicated to the relief of fear, pain, and suffering of all animals and to the concept of respect for all life. It is the largest animal welfare organization in the country.

Membership: 70,000

Funding: Membership dues and gifts.

Publications: *HSUS News* (quarterly); *Humane Education* (quarterly); *Shelter Sense* (bimonthly); list available on request.

E.F. HUTTON & CO., INC.   (6)
1 Battery Park Plaza
New York, New York   10004

Registered Lobbyists: George Bristol
1106 West Avenue
Austin, Texas   78700

A.W. Craig Hackler
1120 Connecticut Avenue NW, Suite 1128
Washington, DC   20036

Kutack, Rock, & Hule
1650 Farnam Street
Omaha, Nebraska   68102

INDEPENDENT BAKERS ASSOCIATION   (6)
3255 O Street NW, P.O. Box 3731
Washington, DC   20007   202/223-2325

Founded: 1967

Executive Director: Robert N. Pyle

The Independent Bakers Association is an association of small and medium-size wholesale bakers, who produce about 45 percent of the nation's wholesale bakery products, and three bakery cooperatives.

Membership: 168 (140 regular and 28 allied) (1978)

Registered Lobbyist: Robert N. Pyle

Publication: *The Independent*

INDEPENDENT BANKERS ASSOCIATION OF AMERICA   (6)
1168 South Main
Sauk Centre, Minnesota   56378   612/352-6546

Founded: 1930

Washington Office: 1625 Massachusetts Avenue NW
                     Washington, DC   20036   202/265-1921

The Independent Bankers Association is an association of commercial banks of which two-thirds are located in towns of 5,000 or less.

Membership: 7,300 member banks in eighteen major agricultural states.

Registered Lobbyists: Terrence H. Klasky, Joel C. McConnell, Jr.

INDUSTRIAL UNION DEPARTMENT, AFL-CIO   (9)
815 16th Street NW
Washington, DC   20006   202/637-5000

Secretary-Treasurer: Jacob Clayman

The Industrial Union Department of AFL-CIO is comprised of sixty international unions.

Membership: 6 million local members

Funding: Membership dues.

Registered Lobbyists: Marvin Caplan, Jacob Clayman, Joseph Vehlein.

INSTITUTE FOR FOOD AND DEVELOPMENT POLICY   (11)
2588 Mission Street
San Francisco, California   94110   415/648-6090

Founded: 1975

Cofounders: Frances Moore Lappe and Joseph Collins

The Institute for Food and Development Policy is a not-for-profit research, documentation, and education center working in the areas of international agricultural development and hunger problems.

Funding: Sale of publications; grants from Ottinger Foundation, Stern Fund ($15,000, 1977-1978), Samuel Rubin Foundation, Tides Foundation, United Presbyterian Church, Church of the Brethren, Episcopal Church, St. James Episcopal Church of New York, First United Church of Oak Park, Illinois, individual contributions. Will not accept contributions from governments or corporations.

Publications: List available upon request.

INSTITUTE FOR POLICY STUDIES   (11)
1901 Q Street NW
Washington, DC   20009   202/234-9382

Founded: 1963

Director: Bob Borosage

Food Policy: Eleanor LeCain

The Institute for Policy Studies engages in research and publication on the impact of U.S. policies on Third-World countries.

Funding: Foundation grants: Shalan Foundation, $10,500, tax reform, 1976; Field Foundation, general support, $15,000, 1976; New World Foundation, $35,000, 1977, programs of Conference on Alternative State and Local Policies; Stern Fund, $2,000 for education on national security and disarmament, $20,000 for support of the Transnational Institute.

INSTITUTE OF SHORTENING AND EDIBLE OILS, INC.   (6)
1750 New York Avenue NW
Washington, DC   20006   202/296-7960

President: William W. Goodrich

INSTITUTE FOR WORLD ORDER   (11)
11 W. 42d Street
New York, New York   10036   212/575-0055

Founded: 1961

The Institute for World Order is a nonprofit, tax-exempt education and research organization seeking to develop awareness of the need for new systems of world institutions built on human values. It assists in the development of college courses on world food issues.

Funding: Foundation grants and contributions: $13,000 from Lilly Endowment, 1976; $20,000 from Scherman Foundation, 1976; $7,129, Compton Foundation, 1976.

Publications: *Ways and Means*; list of others available on request.

INTERFAITH CENTER ON CORPORATE RESPONSIBILITY   (7)
475 Riverside Drive, Room 566
New York, New York   10027   212/879-2316

Director, Agribusiness Project: Bob Morris

Founded: 1974

The Interfaith Center on Corporate Responsibility is an organization of religious agencies and individuals which monitors the social effects of corporation policies including policies affecting world hunger, malnutrition, and poverty.

Washington Representative
and Registered Lobbyist: James C. Rosapepe
Rosapepe & Associates
101 N. Columbus Street, Room 400
Alexandria, Virginia
22314 703/920-0725

Publications: *The Corporate Examiner, The CIC Brief*

INTERNATIONAL AGRICULTURAL DEVELOPMENT SERVICES (7)
1133 Avenue of the Americas
New York, New York 10036 212/869-8500

President: Sterling Wortman

Executive Officer: A. Colin McClung

The International Agricultural Development Service is engaged in development assistance projects in developing countries through contracts with the U.S. Agency for International Development, private foundations, and foreign governments.

Funding: During 1978, $1,260,000 from Rockefeller Foundation plus $236,731 deferred support from 1977; $30,500 from Agency for International Development for publication of a handbook; Lilly Endowment grant of $148,686 used in 1978, $330,481 remaining for 1979.

Washington Representative
and Registered Lobbyist: Voys, Sater, Seymour, & Pease
Suite 800, 1800 M Street NW
Washington, DC 20035

Publication: *IADS Report* (annual)

INTERNATIONAL APPLE INSTITUTE (6)
2430 Pennsylvania Avenue NW
Washington, DC 20037 202/833-9150

Executive Vice-President: Fred W. Burrows

INTERNATIONAL ASSOCIATION OF ICE CREAM MANUFAC-
TURERS (6)
910 17th Street NW, Suite 1105
Washington, DC 20006 202/296-4250

Founded: 1908

President: Fay R. Wells

The International Association of Ice Cream Manufacturers represents manufacturers of ice cream and other related frozen desserts who produce about 85 percent of all ice cream and similar frozen desserts in the United States.

Membership: 325

Registered Lobbyists: Robert M. Mulligan, Austin T. Rhodes, John F. Speer Jr., Linwood Tipton, Glenn P. Witte.

Publication: *Up to Date* (monthly)

INTERNATIONAL ASSOCIATION OF REFRIGERATED WARE-HOUSES   (6)
THE REFRIGERATION RESEARCH FOUNDATION
7315 Wisconsin Avenue NW, Suite 700W
Washington, DC   20014   202/652-5674

Secretary: Joseph H. Colquitt

INTERNATIONAL COMMODITIES CLEARING HOUSE, LTD.   (6)
Roman Wall House
2 Crutched Friars
London EC3N   2AN
England

Registered Lobbyist: Arnold & Porter
1229 19th Street NW
Washington, DC   20036

INTERNATIONAL FOODSERVICE MANUFACTURERS ASSOCIA-TION   (6)
875 North Michigan Avenue, Suite 3460
Chicago, Illinois   60611

Washington Address: 1025 Connecticut Avenue NW, Suite 900
Washington, DC   20036   202/457-6530

President: Michael J. Licata

Washington Counsel
and Registered Lobbyist: Philip F. Zeidman
Brownstein, Schomer, & Chase

INTERNATIONAL HARVESTER   (6)
401 North Michigan Avenue
Chicago, Illinois   60611

Registered Lobbyists: Thomas L. Trueblood, Brian B. Whalen.

INTERNATIONAL LONGSHOREMEN'S AND WAREHOUSEMEN'S UNION   (9)
1188 Franklin Street
San Francisco, California   94109   415/775-0533

Founded: 1937

Washington Representative
and Registered Lobbyist: Patrick F. Tobin
                                  417 Fourth Street SW
                                  Washington, DC   20001   202/544-4441

The International Longshoremen's and Warehousemen's Union has represented 20,000 workers in Hawaii since 1945 including agreements with fifteen sugar plantations covering 8,000 workers.

Membership: 116,000

Funding: Membership dues.

INTERRELIGIOUS TASK FORCE ON U.S. FOOD POLICY   (7)
110 Maryland Avenue NE
Washington, DC   20002   202/543-2800; 800/424-7292

Chairman: George Chauncey

Founded: 1974

The Interreligious Task Force on U.S. Food Policy is a team of thirty-five Washington-based staff of national religious denominations and groups who collaborate on legislative analysis, policy recommendations, and political strategies as a means of helping the U.S. religious community witness for a responsible U.S. food policy. They speak for themselves and not for the churches and ecumenical agencies that cooperate in their work.

Organizations and Boards Represented: American Baptist Churches, U.S.A.; American Jewish Committee; American Lutheran Church; Christian Church (Disciples of Christ); Church of the Brethren; Episcopal Church; Friends Committee on National Legislation; Jesuit Conference; Lutheran Church in America; Lutheran Church-Missouri Synod; Moravian Church in America; National Council of Churches; Presbyterian Church in the U.S.; Reformed Church in America; Union of American Hebrew Congregations; Unitarian Universalist Association; Unitarian Universalist Service Committee; United Church of Christ; United Methodist Church; United Presbyterian Church in the U.S.A.; Bread for the World; Center of Concern Network.

Publications: *Hunger, National Impact, Food Policy Notes*

IOWA BEEF PROCESSORS, INC.   (6)
Dakota City, Nebraska   68731

Registered Lobbyists: Doub, Purcell, Muntzing, & Hansen
                        1775 Pennsylvania Avenue NW
                        Washington, DC   20006

                        Francis O. McDermott
                        1750 K Street NW, Suite 1110
                        Washington, DC   20006

KANSAS FARM BUREAU LIFE INSURANCE CO.   (6)
2321 Anderson Avenue
Manhattan, Kansas   66502

Registered Lobbyist: Sutherland, Asbill, & Brennan
                       1666 K Street NW
                       Washington, DC   20006

KELLOGG CO.   (6)
235 Porter Street
Battle Creek, Michigan   49016

Registered Lobbyists: Moss, Frink, & Franklin
                        600 New Hampshire Avenue NW, Suite 480
                        Washington, DC   20037

                        James W. Riddell

**KENTUCKY FARM BUREAU MUTUAL INSURANCE CO. AND
FARM BUREAU INSURANCE CO.**   (6)
120 South Hubbard Lane
Louisville, Kentucky   40207

Registered Lobbyist: Sutherland, Asbill, & Brennan
                       1666 K Street NW
                       Washington, DC   20006

KIKKOMAN FOODS, INC.   (6)
Walworth, Wisconsin   53184

Registered Lobbyist: Thomas G. Godfrey
                       Elkhorn, Wisconsin

KRAUSE MILLING CO.   (6)
P.O. Box 1156
Milwaukee, Wisconsin   53201

Registered Lobbyist: Williams & Jensen
                        1130 17th Street NW
                        Washington, DC   20036

KROGER CO.   (6)
1014 Vine Street
Cincinnati, Ohio   45202

Registered Lobbyist: Manly Molpus
                        Arnold & Porter
                        1229 19th Street NW
                        Washington, DC   20036

LAND O'LAKES, INC.   (3)
614 McKinley Place
Minneapolis, Minnesota   55413

Registered Lobbyist: E.A. Jaenke and Associates
                        1735 I Street NW, Suite 610
                        Washington, DC   20006

LEAGUE OF WOMEN VOTERS OF THE UNITED STATES   (7)
1730 M Street NW
Washington, DC   20036   202/296-1770

President: Ruth Clusen

Founded: 1920

The League of Women Voters of the United States is a nonpartisan political
action and study organization of women and men working to increase participation in government and substandard education and housing.

Membership: 136,000 in 1,350 state and local organizations

Registered Lobbyists: Laureen E. Andrews, Catherine B. Deely, Sarah M.
                        Laird, Lloyd Leonard, Joan E. Twiggs; Arent,
                        Fox, Kinter, Plotkin & Kahn

Publications: List available on request.

Funding: Grant from Ford Motor Co. Fund of $6,500 (1976); $25,000
from Rockefeller Brothers Fund (1976) for Asian program of developing
women's skills.

LEGAL SERVICES CORPORATION   (7)
733 15th Street NW
Washington, DC   20005   202/376-5100

President: Dan J. Bradley

Executive Vice-President: E. Clinton Bamberger, Jr.

Founded: 1975

The Legal Services Corporation is a private, nonprofit organization established by Congress in 1974 to provide financial support for legal assistance to the poor in civil matters. It is the successor to the former Office of Economic Opportunity poverty law program that was started in 1965. The federally funded legal services program was removed from the executive branch after it became apparent in the late 1960s and early 1970s that a structural change was necessary to insulate legal services for the poor from partisan political pressures.

Funding: Congressional appropriations; federal appropriation, $205 million for fiscal year 1978, $125 million for 1977.

Grantees: Grants to 335 legal services programs in 900 neighborhood offices in fifty states, District of Columbia, Puerto Rico, the Virgin Islands, and Micronesia. Approximately 5,080 lawyers and 2,377 paralegals work in these offices. The corporation also supports training, research, clearinghouse activities, and technical assistance to lawyers, paralegals, and other staff who work for local legal services programs so they can provide the highest quality legal services to the poor.

Registered Lobbyist: Judith Riggs (registered May 1976); Alice Daniel
                      (April 1977); Quentin L. Burgess.

Publications: *Legal Services Corporation News* (bimonthly)

LIVESTOCK MARKETING ASSOCIATION   (6)
4900 Oak Street
Kansas City, Missouri   64112

Registered Lobbyist: Robert M. Cook

LONDON COMMODITY EXCHANGE CO. LTD.   (6)
Cereal House
58 Mark Lane
London, EC34   7NE
England

Registered Lobbyist: Arnold & Porter
                      1229 19th Street NW
                      Washington, DC   20036

THE LOUISIANA LAND & EXPLORATION CO.   (5)
P.O. Box 60350
New Orleans, Louisiana   70160

LUMMI TRIBE OF INDIANS   (12)
2616 Kwina Road
Bellingham, Washington   98225

Registered Lobbyist: Zionty, Pirtle, Morisset, Ernstoff, & Chestnut
                         208 Pioneer Building, 600 First Avenue
                         Seattle, Washington   98104

LUTHERAN WORLD RELIEF   (7)
315 Park Avenue South
New York, New York   10010   212/677-3950

Washington Office: 475 L'Enfant Plaza West, SW Suite 2720
                     Washington, DC   20024   202/484-3959

Executive Secretary: Bernard Confer

Founded: 1945

Lutheran World Relief provides financial, material, and personnel support
to assist needy people throughout the United States in disaster and emergen-
cies as well as in long-term development projects.

Membership: Represents three U.S. Lutheran Church organizations.

MAKAH TRIBAL COUNCIL   (12)
P.O. 115
Neah Bay, Washington   98357

Registered Lobbyist: Rebecca D. Shapiro & Associates
                       111 C Street SE
                       Washington, DC 20003

MARS, INC.   (6)
1651 Old Meadow Road
McLean, Virginia   22101

Registered Lobbyist: William J. Colley
                       Patton, Boggs, & Blow
                       1200 17th Street NW
                       Washington, DC   20036

MCDONALD'S CORP.   (6)
1 McDonald's Plaza
Oak Brook, Illinois   60521

Registered Lobbyists: Clifford H. Raber, Clayton C. Taylor.

MEAT IMPORTERS COUNCIL OF AMERICA, INC.   (6)
1 Penn Plaza
New York, New York   10001   212/594-2348

Washington Office: 1901 N. Fort Myer Drive
                     Arlington, Virginia   22209

Registered Lobbyists: William C. Morrison, John E. Ward
                        Barnes Richardson & Colburn
                        1919 H. Street NW
                        Washington, DC   20006

MEAT PRICE INVESTIGATORS ASSOCIATION   (7)
P.O. Box 66
Des Moines, Iowa   50301

The Meat Price Investigators Association is a registered lobby for the purpose of supporting legislation that would overturn the Illinois *Brick* decision and correct meat pricing practices.

Registered Lobbyist: Glenn Freie

MEAT PRODUCTS GROUP, AMERICAN IMPORTERS ASSOCIATION   (6)
420 Lexington Avenue
New York, New York   10017

Registered Lobbyist: Berry, Epstein, Sandstrom, & Blatchford
                       1700 Pennsylvania Avenue NW
                       Washington, DC   20006

MERCK AND CO., INC.   (6)
P.O. Box 2000
Rahway, New Jersey   07065

Registered Lobbyists: William W. Bailey
                        1050 17th Street NW, Suite 1050
                        Washington, DC   20036

                        Robert R. Hurt

MERRILL, LYNCH, PIERCE, FENNER, & SMITH, INC. (6)
One Liberty Plaza
New York, New York 10006

Registered Lobbyist: Desautels Associates, Inc.
1725 K Street NW, Suite 811
Washington, DC 20006

METLAKATLA INDIAN COMMUNITY (12)
P.O. Box 8
Metlakatla, Arkansas 99926

Registered Lobbyist: Zionty, Pirtle, Morisset, Ernstoff, & Chestnut
208 Pioneer Building, 600 First Avenue
Seattle, Washington 98104

MEXICAN NATIONAL CONFEDERATION OF LIVESTOCK PRO-
DUCERS (6)
3200 16th Street
Chichuahua, Mexico

Registered Lobbyist: Dell, Craighill, Fentress, & Benton
888 17th Street NW, Suite 1200
Washington, DC 20006

MFA MUTUAL INSURANCE CO. (6)
1817 West Broadway
Columbia, Missouri 65201

Registered Lobbyist: Arnold & Porter
1229 19th Street NW
Washington, DC 20036

MID-AMERICA DAIRYMEN, INC. (3)
P.O. Box 1837 S.S. Station
Springfield, Missouri 65805 417/865-9641

Founded: 1968

Executive Vice President and General Manager: Gary Hanman

Mid-America Dairymen, Inc., is a regional dairy cooperative which performs a total marketing and manufacturing operation for the dairy farmers
who own and control the enterprise.

Membership: 10,673 (1978)

Government Relations: Works through National Milk Producers Federation and the National Council of Farmer Cooperatives.

Publication: *Mid-Am Reporter*

Net Sales Revenues: $770,446,269 (1978)

MIDCONTINENT FARMERS ASSOCIATION (MISSOURI FARMERS ASSOCIATION) (1)
201 South Seventh Street
Columbia, Missouri 65201   314/874-5111

Founded: 1914

Washington Representative: E.A. Jaenke & Associates
                            1735 I Street NW
                            Washington, DC 20006

President: Eric G. Thompson

Midcontinent Farmers Association originated as Missouri Farmers Association with cooperative stores and marketing services to its members. In national legislative efforts it has joined with other farm and commodity groups to work for preservation of the family farm, full-parity prices for producers, and cooperation with government to improve markets and incomes for farmers.

Membership: 175,000 (1979) in Missouri and nearby states.

Funding: Membership and payments from members for services through affiliated companies and cooperatives.

Registered Lobbyists: L.C. Carpenter (until August 1979); E.A. Jaenke & Associates.

Publication: *Today's Farmer*

MIGRANT LEGAL ACTION PROGRAM, INC.   (7)
806 15th Street NW
Washington, DC 20005   202/347-5100; 800/424-9425

Executive Director: Raphael Gomez

Founded: 1970

The Migrant Legal Action Program, Inc., is a national support center providing direct assistance to Legal Services offices on migrant and seasonal farm worker issues and advocates directly for farm workers on national policy matters. Activities include litigation support, national policy representation, training for attorneys on migrant matters, and preparation of manuals and maintenance of a law library and research files.

Funding: Legal Services Corporation, direct grant $482,354 in 1978. Approximate 1979 total budget: $6.2 million. McKnight Foundation, $5,000, 1976.

Employees: Eleven attorneys, office manager, paralegal, and general support staff.

Registered Lobbyist: Burton D. Fretz

Publication: *Washington Report*

MILK INDUSTRY FOUNDATION   (6)
1910 17th Street NW, Suite 1105
Washington, DC   20006   202/296-4250

Founded: 1916

The Milk Industry Foundation is the industry association representing fluid-milk processors and distributors located throughout the United States who process and distribute about 75 percent of the fluid milk and fluid-milk products consumed in the United States.

Membership: 500

Registered Lobbyists: Robert M. Mulligan, Austin T. Rhodes, John F.
                        Speer, Jr., Linwood Tipton, and Glenn Witte.

Publication: *Up to Date* (monthly)

MILLERS' NATIONAL FEDERATION   (6)
1776 F Street NW
Washington, DC   20006   202/452-0900

President: Wayne E. Swegle

MINNEAPOLIS GRAIN EXCHANGE   (6)
400 South 4th Street
Minneapolis, Minnesota   55415   612/338-6212

Founded: 1881

Executive Vice-President: Alvin W. Donahoo

The Minneapolis Grain Exchange is the world's largest cash grain market. Its members are commission houses, grain brokers, county and terminal elevator managers, processors, millers, and exporters of grain.

Membership: 420

MISSISSIPPI FARM BUREAU MUTUAL INSURANCE CO.   (6)
Jackscn, Mississippi   39205

Registered Lobbyist: Sutherland, Asbill, & Brennan
                       1666 K Street NW
                       Washington, DC   20006

MOBAY CHEMICAL CORP.   (6)
P.O. Box 4913, Hawthorn Road
Kansas City, Missouri   64120

Registered Lobbyist: James T. Conner
                       1140 Connecticut Avenue NW
                       Washington, DC   20036

MODESTO IRRIGATION DISTRICT   (10)
1231 11th Street
Modesto, California   95352

Registered Lobbyist: White, Fine, Verville
                       1156 15th Street NW, Suite 302
                       Washington, DC   20005

MONSANTO CO.   (6)
800 North Lindbergh Boulevard
St. Louis, Missouri   63166

Washington Address: 1101 17th Street NW, Suite 604
                      Washington, DC   20036

Registered Lobbyists: David S.J. Brown, James R. Enyart, John F.
                        Hussey, Sam Pickard, Lloyd D. Shand, Earl C.
                        Spurrier.

NABISCO, INC.   (6)
100 DeForest Avenue
East Hanover, New Jersey   07936

Registered Lobbyist: Wayne C. Anderson

NATIONAL AGRICULTURAL AVIATION ASSOCIATION   (6)
National Press Building, Suite 459
Washington, DC   20004   202/638-0542

Founded: 1967

Executive Director: Farrell Higbee

The National Agricultural Aviation Association is an organization of operators of aerial spraying equipment, including large farmers who own such equipment. Members operate about 86 percent of the aircraft used in agricultural activity.

Membership: 1,216 operators, pilots, allied firms, and international members.

Registered Lobbyist: Harold Collins

NATIONAL AGRICULTURAL CHEMICALS ASSOCIATION   (6)
1155 11th Street NW, Suite 514
Washington, DC   20005   202/296-1585

Founded: 1933

President: Jack D. Early

The National Agricultural Chemicals Association is the national association of the manufacturers and formulators of pest control products employed in agricultural production. Members are companies which produce and sell virtually all the technical pesticide materials' active ingredients in, and a large percentage of the formulated products registered for, use in the United States.

Membership: 122, of which 14 are classified as associate members (1978).

Registered Lobbyists: Doub, Purcell, Muntzing, & Hansen; Jack D. Early.

Publication: *Actionews* (biweekly)

NATIONAL ASSOCIATION OF COUNTY AGRICULTURAL STABI-
LIZATION AND CONSERVATION SERVICE OFFICE EMPLOYEES
(NASCOE)   (10)
Gettysburg, Pennsylvania   17325

Founded: 1959

President: Neal Phillips
            Box 250
            Halifax, North Carolina   27839

The National Association of County ASCS Office Employees is a voluntary organization of county employees whose purpose is to represent the welfare of its members.

Membership: 96 percent of the 8,245 employees (1977)

Publication: *NASCOE Letter*

NATIONAL ASSOCIATION OF CONSERVATION DISTRICTS   (8)
(Formerly National Association of Soil Conservation Districts)
1025 Vermont Avenue NW, Room 1105
Washington, DC   20005   202/347-5995

Executive Vice President: Neil Sampson

Founded: 1946

The National Association of Conservation Districts is an organization of farmers and landowners working to conserve land, water, forests, wildlife, and related natural resources through 3,000 local soil and water and natural resource conservaton districts in fifty states, Puerto Rico, and the Virgin Islands.

Membership: 3,500

Publication: *Tuesday Letter*

NATIONAL ASSOCIATION OF CONVENIENCE STORES   (6)
5205 Leesburg Pike, Suite 311
Falls Church, Virginia   22041

Registered Lobbyist: State and Federal Associates, Inc.
                        1101 15th Street NW, S-311
                        Washington, DC   20005

NATIONAL ASSOCIATION OF COUNTIES   (10)
1735 New York Avenue NW
Washington, DC   20006   202/785-9577

Founded: 1935

Executive Director: Bernard F. Hillenbrand

The National Association of Counties is a nonprofit organization concerned with mutual problems and public issues that affect county governments.

Membership: Approximately 1,800

Publications: *County News*, *County Employment Reporter*, others available.

NATIONAL ASSOCIATION OF FARMER ELECTED COMMITTEE-MEN   (5)

Founded: 1965

President: Ned Hundstad
                    Bath, South Dakota   57424

Secretary-Treasurer: Ray Wax
                                    Newman, Illinois   61942   217/837-2533

The farmer elected committeemen are local farmers who serve as advisors to local and state Agricultural Stabilization and Conservation Service offices in administering the price support and grain storage programs. "We represent the farmers before the government and we represent the government fairly before the farmers."

Membership: 12,000

Registered Lobbyists: Tom B. Cunningham, Ed Bowmon, Billy League, Ray Wax.

Publication: *NAFEC Newsletter* (six times a year)

NATIONAL ASSOCIATION OF FARMWORKER ORGANIZATIONS   (7)
1329 E Street NW, Suite 1145
Washington, DC   20004   202/347-2407; 800/424-5100

Executive Director: F. Thomas Jones

Founded: 1973

The National Association of Farmworker Organizations is a nonprofit organization of forty migrant and seasonal farm worker organizations focusing on advocating for the civil and labor rights of migrant and seasonal farm workers.

Membership: 54 farm worker organizations in thirty-eight states, including twenty membership organizations.

Funding: 1977-1978: $1 million, Community Services Administration, energy and weatherization; $250,000, CSA, national information network; $150,000, CSA, national health plan; $100,000, CSA, community food and nutrition program; $100,000, Campaign for Human Development, U.S. Catholic Conference; membership, $30,000. Total budget: $1,630,000.

Registered Lobbyists: Organization registration, January 1978.

Publication: *The National Farmworker*, list of other available publications on request.

NATIONAL ASSOCIATION OF FEDERAL VETERINARIANS   (10)
1522 K Street NW, Suite 836
Washington, DC   20005   202/223-3590

The National Association of Federal Veterinarians is an organization of professional veterinarians employed by the federal government.

Membership: 1700

Washington Representative
and Registered Lobbyists: William Hughes, R.E. Omohundro.

Publication: *Federal Veterinarian*

NATIONAL ASSOCIATION FOR HUMANE LEGISLATION, INC.   (7)
P.O. Box 11675
St. Petersburg, Florida   33733

Acting President: Mrs. William A. (Charlotte) Parks

The National Association for Humane Legislation, Inc., is a national organization concerned with legislation that affects humane treatment of animals.

Registered Lobbyist: Organization, first quarter 1979

NATIONAL ASSOCIATION OF MARGARINE MANUFACTURERS   (6)
1725 K Street NW, Suite 1202
Washington, DC   20006

Registered Lobbyist: Siert F. Riepma

NATIONAL ASSOCIATION OF MEAT PURVEYORS, INC.   (6)
293A Agawam Drive
Stratford, Connecticut   06497

Washington Address: 2020 K Street NW, Suite 420
                      Washington, DC   20006   202/833-8078

Washington Representative: Peter H. Petersen

NATIONAL ASSOCIATION FOR MILK MARKETING REFORM   (6)

Registered Lobbyist: Donald A. Randall
                      1625 K Street NW, Suite 1205
                      Washington, DC   20006

NATIONAL ASSOCIATION OF RETAIL GROCERS OF THE U.S.   (6)
11800 Sunrise Valley
Reston, Virginia   22091   703/860-3300

Founded: 1893

President: Frank Register

The National Association of Retail Grocers is the national trade association of retail grocers.

Membership: 35,000 retail members in forty affiliated state and sixty-seven local and regional organizations.

Registered Lobbyist: Frank D. Register

Publications: List on request.

NATIONAL ASSOCIATION OF STATE DEPARTMENTS OF AGRICULTURE   (10)
1616 H Street NW
Washington, DC   20006   202/628-1566

Founded: 1915

President: James A. Graham

Membership: 50 state departments of agriculture.

NATIONAL ASSOCIATION OF STATE UNIVERSITIES AND LAND-GRANT COLLEGES   (10)
1 DuPont Circle
Washington, DC   20036   202/293-7120

Founded: 1871

President: Robert Clodius

Director, Government Relations: Russell McGregor

The National Association of State Universities and Land-Grant Colleges is an organization representing the land-grant universities and certain other state universities.

Membership: 144 colleges and universities

Publication: *Circular Letter*

NATIONAL ASSOCIATION OF WHEAT GROWERS   (2)
415 Second Street NE, Suite 300
Washington, DC   20015   202/582-7000

Founded: 1950

Executive Vice-President: Jerry Rees

The National Association of Wheat Growers is a national organization of wheat growers affiliated with sixteen state associations and producing 85 percent of the nation's wheat.

Membership: 80,000 (estimated 1979)

Registered Lobbyists: Jerry Rees, Carl Schwensen, Craig Hackler.

Publication: *Wheat Grower* (monthly)

NATIONAL AUDUBON SOCIETY   (8)
1511 K Street NW   950 Third Avenue
Washington, DC   20036   New York, New York   10022
202/466-6600   212/832-3200

Founded: 1905

President and Senior Council: Elvis J. Stahr

The National Audubon Society is one of the nation's oldest and largest conservation organizations in the United States with a special interest in protection of natural resources.

Membership: 360,000 members and 300 chapters

Registered Lobbyists: Michael R. Zagata, Marcia Ann Graham, Stephen
                                     Young.

Publications: List available on request.

Funding: Memberships; gifts; grant from Rockefeller Brothers Fund, $200,000, to evaluate society's environmental education programs and general budgetary support of these programs, 1977.

NATIONAL BAKERY SUPPLIERS ASSOCIATION   (6)
1625 K Street NW
Washington, DC   20006   202/658-5530

Counsel: Wayne K. Hill

NATIONAL BEER WHOLESALERS' ASSOCIATION OF AMERICA   (6)
5205 Leesburg Pike
Falls Church, Virginia   22041   703/578-4300

NATIONAL BROILER COUNCIL   (6)
1155 15th Street NW
Washington, DC   20005   202/296-2622

Founded: 1954

President: George B. Watts

The National Broiler Council is a nonprofit trade association representing producers and processors of approximately 75 percent of broiler-fryer chickens produced in the United States.

Membership: 125 to 150 companies

Registered Lobbyists: Collier, Shannon, Rill, Edwards, & Scott; Marilee Menard; George B. Watts.

Publication: *NBC Washington Report*

NATIONAL CANDY WHOLESALERS ASSOCIATION, INC.   (6)
1430 K Street NW, Suite 1000
Washington, DC   20005   202/393-6733

Registered Lobbyist: Russell L. Shipley, Jr., Raymond J. Foley.

NATIONAL CATHOLIC RURAL LIFE CONFERENCE   (7)
4625 N.W. Beaver Drive
Des Moines, Iowa   50322   515/274-1581

Founded: 1923

Washington Office: 1312 Massachusetts Avenue NW
                     Washington, DC   20005
                     202/659-6839

President: Maurice J. Dingman

The National Catholic Rural Life Conference is concerned with the responsible development and just distribution of the earth's resources. They have special interest in land, food, and community development issues.

Membership: Represents all citizens, not just farmers.

Publication: *Catholic Rural Life*; *Washington Memorandum*

NATIONAL CATTLEMEN'S ASSOCIATION   (2)
1001 Lincoln Street
Denver, Colorado   80201   303/861-1904

Founded: 1977

Washington Office: 425 13th Street NW, Suite 1020
                     Washington, DC   20004   202/347-0228

President: Richard A. McDougal
             Lovelock, Nevada   89419

Vice-President, Government Affairs: C.W. McMillan

The National Cattlemen's Association is an association of cattle producers and feeders with sixty-five affiliated state and national groups. The National Livestock Feeders Association merged with American National Cattlemen's Association in 1977.

Membership: 280,000

Registered Lobbyists: Thomas A. Davis and Michael R. McLeod, Davis & McLeod; J. Burton Eller, Jr.; C.W. McMillan; Ronald A. Michieli.

Publication: *Beef Business Bulletin*

NATIONAL CENTER FOR APPROPRIATE TECHNOLOGY   (7)
P.O. Box 3838   815 15th Street NW
Butte, Montana   59701   Washington, D.C.   20005
406/723-6533   202/347-9193

Executive Director: Edwin C. Kepler

The National Center for Appropriate Technology is a research and information center working on food production, solar technology, and methane generation. It is an independent, nonprofit corporation.

Funding: Community Services Administration, 1978-1979, $3,218,000.

NATIONAL CHILD NUTRITION PROJECT   (7)
46 Bayard Street
New Brunswick, New Jersey   08901   201/846-1161

President: Barbara Zang

Founded: 1972

The National Child Nutrition Project is a nonprofit organization which seeks to improve and expand federal food program operations.

Employees: 6

Funding: Community Services Administration, $118,514 in 1978-1979; Meyer foundation, $10,000, 1975; sale of publications.

Publication: *Food Action*; list of others available on request.

NATIONAL CONFECTIONERS ASSOCIATION   (6)
36 South Wabash Avenue
Chicago, Illinois   60603   312/372-1492

Founded: 1884

Washington Representative, Registered Lobbyist,
President, and General Counsel: James E. Mack
                                  5101 Wisconsin Avenue
                                  Suite 504
                                  Washington, DC 20016
                                  202/966-7888

The National Confectioners Association is the national trade association of
candy and confectionary manufacturers, producing about 95 percent of the
total U.S. consumption.

Membership: 350

Publication: *Monthly Confection News*

NATIONAL CONFERENCE OF STATE LEGISLATURES   (10)
444 N. Capitol
Washington, DC   20002   202/624-5400

Founded: 1975

Executive Director: Earl MacKay

Membership: All the state legislatures, 7,482.

Publication: *State Legislature, Dateline*

NATIONAL CONGRESS OF AMERICAN INDIANS   (7)
1430 K Street NW
Washington, DC   20036   202/347-9520

Director Community Development Programs: Teresa Carmondy

Founded: 1944

The National Congress of American Indians represents all American Indian
tribes. One of their major concerns is federal food programs for Indians.

Registered Lobbyists: Some individual tribes have employed lobbyists to
                        represent them.

NATIONAL CONGRESS OF PARENTS AND TEACHERS (National
PTA)   (7)
700 N. Rush Street
Chicago, Illinois   60611   312/787-0977

Founded: 1897

Executive Director: Becky Schergens

The National PTA is a national advocacy organization working for improvements in quality of education and quality of life for young people.

Membership: 6,100,000 individuals in local and state organizations

Registered Lobbyist: Ann P. Kahn

Publication: *PTA Today* (nine times a year)

NATIONAL CONSUMERS LEAGUE (Including National Consumers Congress)   (7)
1522 K Street NW, Suite 406
Washington, DC   20036   202/797-7600

Executive Vice-President: Sandra Willett

Founded: 1899

The National Consumers League is a registered lobby concerned with a variety of interests dealing with consumers and related legislation, including federal funding of meals on wheels and food stamps.

Membership: 600 individuals, 500 firms (1979)

Registered Lobbyists: Sandra L. Willett, Ann Harrison Clark, April D. Moore, Barbara K. Pequet.

Funding: Membership dues; federal agency contracts and grants dealing with standard setting, consumer education, nutrition labeling.

Publication: *NCL Bulletin*, list of other publications available upon request.

NATIONAL CORN GROWERS ASSOCIATION   (2)
8450 Hickman, Suite 23
Des Moines, Iowa   50265   515/225-8840

Founded: 1959

President: Russel Arndt
               LaCrosse, Indiana   46348   219/754-2120

Executive Vice-President: Melvin "Mike" Hayenga

The National Corn Growers Association is comprised of corn growers in fifteen affiliated state associations. It is a member of the U.S. Feed Grains Council, an industrywide group established to expand foreign markets for feed grains.

Membership: 9,000

Publication: *Corn Talk*

NATIONAL COTTON COUNCIL OF AMERICA (6)
P.O. Box 12285
Memphis, Tennessee 38112   901/274-9030

Founded: 1939

Washington Office: 1030 15th Street NW
                   Washington, DC 20005   202/833-2943

President: Lon Mann (1978)

The National Cotton Council is the central organization representing seven segments of the raw cotton industry. It is a representative body composed of 290 delegates selected by cotton growers, ginners, cooperatives, warehousemen, merchants, cottonseed crushers, and manufacturers through their own state, regional, and national organizations.

Registered Lobbyists: Charles Bragg, Philip C. Burnett, Carl C. Campbell, Macon T. Edwards, David C. Hull, Randall T. Jones, Carlton H. Power, Earl W. Sears, Albert R. Russell, LaVerne Still.

Publications: Various studies and reports dealing with the cotton industry.

NATIONAL COUNCIL OF AGRICULTURAL EMPLOYERS (5)
237 Southern Building
1425 H Street NW
Washington, DC 20005

Registered Lobbyist: Perry R. Ellsworth

NATIONAL COUNCIL OF FARMER COOPERATIVES (3)
1800 Massachusetts Avenue, Suite 604
Washington, DC 20036   202/659-1525

Founded: 1929

President: Kenneth D. Naden

The National Council of Farmer Cooperatives is a national association representing all types of farmer-owned and controlled cooperatives.

Membership: 5,800 cooperatives with nearly 3 million members; 105 regional cooperatives, 32 state councils.

Registered Lobbyists: Bill Brier, Donald A. Frederick, Donald E. Graham, Robert N. Hampton, Donald K. Hanes, Charles Hartmen, Glen D. Hofer, James S. Krzyminski, Edward L. Merrigan, Kenneth D. Naden, R. Thomas Van Arsdall, Paul S. Weller.

Publication: *Washington Situation*

NATIONAL COUNCIL OF SENIOR CITIZENS (7)
1511 D Street NW
Washington, DC 20005   202/638-4351

President: James Carbray

Executive Director: William R. Hutton

Founded: 1961

The National Council of Senior Citizens is a federation of senior citizens' groups and individuals interested in the welfare of older people in the United States.

Membership: 22 state councils of senior citizens; 204,612 individuals from eleven national labor unions.

Funding: Estimated for 1979: individual memberships $808,000; contracts and grants from U.S. Department of Labor, Administration on Aging, and other government programs, $700,000; contributions from AFL-CIO and other labor groups, $230,000; sale of publications, $21,000.

Publication: *Retirement Newsletter* (monthly)

Registered Lobbyists: Richard M. Millman, Millman & Greenberg.

NATIONAL DRY BEAN COUNCIL (6)
1030 15th Street NW, Suite 840
Washington, DC 20005   202/466-2804

Washington Representative: Donald G. Lerch, Jr.

NATIONAL FAMILY FARM COALITION (7) (National Family Farm Education Project)
918 F Street, 2nd Floor
Washington, DC 20005   202/638-6848

Coordinators: Catherine Lerza, Robin Rosenbluth

Founded: 1978

The National Family Farm Coalition was organized to provide legislative support for the Family Farm Development Act introduced by Congressmen Richard Nolan and George Brown. It includes citizen, consumer, and environmental groups.

Membership: 90 local organizers, mailing list around 2,000 (1979), but not all members.

Funding: Grants from United Methodist Church, United Church of Christ, United Methodist Women; other contributions from organizations and individuals. Grant to National Family Farm Education Project from Community Services Administration, 1979, to publish Family Farm Monitor, quarterly newsletter.

Publication: Available on request.

NATIONAL FARM COALITION   (5)

Founded: 1970

Spokesman: Fred Heinkel, Former President, Midcontinent Farmers Association, Columbia, Missouri.

The Coalition is an informal alliance of thirty-six general commodity and cooperative farm organizations leaders (national, state, and local) representing more than 1 million agricultural producers.

Membership: (1977) The National Grange; National Association of Wheat Growers; National Farmers Organization; National Milk Producers Federation; National Corn Growers Association; Midcontinent Farmers Association; FAR-MAR-CO, Inc.; Land O'Lakes, Inc.; Farmers Union Grain Terminal Association; Farmers Union Central Exchange (CENEX); Grain Soybean Growers of America; National Rice Growers Association; American Rice, Inc.; National Association of Farmer Elected Committeemen; National Peanut Growers Group; North Carolina Peanut Growers Association; Virginia Peanut Growers Association; Southwestern Peanut Growers Association; Georgia Peanut Commission; GFA Peanut Association; Texas Peanut Producers Board; Oklahoma Peanut Growers Association; South Carolina Peanut Board; New Mexico Peanut Growers Association; Florida Peanut Council; National Wool Growers Association; United Grain Farmers of America; Farmers Cooperative Council of North Carolina; Virginia Council of Farmer Co-ops; Webster County Farmers Organization; Farmers Union Marketing and Processing Association; TransPecos Cotton Association; Rolling Plains Cotton Growers, Inc.; Farmers Grain Cooperative, Ogden, Utah.

NATIONAL FARMERS ORGANIZATION (1)
Corning, Iowa   50841   515/322-3131

Founded: 1955

Washington Office: Suite 2250, 457 L'Enfant Plaza
                     Washington, DC 20024   202/484-7075

President: DeVon Woodland

Director of Washington Office and Registered Lobbyist: Charles Frazier

The National Farmers Organization membership is open to farmers and
ranchers. It is committed to the collective-bargaining concept authorized in
the Capper-Volstead Act of 1922. It believes in the principle of farmers
striking or holding their products to obtain fair prices as long as such action
remains within legal bounds. Collective bargaining with buyers of farm
products is emphasized as the means of helping their members in preference
to government assistance.

Membership: Not publicly reported; 30,000 to 40,000 (estimated 1979).

Funding: Membership dues and check-off payments from members for
marketing services carried out by the organization.

Publication: *NFO Reporter*

NATIONAL FARMERS UNION (Also National Farmers Educational and
Cooperative Union)   (1)
12025 East 45th Avenue
P.O. Box 39251
Denver, Colorado   80239   303/371-1760

Founded: 1902

Washington Office: 1012 14th Street NW
                     Washington, DC 20005   202/628-9774

President: Tony Dechant (until March 1980)

Secretary and Economist: Robert Lewis (Washington, D.C.)

Legislative Director: Reuben Johnson

Farmers Union members are dedicated to preservation of the democratic
ideals set forth in the Constitution, the family farm or ranch as the keystone
of a highly successful agricultural system, and support of policies that are
aimed toward achieving full-parity prices for farm products.

Membership: 260,000 (1979); organizations in thirty states.

Funding: Membership dues, payments from members for direct services or through affiliated companies and cooperatives, operation of Green Thumb Program under contract with U.S. Department of Labor.

Registered Lobbyists: Tony Dechant, Reuben L. Johnson, Ruth E. Kobell, Robert G. Lewis, Robert J. Mullins, Morris Woodrow Wilson.

Publication: *National Farmers Union's Washington Newsletter*

NATIONAL FARM & POWER EQUIPMENT DEALERS ASSOCIATION   (6)
10877 Watson Road
St. Louis, Missouri   63127   314/821-7220

Registered Lobbyist: Frank R. Wolf
1901 North Moore Street, Suite 804
Arlington, Virginia   22209

NATIONAL FEDERATION OF FISHERMEN   (6)
919 18th Street NW, No. 820
Washington, DC   20006

Registered Lobbyist: Richard N. Sherood, Wilcox & Sherood
1899 L Street NW, No. 705
Washington, DC   20036

NATIONAL FEDERATION OF INDEPENDENT BUSINESS   (6)
150 W. 20th Avenue
San Mateo, California   94403   415/341-7441

Founded: 1943

Washington Office: 490 L'Enfant Plaza East, SW Suite 3206
Washington, DC   20024   202/554-9000

President: Wilson S. Johnson

Washington Counsel: James D. 'Mike' McKevitt

The National Federation of Independent Business is the nation's largest individual membership business organization working as a spokesman for the small and independent business.

Membership: 558,000 (1978)

Registered Lobbyists: George Burger, Kathleen A. Clarken, Covington & Burling, Sally L. Douglas, James D. McKevitt, John Motley, Janice N. Somers, Carol Ann Ward.

Publication: *Mandate* (monthly); other special reports on economic and business issues.

NATIONAL FISHERIES INSTITUTE (6)
1101 Connecticut Avenue NW, Suite 700
Washington, DC 20036   202/857-1110

Founded: 1945

Director of Government Relations: Gustave Fritschie

The National Fisheries Institute is the national trade association of individuals and firms who harvest, process, and distribute fish and seafood products.

Membership: 833

Registered Lobbyists: Gustave Fritschie, Lee Weddig.

Publication: *The Flashes* (weekly)

NATIONAL FISH MEAL AND OIL ASSOCIATION (6)
1100 17th Street NW, Suite 411
Washington, DC 20036   202/785-0227

Executive Director: Thomas E. Reynolds

NATIONAL FOOD BROKERS ASSOCIATION (6)
The NFBA Building
1916 M Street NW
Washington, DC 20036

President: Mark M. Singer

Registered Lobbyist: Bison and Wenning

NATIONAL FOOD PROCESSORS ASSOCIATION (Formerly National Canners Association) (6)
1133 20th Street NW
Washington, DC 20036   202/331-5900

Founded: 1907

President: Charles J. Carey

The National Food Processors Association is a nonprofit trade association of firms that produce 90 percent of the canned foods in the United States.

Membership: 700

Registered Lobbyists: Claude D. Alexander, Claudia R. Fuquay, Richard
                        W. Murphy, M. Kathryn Nordstrom, Mary Sophos.

Publication: *Information Letter* (weekly)

NATIONAL FROZEN FOOD ASSOCIATION, INC.   (6)
1 Chocolate Avenue, P.O. Box 398
Hershey, Pennsylvania   17003   717/534-1601

Registered Lobbyist: Michael J. Guiffrida

NATIONAL GRAIN AND FEED ASSOCIATION   (6)
500 Folger Building
P.O. Box 28328
725 15th Street NW
Washington, DC   20005   202/783-2024

Founded: 1896

Executive Vice-President: Alvin E. Oliver

The National Grain and Feed Association is an association of grain and
feed dealers, county elevators, terminal elevators, processing and exporting
firms in forty-eight states.

Membership: 1,200 members including forty-eight affiliated state and
regional grain and feed associations with combined association membership
of 12,000 firms.

Registered Lobbyists: William J. Keating, Alvin E. Oliver.

Publication: *Directory Yearbook* (annual), *National Newsletter* (weekly)

NATIONAL GRAIN TRADE COUNCIL   (6)
725 15th Street NW
Washington, DC   20005   202/783-8945

President: William F. Brooks

NATIONAL GRANGE   (1)
1616 H Street NW
Washington, DC   20006   202/628-3507

Founded: 1867

Master: Edward Andersen

Legislative Director: Robert Frederick

The National Grange is more than a farm organization. Its purpose is to serve the total interest of the rural community. It supports preservation and protection of the family-owned and -operated farm; a return for labor, management, risk, and investment in a reasonable relationship to other segments of the economy; development of domestic and foreign markets for U.S. farm products; commodity programs which provide producers and workers competitive advantage and freedom to operate within the framework of "freedom under law"; and sound land management.

Membership: 500,000 in forty-one states and 7,000 local communities (1977).

Funding: Membership dues.

Registered Lobbyists: Robert Frederick, David Lambert, John W. Scott.

Publication: *Legislative Policies* (annual), *Grange Newsletter* (monthly)

NATIONAL INDEPENDENT MEAT PACKERS ASSOCIATION   (6)
734 15th Street NW
Washington, DC   20005   202/347-1000

Founded: 1942

President: John Mohay

The National Independent Meat Packers Association is a trade association of meat packing companies with major interests in beef.

Membership: 320 packing companies, 150 associate members

Publication: *NIMPA Bulletin*

NATIONAL INSTITUTE OF OILSEED PRODUCTS   (6)
1725 K Street NW
Washington, DC   20006   202/233-5475

Washington Representative: Douglas Dies

NATIONAL LABOR MANAGEMENT FOUNDATION   (6)
200 W. Chestnut Street
Louisville, Kentucky   40202   502/587-0637

Founded: 1947

Washington Office: 1901 L Street NW
                              Washington, DC   20036   202/296-8577

President: S. Rayburn Watkins

The National Labor Management Foundation is a nonpartisan, nonprofit education and information organization, serving business and industrial firms in fifty states comprising small employers of business and industrial firms in fifty states.

Membership: 3,000 firms

Registered Lobbyists: Philip W. Hamilton,
                                    Wilson E. Hamilton & Associates Inc.

Publication: *On the Labor Front* (newsletter)

NATIONAL LAND FOR PEOPLE   (7)
2348 Cornelia
Fresno, California   93711   209/233-4727

Founded: 1974

Coordinator: George Ballis

National Land for People is a nonprofit organization of citizens united to obtain enforcement of the 160-acre limitation on farm size established for federal water projects under the Reclamation Act of 1902, to promote family farming and land redistribution.

Membership: 1,100

Funding: Membership dues and contributions. Foundation grant to National Land for People Foundation for research, education, and litigation and public policy on land ownership, Akbar Foundation, $20,000, 1977; from Rosenberg Foundation, $25,000 in 1976 and $10,000 in 1977; Stern Fund, $30,000, general support, 1977-1978; Shalan Foundation, $5,000 in 1979.

Publication: *NLP Newsletter*

NATIONAL LIMESTONE INSTITUTE   (6)
3251 Old Lee Highway, Suite 501
Fairfax, Virginia   22030   703/273-8517

Founded: 1945

President: Robert M. Koch

The National Limestone Institute is a lobbying organization representing limestone companies producing agricultural and crushed limestone.

Membership: 570

Registered Lobbyists: Jerome J. Breitler; Francis J. Boyd, Jr.; Michael P.

DeBlois; Gordon H. Fry; Richard Haas; Christopher
G. Hankin: Stephen B. Hellum; Phillip G. Hough;
Robert M. Koch; Robert M. Koch, Jr.; Eric D.
Lindemann; Keven McAfee; Samuel Omasta;
Patton, Boggs, & Blow; Randall Rawson; Craig G.
Thibaudeau, Michael P. Neumann.

Publication: Membership letter

NATIONAL MACARONI MANUFACTURERS ASSOCIATION   (6)
P.O. Box 336
Palatine, Illinois   60037

Registered Lobbyist: Leighton, Conklin, & Lemov
2033 M Street NW, Suite 800
Washington, DC   20036

NATIONAL MILK PRODUCERS FEDERATION   (3)
30 F Street NW
Washington, DC   20001   202/393-8151

Founded: 1916

President: William A. Powell

Secretary and Manager, Washington Office: Patrick B. Healy

The National Milk Producers Federation is a national federation of dairy
marketing cooperatives which market a substantial percentage of the milk
produced in the United States. Its purpose is to provide dairy farmer
cooperatives with an opportunity to participate in the formation of national
public policy aimed at maintaining and improving the economic well-being
of dairy farmers and their cooperatives, thus ensuring the nation's consumers an adequate supply of wholesome milk and dairy products.

Membership: 600 cooperative dairy marketing associations

Registered Lobbyists: Neal Bjornson, Susan Fridy, Patrick Healy, Lynn
Stalbaum.

Publication: *NMPF News for Dairy Co-Ops*

NATIONAL NUTRITIONAL FOODS ASSOCIATION   (6)
7727 South Painter Avenue
Whittier, California   90602   213/945-2669

Washington Representative
and Registered Lobbyist: Bernard Fensterwald & Associates
2101 L Street NW
Washington, DC   20037

Founded: 1936

The National Nutritional Foods Association is a nonprofit trade association representing manufacturers, wholesalers, distributors, and retailers of health foods and health food products.

Membership: 3,000 (estimated)

NATIONAL ORGANIZATION FOR RAW MATERIALS, INC.
(NORM)   (5)
(Formerly, National Raw Materials Council)
220 10th Avenue
Granite Falls, Minnesota   56241   612/564-2555

Founded: 1969

Washington Office: 200 C Street SE
                                Washington, DC   20003   202/547-6300

President: Arnold E. Paulson

A group organized for research, education, legislation, and public information to emphasize the basic wealth of agriculture and rural communities is dependent on the value of the basic raw materials produced by agriculture, forestry, fisheries, and mining.

Membership: Uncertain

Publication: *NORM*

NATIONAL PEANUT COUNCIL   (6)
1000 16th Street NW, Suite 506
Washington, DC   20036   202/659-5656

President: John M. Martin

NATIONAL PEANUT GROWERS GROUP   (2)

Founded: 1974

Chairman, Steering Committee: H. Emmett Reynolds
                                                    Arabi, Georgia   912/273-5563

A federation of state peanut growers' organizations: Alabama Peanut Growers, Georgia Peanut Commission, GFA Peanut Association, Florida Peanut Growers Association, New Mexico Peanut Growers Association, North Carolina Peanut Growers Association, Oklahoma Peanut Growers Association, Oklahoma Peanut Commission, Peanut Growers Cooperative Marketing Association, South Carolina Peanut Board, Southwestern Peanut Growers' Association, Texas Peanut Producers Board, and Virginia Peanut Growers Association, Inc. It operates through a twelve-member board and a technical committee to handle legislative matters.

Membership: 60,000 (1979)

NATIONAL PEST CONTROL ASSOCIATION   (6)
8150 Leesburg Pike, Suite 1100
Vienna, Virginia   22180   703/790-8300

Founded: 1930s

Senior Director, Research: Jefferson D. Keith

The National Pest Control Association is a nonprofit trade association of
the pest control industry.

Membership: 30,000 professionals

Registered Lobbyists: Berry, Epstein, Sandstrom, & Blatchford; Jack
                       Grimes; Jefferson D. Keith; Tom E. Persky; Philip
                       J. Spear.

Publications: *Association Affairs* (monthly); reports relating to various
business and government affairs.

NATIONAL PLANNING ASSOCIATION   (11)
1606 New Hampshire Avenue NW
Washington, DC   20009   202/265-7685

Founded: 1934

President: Arthur J.R. Smith

Agriculture Committee Chairman: Lauren K. Soth

The National Planning Association is a private, nonprofit, nonpolitical
organization that carries on research and policy formulation in the public
interest for the purpose of getting diverse groups to work together to nar-
row areas of controversy and broaden areas of agreement.

Membership: 1,000

Publications: List available upon request.

NATIONAL PORK PRODUCERS COUNCIL   (2)
4715 Grand Avenue
Des Moines, Idaho   50312   515/277-6419

Founded: 1954

President: William Buller
            Brookings, South Dakota   57006

Executive Vice-President: Orville Sweet

Washington Representative and
Director of Government Affairs: C. Donald Van Houweling

A national organization of thirty-five state pork producers' associations
whose purpose is to promote the interest of pork producers.

Membership: 85,000 (1979)

NATIONAL POTATO COUNCIL   (6)

Registered Lobbyist: James H. Lake
                        1101 Connecticut Avenue NW, Suite 800
                        Washington, DC   20036

NATIONAL RURAL CENTER   (7)
1828 L Street NW
Washington, DC   20036   202/331-0258

Regional Offices: Atlanta, Georgia, and Austin, Texas

President: John M. Cornman

Founded: 1976

The National Rural Center is an independent, nonprofit organization
created to develop and advocate policy alternatives and to provide information which can help rural people and their communities achieve full potential.

Funding: Grants from U.S. Department of Agriculture; National Science
Foundation, fiscal year 1980, $49,486; Lilly Endowment, $8,800, 1977;
Ford Foundation, $25,000, 1977; Ford Foundation, $20,000, 1977; Rockefeller Brothers Fund, $57,000 in 1976 and $75,000 in 1977; Clark Foundation; estate of Winthrop Rockefeller.

Publications: List available upon request.

NATIONAL RURAL ELECTRIC COOPERATIVE ASSOCIATION   (3)
1800 Massachusetts Avenue NW
Washington, DC   20036   202/857-9500

Founded: 1942

Executive Vice-President and General Manager: Robert D. Partridge

The Association is a private membership organization of rural electric
systems generating and transmission cooperatives, rural public power

districts, state rural electric organizations, and cooperative groups working in the rural electrification field. Its major purposes are to protect their interests and work toward the common goal of strengthening and improving rural electrification.

Membership: 1,000 rural electric systems which provide electric power to more than 25 million people in forty-five states, including 2,500 of the nation's 3,100 counties.

Registered Lobbyists: Becky Bogard, John Davenport, Morgan D. Dubrow, Lowell J. Endahl, Joseph S. Ives, Bradley R. Koch, Michael J. Molony, William E. Murray, Robert W. Nelson, Robert D. Partridge, Tony Perkins, William S. Roberts, Charles A. Robinson, Jr., Wally Rustad, Wallace F. Tillman, Carolyn Herr Watts, Charlotte M. Wilmer.

Publications: *Rural Electrification Magazine* (monthly), *Rural Electric Newsletter* (weekly), *Management Quarterly*

NATIONAL RURAL HOUSING COALITION   (7)
1346 Connecticut Avenue NW
Washington, DC   20036   202/296-4944

Founded: 1969

Chairman of the Board: Aaron E. Henry

The National Rural Housing Coalition is a nonprofit, nonpartisan coalition of rural-oriented organizations, churches, labor unions, antipoverty organizations, minority groups, universities, and government agencies. As a public interest lobby, it is dedicated to improving the quality of low-income rural housing.

Funding: Financed by dues and gifts from members and friends.

NATURAL RESOURCES DEFENSE COUNCIL   (8)
2345 Yale Street   122 E. 42d Street
Palo Alto, California   94306   New York, New York   10017
415/327-1080   212/869-0150

Founded: 1970

Washington Office: 915 15th Street NW
                     Washington, DC   20005   202/737-5000

Executive Director: John H. Adams (New York)

The Natural Resources Defense Council is a nonprofit, nationwide membership organization of scientists and lawyers contributing to enforcement of the nation's conservation laws.

Membership: 20,000

Funding: Membership dues; foundation grants: Rockefeller Brothers Fund, $150,000 for general budgetary support, 1977; Gerbode Foundation, $5,000, 1976; Clark Foundation, $25,000, 1976; Noble Foundation, $25,000, 1976; Sherman Foundation, $20,000, 1975; Shalan Foundation, $10,000, 1979.

Registered Lobbyists: Richard Ayres, James Taylor Banks, Thomas J. Barlow, John Roger Beers, Frances G. Beinecke, Judith Lynn Campbell Bird, Faith Thompson Campbell, Marcia Cleveland, Sarah Chasis, Terry R. Lash, Anthony Z. Roisman, Ross Sandler, S. Jacob Scherr, David Schoenbrod, Johanna H. Wald.

Publications: *NRDA Newletter*, list available upon request.

NATIONAL RESTAURANT ASSOCIATION   (6)
1 IBM Plaza, Suite 2600
Chicago, Illinois   60611   312/787-2525

Washington Office: 1850 K Street NW, Suite 850
Washington, DC   20006

Registered Lobbyists: Sheila MacDonald Bamberger, Douglas P. Bennett, Peter J. Hapworth, Robert B. Neville, and A. Kolbert Schrichte.

NATIONAL RETIRED TEACHERS ASSOCIATION & AMERICAN ASSOCIATION OF RETIRED PERSONS   (7)
1909 K Street NW
Washington, DC   20049   202/872-4700

Executive Director: Cyril Brickfield

Founded: 1947 and 1958, respectively

The National Retired Teachers Association and the American Association of Retired Persons are national membership organizations with interests in a broad range of issues affecting retired persons.

Membership: Over 12,000,000

Registered Lobbyists: Thomas C. Borzilleri; Thomas Elvood; Jauri Ann
                        Fiori; Peter W. Hughes; John Martin; Faye Mench;
                        James M. Hacking; Fred W. Wegner; Cyril F.
                        Brickfield; Miller, Singer, Michaelson, Brickfield,
                        & Raives.

Publication: *NRTA Journal, Modern Maturity, Dynamic View for 50 &
               Over, AARP News Bulletin*

NATIONAL SHRIMP CONGRESS   (6)
1225 19th Street NW, Suite 700
Washington, DC   20036   202/785-2130

Executive Director: William Nelson Utz

NATIONAL SOFT DRINK ASSOCIATION   (6)
1101 16th Street NW
Washington, DC   20036   202/833-2450

Registered Lobbyists: Thomas F. Baker

                        Thomas A. Daly

                        Dwight C. Reed

                        Christopher Nolde

                        Williams & Jensen
                        1101 Connecticut Avenue NW, No. 500
                        Washington, DC   20036

NATIONAL SOYBEAN CROP IMPROVEMENT COUNCIL   (6)
211 S. Race Street
Urbana, Illinois   61801   217/367-0412

Founded: 1948

Washington Office: 1800 M Street NW
                     Washington, DC   20036   202/223-8285

Managing Director: Robert Judd

The National Soybean Crop Improvement Council was organized by the
soybean processing industry to promote production and improvement of
soybeans.

Membership: None; operates with thirty-one-person advisory board of
agronomists, government agriculture officials, commercial breeders, and
American Soybean Association representatives.

Publication: *Soybean News* (three times a year)

NATIONAL SOYBEAN PROCESSORS ASSOCIATION   (6)
1800 M Street NW, Suite 1030
Washington, DC   20036   202/452-8040

Founded: 1930

President: Sheldon J. Hauck

The National Soybean Processors association is the trade association of the soybean processing industry. It is the parent organization of the National Soybean Crop Improvement Council. Member firms process 95 percent of the soybeans processed in the United States.

Membership: 29 firms operating 85 processing centers.

Publication: *Weekly Review*

NATIONAL TRIBAL CHAIRMEN'S ASSOCIATION   (7)
1701 Pennsylvania Avenue NW
Washington, DC   20006

The National Tribal Chairmen's Association is an association of the elected or appointed chairmen, presidents, governors, or chiefs of the federally recognized Indian tribes of the United States and the Alaska native regional corporations.

Membership: 190 tribes representing about 90 percent of the 800,000 American Indians and Alaska natives.

Founded: 1971

NATIONAL TURKEY FEDERATION   (6)
11800 Sunrise Valley Drive
Reston, Virginia   22090   703/860-0120

Founded: 1939

Executive Vice-President: G.L. Walts

The National Turkey Federation is a national trade association representing the turkey industry in the United States. Members include producers, breeders, breeder flockowners, hatchermen, processors and marketers, and firms supplying goods and services to these groups.

Membership: 2,300

Registered Lobbyist: Organization registered 1978.

Publication: *NTF Newsletter*

NATIONAL URBAN LEAGUE   (7)
500 E. 62d Street
New York, New York   10021   212/644-6600

Washington Office: 2100 M Street NW
                     Washington, DC   20036   202/644-6600

President: Vernon Jordan

Founded: 1911

The National Urban League works for the welfare of minorities. Its legislative concerns include poverty programs, community issues, and food assistance programs.

Membership: 115 affiliated organizations

Publication: *The National Urban Leagues News* (quarterly)

NATIONAL WELFARE FRAUD ASSOCIATION   (10)
Suite 1430, 666 N. Lake Shore Drive
Chicago, Illinois   60611   312/944-4610   (Secretariat and mailing)

President: Carl Chase, Jr.
             P.O. Box 11306, Capitol Station
             Columbia, South Carolina   29211

The National Welfare Fraud Association is an organization of local, state, and federal officials who administer welfare programs on a daily basis and who prosecute fraud cases.

NATIONAL WILDLIFE FEDERATION   (8)
1412 16th Street NW
Washington, DC   20036   202/797-6800

Executive Vice-President: Thomas L. Kimball

Founded: 1936

The National Wildlife Federation is a nonprofit, conservation education organization dedicated to arousing public awareness of the need for wise use, proper management, and conservation of the natural resources on which all life depends.

Membership: 3,500,000 with affiliates, local groups, supporters, nationwide.

Publications: List available upon request.

Funding: Membership, publications, fund-raising efforts; foundation grants: $5,000, Gerbode Foundation, 1976; $25,000, Clark Foundation, 1976; $20,000, Scherman Foundation, 1975; Rockefeller Brothers Fund, $150,000 for general budgetary support, $15,000 to examine threatened forest resources in tropical countries, $75,000 to study ways to improve management of transportation in New York City area, 1977.

NATIONAL WOOL GROWERS ASSOCIATION   (2)
600 Crandall Building
Salt Lake City, Utah   84101   801/363-4483

President: Marvin Cronberg

Founded: 1865

Washington Office: Suite 5
                     1776 F Street NW
                     Washington, DC   20006   202/293-1160

The National Wool Growers Association is a national organization of sheep and wool producers.

Washington Representative
and Registered Lobbyist: Hamel, Park, McCabe, & Saunders

Membership: 23 associations

THE NAVAJO NATION   (12)
Window Rock, Arizona   86515

Registered Lobbyist: Joseph S. Miller
                       19 Third Street NE
                       Washington, DC   20002

NETWORK   (7)
1029 Vermont Avenue NW, Suite 650
Washington, DC   20005   202/347-6200

Founded: 1971

Executive Director: Carol Coston

Network is a Catholic social justice lobby concerned about issues that affect "people who are poor, powerless and marginalized."

Funding: Donations, sale of publications, services performed.

Publications: *NETWORK Newsletter* and *NETWORK Quarterly*

Registered Lobbyist: Carol Coston (Common Cause)

NEW ENGLAND FISH CO.   (6)
Pier 89
Seattle, Washington   98119

Registered Lobbyist: Beveridge, Fairbanks, & Diamond
                         One Farragut Square South
                         Washington, DC   20006

NEW YORK COTTON EXCHANGE   (6)
New York, New York

Founded: 1870

President: J. Wm. Donaghy

The New York Cotton Exchange was the contract market for trading in cotton. Members include those engaged in trading in cotton futures. It has not been active since 1976.

THE NEZ PERCE TRIBE   (12)
Lapwai, Idaho

Registered Lobbyist: Fried, Frank, Harris, Shriver, & Kampelman
                         600 New Hampshire NW
                         Washington, DC   20037

NORTH AMERICAN EXPORT GRAIN ASSOCIATION   (6)
1800 M Street NW, Suite 610
Washington, DC   20036   202/223-8285

Founded: 1917

Executive Director: Joseph Halow

The North American Export Grain Association is an organization of grain exporters who continue to seek markets for U.S. grains and provide the facilities and servicing for export of most U.S. grain abroad. Members handle 90 percent of the total U.S. grain exports.

Membership: 31 (1979)

Registered Lobbyist: Joseph Halow

Publication: *Legislative Report*

NORTH AMERICAN GAME BREEDERS & SHOOTING PRESERVE
ASSOCIATION   (8)
Gooselake, Iowa   52750

Founded: 1956

Washington Representative
and Registered Lobbyist: Williams & Jensen
                                1101 Connecticut Avenue
                                Washington, DC   20035

Membership: 600 to 700

NORTHERN CHEYENNE INDIAN TRIBE   (12)
P.O. Box 128
Lame Deer, Montana   59043

Registered Lobbyist: Zionty, Pirtle, Morisset, Ernstoff, & Chestnut
                        208 Pioneer Building, 600 First Avenue
                        Seattle, Washington   98104

OCEAN SPRAY CRANBERRIES, INC.   (6)
Plymouth, Massachusetts   02360

Registered Lobbyist: George C.P. Olsson
                        25 Clifford Road
                        Plymouth, Massachusetts   02360

OGLALA SIOUX TRIBE OF THE PINE RIDGE RESERVATION   (12)
Pine Ridge, South Dakota   57770

Registered Lobbyist: Fried, Frank, Harris, Shriver, & Kampelman
                        600 New Hampshire Avenue
                        Washington, DC   20037

OGLETHORPE ELECTRIC MEMBERSHIP CORP.   (3)
3951 Snapfinger Parkway
Decatur, Georgia   30035

Washington Address: 1666 K Street
                      Washington, DC   20006

Registered Lobbyists: Sutherland, Asbill, & Brennan
                        3100 First National Bank Tower
                        Atlanta, Georgia   30303

OKLAHOMA ASSOCIATION OF ELECTRIC COOPERATIVES   (3)
P.O. Box 11047
Oklahoma City, Oklahoma   73111

Registered Lobbyist: Ed Edmondson
                       P.O. Box 11
                       Muskogee, Oklahoma   74401

ORGANIZATION OF PROFESSIONAL EMPLOYEES OF THE U.S.
DEPARTMENT OF AGRICULTURE   (10)
Room 1247 South Building
U.S. Department of Agriculture
Washington, DC   20250   202/447-4898

Founded: 1929

Washington Representative
and Registered Lobbyist: Walter W. John

The Organization of Professional Employees of the Department of
Agriculture is the representative of the employees of the USDA at the White
House, Congress, Office of Personnel Management, Merit Systems Protection Board, the Secretary of Agriculture, and top management of USDA
agencies.

Membership: 8,000

ORKIN EXTERMINATING CO.   (6)
2170 Piedmont Road NE
Atlanta, Georgia   30324

Registered Lobbyist: Robert M. Russell
                       Berry, Epstein, Sandstrom, & Blatchford
                       1700 Pennsylvania Avenue NW
                       Washington, DC   20006

OVERSEAS DEVELOPMENT COUNCIL   (7)
1717 Massachusetts Avenue NW
Washington, DC   20036   202/234-8701

President: James P. Grant

Founded: 1969

Overseas Development Council is a private, independent, nonprofit
organization that seeks to increase understanding of problems confronting
developing countries.

Funding: 1978 budget of $1,375,000 from contributions from business firms and foundations, project grants and contracts, sales of publications, and reimbursements for services.

Publications: List available upon request.

PACIFIC SEAFOOD PROCESSORS ASSOCIATION   (6)
1600 South Jackson Street
Seattle, Washington   98144

Registered Lobbyist: Preston, Thorgrimson, Ellis, Holman & Fletcher
1776 F Street NW, Suite 201
Washington, DC   20006

PALM BEACH-BROWARD FARMERS COMMITTEE FOR LEGISLA-
TIVE ACTION   (2)
P.O. Box 396
Boynton Beach, Florida   33435

Registered Lobbyist: Van Ness, Feldman, & Sutcliffe
1220 19th Street NW, Suite 500
Washington, DC   20036

PEANUT BUTTER AND NUT PROCESSORS ASSOCIATION   (6)
(Formerly Peanut Butter Manufacturers & Nut Salters Association)
5101 Wisconsin Avenue NW, Suite 504
Washington, DC   20016   202/966-7888

Founded: 1969

Managing Director and General Counsel: James E. Mack

The Peanut Butter and Nut Processors Association is the trade association of firms who produce peanut butter, peanut butter sandwiches, salted and other packaged nuts. Members process 95 percent of the U.S. edible-peanut consumption.

Membership: 73 manufacturers, 100 associate (suppliers)

Registered Lobbyist: James E. Mack

Publication: Bulletins when needed.

PENNSYLVANIA FOOD PROCESSORS ASSOCIATION   (6)

Registered Lobbyists: Thomas R. Hendershot

Obermayer, Rebmann, Maxwell, & Hippel
2001 I Street NW, Suite 500
Washington, DC   20006

PEPSICO INC.   (6)
Purchase, New York   10577

Registered Lobbyists: Douglas P. Bennett
                       499 S. Capital Street SW, No. 407
                       Washington, DC   20003

                       Patton, Boggs, & Blow
                       1200 17th Street NW
                       Washington, DC   20036

PERDUE FARMS, INC.   (5)
P.O. Box 1537
Salisbury, Maryland   21801

Registered Lobbyist: Covington & Burling
                       888 16th Street NW
                       Washington, DC   20006

PESTICIDE FORMULATORS ASSOCIATION (PESTICIDES PROD-
UCTS ASSOCIATION)   (6)

Founded: 1975

Washington Representative: Graham Purcell
                            Doub, Purcell, Muntzing, & Hansen
                            1775 Pennsylvania Avenue NW
                            Washington, DC   20006

The Pesticide Formulators Association is an organization of small to
intermediate-size companies who manufacture and/or formulate pesticides
for a wide variety of uses, including animal health, agricultural, household,
garden, and structural pest control.

PET FOOD INSTITUTE   (6)
1101 Connecticut Avenue NW, Suite 700
Washington, DC   20036   202/857-1100

Director, Regulatory Affairs: Susan K. Finn

PFIZER, INC.   (6)
1700 Pennsylvania Avenue NW
Washington, DC   20006

Registered Lobbyists: Calvin J. Collier
                       Hughes, Hubbard, & Reed
                       1600 L Street NW
                       Washington, DC   20035

Stephen R. Conafay
1700 Pennsylvania Avenue NW
Washington, DC   20006

John H. Holloman, III
O'Connor & Hannan
1747 Pennsylvania Avenue NW
Washington, DC   20006

Raymond R. Krauze

Phillip A. Lacovara

Charles J. Micoleau
Curtis, Thaxter, Corey, Lipez, & Stevens
One Canal Plaza
Portland, Maine   04112

Robert L. Shafer

PICKLE PACKERS INTERNATIONAL INC.   (6)
1625 K Street NW
Washington, DC   20006   202/628-5530

General Counsel: Walter E. Byerley

PILLSBURY CORP.   (6)
608 Second Avenue South
Minneapolis, Minnesota   55402

Registered Lobbyists: Patton, Boggs, & Blow
1200 17th Street NW
Washington, DC   20036

Williams & Jensen
1101 Connecticut Avenue NW
Washington, DC   20036

PINEAPPLE GROWERS OF HAWAII   (2)
1902 Financial Plaza
Honolulu, Hawaii   96813

Washington Representative
and Registered Lobbyist: Covington & Burling

PIONEER HI-BRED INTERNATIONAL, INC.   (6)
1206 Mulberry Street
Des Moines, Iowa   50308

Registered Lobbyist: O'Connor & Hannan
                         1747 Pennsylvania Avenue NW, Suite 600
                         Washington, DC   20006

PLAINS COTTON GROWERS, INC. (2)
P.O. Box 3640
Lubbock, Texas   79452

Registered as lobbyists: 1978

POTATO CHIP/SNACK FOOD ASSOCIATION (6)
914 Euclid Office Plaza
26250 Euclid Avenue
Euclid, Ohio   44132

Registered Lobbyists: State and Federal Associates, Inc.
                         1101 15th Street NW
                         Washington, DC   20005

                         Lawrence E. Burch

                         Susan Magau

POULTRY AND EGG INSTITUTE OF AMERICA (6)
1815 N. Lynn Street, Suite 801
Arlington, Virginia   22209   703/522-1363

Founded: 1873 as American Poultry Association. Merged with Northeastern Poultry Producers Council in 1978, with Institute of American Poultry Industries and American Poultry and Hatchery Federation in 1971.

President: Don C. Beaver

Executive Vice-President: Lee Campbell

The Poultry and Egg Institute of America is the only national poultry and egg trade association representing all segments of the industry—production, handling, processing, and distribution.

Membership: 2,422 (1978)

Government Relations Staff: Richard Ammon, Lee Campbell, Paul Korody, Denise-Marie Zaraska.

Publications: *Poultry Times, Consumer Affairs Update* (monthly)

PROCTOR & GAMBLE MANUFACTURING CO. (6)
301 East Sixth Street
Cincinnati, Ohio   45202

Washington Address: 1801 K Street NW
                       Washington, DC   20006

Registered Lobbyists: Edwin L. Behrens
                        Bryce N. Harlow
                        Walter A. Hasty
                        Charls Leppert, Jr.
                        Jane Fawcett-Hoover
                        Mike Manatos
                        Charls E. Walker Associates, Inc.
                        1730 Pennsylvania Avenue NW
                        Washington, DC   20006

PROTEIN GRAIN PRODUCTS INTERNATIONAL   (6)
1030 15th Street NW, Suite 760
Washington, DC   20005   202/785-2052

President: Robert D. Fondahn

PUEBLO OF LAGUNA   (12)
Laguna, New Mexico   87026

Registered Lobbyist: Fried, Frank, Harris, Shriver, & Kampelman
                        600 New Hampshire Avenue NW
                        Washington, DC   20037

QUILEUTE INDIAN TRIBE   (12)
P.O. Box 279
LaPush, Washington   98350

Registered Lobbyist: Zionty, Pirtle, Morisset, Ernstoff, & Chestnut
                        208 Pioneer Building, 600 First Avenue
                        Seattle, Washington   98104

QUINAULT INDIAN NATION   (12)
P.O. Box 1118
Taholah, Washington   98587

Registered Lobbyist: Rebecca D. Shapiro & Associates
                        111 C Street SE
                        Washington, DC   20003

RACHEL CARSON TRUST FOR THE LIVING ENVIRONMENT,
INC.   (8)
8940 Jones Mill Road
Washington, DC   20015   301/652-1877

Founded: 1965

Executive Director: Shirley Briggs

The Rachel Carson Trust for the Living Environment is an international clearinghouse of information on ecology of the environment for both scientists and laymen primarily concerned with chemical contamination as it affects human and environmental health.

Funding: Gifts, endowment income, and contributions.

Publications: List available upon request.

RALSTON-PURINA CO.   (6)
Checkerboard Square
St. Louis, Missouri   63188

Registered Lobbyists: Charles E. Ehrhart
                        1800 K Street NW, Suite 924
                        Washington, DC   20006

                        Patton, Boggs, & Blow
                        1200 17th Street NW
                        Washington, DC   20036

                        Judith A. Pond

RESOURCES FOR THE FUTURE   (11)
1755 Massachusetts Avenue NW
Washington, DC   20036   202/462-4400

Founded: 1952

President: Emory Castle

Resources for the Future is a research organization which examines issues relating to resources and the environment, including food and energy relationships.

Funding: Foundation grants, contracts, contributions; National Science Foundation, four projects, $130,611 in fiscal year 1980; Ford Foundation, $3 million, 1978; total revenue in 1978 was $6,924,844.

Publications: *Resources* (quarterly); list of books available upon request.

RETAIL BAKERS OF AMERICA   (6)
Presidential Building, Suite 250
6525 Belcrest Road
Hyattsville, Maryland   20782   301/277-0990

Executive Vice-President: Richard C. Gohla

Registered Lobbyists: Richard C. Gohla, Gerard Paul Panaro, William A. Quinlan.

R.J. REYNOLDS INDUSTRIES, INC.   (6)
P.O. Box 2959
Winston-Salem, North Carolina   27102

Registered Lobbyists: Paul C. Bergson

Frank D. Gorham, III

Howard Pyle, III
1150 Connecticut Avenue NW, Suite 805
Washington, DC   20036

Ragan & Mason
900 17th Street NW
Washington, DC   20006

RICELAND FOODS   (3)
Stuttgart, Arkansas   72160   501/673-5500

President: Wilfred Carle

Vice-President: Richard E. Bell (Assistant Secretary of Agriculture
1974-1976)

Riceland Foods is a farmer owned and controlled marketing cooperative
with members in Arkansas, Louisiana, Mississippi, Tennessee, and
Missouri. It handles about 20 percent of the total U.S. rice production and
about 60 percent in Arkansas. Soybeans are also an important part of its
business.

Membership: 5,000

RICE MILLERS ASSOCIATION   (6)
2001 Jefferson Davis Highway
Arlington, Virginia   22209   703/920-1281

Founded: 1899

Executive Vice-President: Stephen Gabbert

The Rice Millers Association is an organization of independently owned
and cooperative millers which process 80 percent of the U.S.-grown rice and
about 96 percent of the Southern production.

Membership: 32

Publication: *Movement of Rice* (monthly)

ROSEBUD SIOUX TRIBE   (12)
Rosebud, South Dakota   57570

Registered Lobbyist: Fried, Frank, Harris, Shriver, & Kampelman
                        600 New Hampshire Avenue NW
                        Washington, DC   20037

ROSENTHAL & CO.   (6)
141 West Jackson Boulevard
Chicago, Illinois   60604

Registered Lobbyist: Robert C. Lower
                        Alston, Miller, & Gaines
                        1200 C&S National Bank Building
                        Atlanta, Georgia   30303

RURAL AMERICA, INC.   (7)
1346 Connecticut Avenue NW
Washington, DC   20036   202/659-2800

Executive Director: David Raphael

Chairman: George Ballis, Fresno, California

Founded: 1975 (Merged with Rural Housing Alliance in 1977)

Rural America is a nonprofit, tax-exempt, membership organization which
seeks, through research, technical assistance, education, and advocacy, to
ensure rural people equity in the formation and implementation of public
policies and programs.

Membership: 2,315 (1979)

Funding: Total receipts for year ending June 1979 were $6,875,087.
Department of Labor, $6,401,775; Community Services Administration,
$311,106; Department of Health Education and Welfare, $20,000; Department of Housing and Urban Development, $37,500; Department of Energy,
$5,876; Field Foundation, $10,000; Youth Project, $2,500; Ottinger Foun-
dation, $2,500; dues and contributions, $83,839. In October 1979, Community Services Administration provided $20,000 to help get low income
people to testify at 10 regional hearings on the "Structure of Agriculture".

RURAL AMERICAN WOMEN, INC.   (7)
1522 K Street, Suite 700
Washington, DC   20005   202/785-4700

President: Jane Threatt

Founded: 1977

Rural American Women is a nonprofit organization dedicated to the belief that 32 million rural women in the United States share a host of common problems which must be articulated by the women themselves and brought to the forefront of the country's consciousness. Its purpose is to organize rural women to work together through legislative and voluntary action to develop their individual capabilities, contribute to family welfare, and improve their communities.

Membership: 22,000 (1979)

Staff: Two paid employees in Washington office; President serves without regular salary.

Publication: *News from Rural American Women, Inc.* (bimonthly)

THE RURAL COALITION   (7)
1828 L Street NW
Washington, DC   20036   202/331-1230

Founded: Organization underway in 1979

The Rural Coalition is a coalition of national public interest groups with special concerns for the rural poor and disadvantaged and development of rural communities.

Membership: About 50 organizations

Funding: Membership contributions, foundations

SALT RIVER PROJECT   (5)
P.O. Box 1980
Phoenix, Arizona   85001

Registered Lobbyist: D. Michael Rappoport

SALYER LAND CO.   (5)
P.O. Box 488
Corcoran, California   93212

Washington Address: 1707 L Street NW, Suite 650
                      Washington, DC   20036

Registered Lobbyist: H. Wesley McAden

SCHNITTKER & ASSOCIATES   (11)
1339 Wisconsin Avenue NW
Washington, DC   20007   202/333-7650

Schnittker & Associates is a private research and consulting firm established by John Schnittker, former agricultural economist at Kansas State University and Undersecretary of Agriculture.

G.D. SEARLE & CO.   (6)
P.O. Box 1045
Skokie, Illinois   60076

Registered Lobbyist: Timmons & Co., Inc.
                       1776 F Street NW
                       Washington, DC   20006

THE SENECA NATION OF INDIANS   (12)
Box 231
Salamanaca, New York   14779

Registered Lobbyist: Fried, Frank, Harris, Shriver, & Kampelman
                       600 New Hampshire Avenue NW
                       Washington, DC   20037

SEVEN-UP BOTTLING CO.   (6)
555 Brown Road
St. Louis, Missouri   63141

Registered Lobbyist: Wayne L. Millsap
                       Millsap, Euerman, and Heitman
                       Suite 2300
                       Clayton Inn Center
                       7777 Bonhomme Avenue
                       St. Louis, Missouri   63105

SHAMROCK FOODS CO.   (6)
2228 North Black Canyon
Phoenix, Arizona   85009

Registered Lobbyists: Charles R. Hoover

                        Jennings, Strouss, & Salmon
                        111 West Monroe
                        Phoenix, Arizona   85003

SHELLFISH INSTITUTE OF NORTH AMERICA   (6)
212 Washington Avenue, Suite 9
Baltimore, Maryland   21204   301/821-7860

Executive Director: Everett A. Tolley

SIERRA CLUB   (8)
530 Bush Street
San Francisco, California   94108   415/981-8634

Founded: 1892 by John Muir

Washington Office Director: Brock Evans

Washington Address: 330 Pennsylvania Avenue SE
                      Washington, DC   20003   202/547-1144

Regional Offices: Madison, Wisconsin; New York, New York; An-
chorage, Alaska; Los Angeles, California; Lander, Wyoming; Seattle,
Washington; Santa Fe, New Mexico.

The Sierra Club is a national environmental organization organized to protect and conserve the natural resources of the Sierra Nevada, the United
States, and the world.

Membership: 170,000

Registered Lobbyists: George Alderson, Linda M. Billings, Barbara
                       Blake, Charles M. Slusen, Rhea L. Cohen, Brock
                       Evans, Jonathan P. Ela, Neil B. Goldstein,
                       Jonathan Carl Gibson, Keith Kline, David Levine,
                       J.L. Milne, Gregory Thomas.

Publications: *Sierra Club Bulletin, National News Report*, list of others
available on request.

SOCIETY OF AMERICAN FLORISTS & ORNAMENTAL HOR-
TICULTURISTS (6)
901 North Washington Street
Alexandria, Virginia   22414   703/836-8700

Founded: 1884

Executive Vice President: Jim Wanko

The Society of American Florists and Ornamental Horticulturists is the national trade association of commercial floriculture representing growers,
wholesalers, and allied tradesmen. Through direct members and affiliated
members, they claim to represent 50,000 business firms in a $3.75 billion in-
dustry.

Direct Membership: 7,634 (1978)

Registered Lobbyists: Perry Russ, James E. Wanko, Cook and Hender-
                       son, Michael K. Blevins.

Publications: *American Florist* (monthly), *U.S. Grower* (monthly)

SOCIETY FOR ANIMAL PROTECTIVE LEGISLATION   (7)
P.O. Box 3719, Georgetown Station
Washington, DC   20007   202/337-2332

President: Madeleine Bemelmans

Executive Secretary: John Gleiber

Founded: 1955

The Society for Animal Protective Legislation is a registered lobby devoting all its efforts to enactment of legislation to protect animals.

Funding: Contributions (not tax-deductible)

Registered Lobbyist: As organization

Publications: List available on request.

SOCIETY OF NUTRITION EDUCATION   (11)
2140 Shattuck Avenue
Berkeley, California   94704   415/548-1363

Founded: 1970

The Society of Nutrition Education is an organization of persons trained in nutrition education and professionals in related fields, seeking to increase the effectiveness of nutrition education through publications and exchange of information.

Membership: 4,500

Publication: *Journal of Nutrition Education, SNE Communicator*

SOUTH CAROLINA FARM BUREAU MUTUAL INSURANCE
P.O. Box 124
Cayce, South Carolina   29033

Registered Lobbyist: Sutherland, Asbill, & Brennan
                       1666 K Street NW
                       Washington, DC   20006

SOUTHERN FARM BUREAU CASUALTY INSURANCE CO.   (6)
P.O. Box 78
Jackson, Mississippi   39205

Registered Lobbyist: Sutherland, Asbill, & Brennan
                        1666 K Street NW
                        Washington, DC   20006

SOUTHERN FARM BUREAU LIFE INSURANCE CO.   (6)
P.O. Box 78
Jackson, Mississippi   39205

Registered Lobbyist: Sutherland, Asbill, & Brennan
                        1666 K Street NW
                        Washington, DC   20006

SOUTH FLORIDA TOMATO & VEGETABLE GROWERS ASSOCIA-
TION   (2)
P.O. Drawer B.B.
Homestead, Florida   33030

Registered Lobbyists: Van Ness, Feldman, & Sutcliffe
                        1220 19th Street NW, Suite 500
                        Washington, DC   20036

SOUTHLAND CORPORATION   (6)
2828 N. Haskell Avenue
Dallas, Texas   75204

Registered Lobbyist: Stanley C. Simon
                        Simon & Twambly
                        2 Turtle Creek Village
                        Dallas, Texas   75219

SOUTHWESTERN PEANUT SHELLERS ASSOCIATION   (6)
6815 Prestonshire
Dallas, Texas   75225

Registered Lobbyist: Sydney C. Reagan

SOUTH WEST WINTER VEGETABLE GROWERS ASSOCIATION   (2)
P.O. Box 1670
Immokalee, Florida   33934

Registered Lobbyist: Van Ness, Feldman, & Sutcliffe
                        1220 19th Street NW, Suite 500
                        Washington, DC   20036

SPERRY RAND CORP.   (6)
3333 Pilot Knob Road
St. Paul, Minnesota   55121

Registered Lobbyist: O'Connor & Hannan
                       1747 Pennsylvania Avenue NW
                       Washington, DC   20006

A.E. STALEY MANUFACTURING CO.   (6)
2200 Eldorado Street
Decatur, Illinois   62525

Registered Lobbyist: Dale Sherwin
                       888 17th Street NW, Suite 902
                       Washington, DC   20006

STANDARD BRANDS, INC.   (6)
625 Madison Avenue
New York, New York   10022

Washington Address: 1899 L Street NW, Suite 505
                      Washington, DC   20035

Registered Lobbyists: Covington & Burling
                        888 16th Street NW
                        Washington, DC   20006

                        Robert P. Gardner

STANDING ROCK SIOUX TRIBE   (12)
Fort Yates, North Dakota   58538

Registered Lobbyist: Sonosky, Chambers, & Sachse
                       2030 M Street NW
                       Washington, DC   20036

STEAK & ALE RESTAURANTS OF AMERICA, INC.   (6)
12890 Hillcrest Road
Dallas, Texas   75230

Registered Lobbyist: Richard B. Berman

THE SUGAR ASSOCIATION OF AMERICA INC.   (6)
1511 K Street NW, Suite 1017
Washington, DC   20005   202/628-0189

President: John W. Tatem, Jr.

Registered Lobbyists: Walter Clinton, Jack McDonald, Roy Jacobsen
Jack McDonald Associates, Inc.
6845 Elm Street, No. 500
McLean, Virginia   22101

SUGAR USERS GROUP   (6)
1660 L Street NW
Washington, DC   20036

Founded: 1959

Chairman: Joseph M. Creed (also Executive Vice-President, Biscuit and Cracker Manufacturers' Association)

The Sugar Users Group is a coalition of trade associations whose members are users of sugar and use about 60 percent of the sugar consumed in the United States.

Membership: American Bakers Association; American Frozen Food Institute; Associated Retail Bakers of America; Association for Dressings and Sauces; Biscuit and Cracker Manufacturers' Association; Chocolate Manufacturers Association of the U.S.A.; Flavor & Extract Manufacturers Association; International Association of Ice Cream Manufacturers; Milk Industry Foundation; National Bakery Suppliers Association; National Association of Fruits, Flavors & Syrups, Inc.; National Preservers' Association, Inc.; National Soft Drink Association; Pickle Packers International, Inc.; Processed Apples Institute.

Registered Lobbyists: Registered with individual associations represented

Ragan & Mason
900 17th Street NW
Washington, DC   20006

SUN MAID RAISIN GROWERS   (3)
1101 Connecticut Avenue NW
Washington, DC   20036   202/457-0120

Registered Lobbyists: Thomas A. Hammer, Nancy L. Smith, Nelson & Harding

SUQUAMISH INDIAN TRIBE   (12)
P.O. Box 556
Suquamish, Washington   98392

Registered Lobbyist: Zionty, Pirtle, Morisset, Ernstoff, & Chestnut
208 Pioneer Building, 600 First Avenue
Seattle, Washington   98104

TADCO ENTERPRISES, INC.   (6)
1625 I Street NW
Washington, DC   20006

Registered Lobbyists: Robert A. Best

Joseph E. Karth
475 L'Enfant Plaza SW, Suite 4400
Washington, DC   20024

Mark A. Siegel
Mark A. Siegel and Associates
734 15th Street NW, Suite 403
Washington, DC   20005

TAIYO FISHERY CO.   (6)
277 Park Avenue
New York, New York   10017

Registered Lobbyist: William J. Kenney
1730 Pennsylvania Avenue NW
Washington, DC   20006

TENNECO INC.   (6)
P.O. Box 2511
Houston, Texas   77001

Washington Address: 490 L'Enfant Plaza East SW
Washington, DC   20024

Registered Lobbyists: Jeffrey A. Fritzlen, James A. Gavin, David R.
Griffen, Robert H. Miller, Michael S. Moe,
James L. Thorne, Michael A. Weiss

TEXAS COUNTY IRRIGATION AND WATER RESOURCES ASSO-
CIATION   (5)
118 West Sixth Street
Guymon, Oklahoma   73942

Registered Lobbyist: Williams & Jensen
1130 17th Street NW
Washington, DC   20036

THE THREE AFFILIATED TRIBES OF THE FORT BERTHOLD
RESERVATION   (12)
New Town, North Dakota   58763

Registered Lobbyist: Wilkinson, Cragun, & Barker
                        1735 New York Avenue NW
                        Washington, DC   20006

TOBACCO ASSOCIATES INC.   (6)
1101 17th Street NW, Suite 912
Washington, DC   20036

TOBACCO INSTITUTE   (6)
1776 K Street NW
Washington, DC   20006   202/457-4873

Founded: 1958

President: Horace R. Kornegay

The Tobacco Institute is the trade association representing the interests of
the tobacco manufacturing industry.

Membership: Philip Morris, Inc.; R.J. Reynolds Industries, Inc.; Liggett
Group, Inc.; Lorillard, Division of Loews Theaters, Inc.; Brown and
Williamson Tobacco Corp.; U.S. Tobacco.

Registered Lobbyists: Earl C. Clements, Franklin B. Dryden, J.C.B.
                        Earlinghuse, Jr., William H. Hecht, Cook and
                        Henderson, Horace R. Kornegay, Roger L.
                        Mezingo, John F. Mills, Fred Panzer.

Publication: *The Tobacco Observer* (monthly)

TOBACCO TAX COUNCIL   (6)
P.O. Box 8269, 5407 Patterson Avenue
Richmond, Virginia   23226

Registered Lobbyist: Martin, Ryan, Haley, & Associates, Inc.
                        1511 K Street NW
                        Washington, DC   20005

TUNA RESEARCH FOUNDATION   (6)
1101 17th Street NW
Washington, DC   20036

Registered Lobbyists: John P. Mulligan

                        Peabody, Rivlin, Lambert, & Myers
                        1150 Connecticut Avenue NW
                        Washington, DC   20036

Van Ness, Feldman, & Sutcliffe
1220 19th Street NW, Suite 500
Washington, DC   20036

TURLOCK IRRIGATION DISTRICT   (10)
P.O. Box 949
333 E. Canal Street
Turlock, California   95380

Registered Lobbyist: White, Fine, & Verville
1156 15th Street NW, Suite 302
Washington, DC   20005

UNCLE BEN'S FOODS   (6)

Registered Lobbyists: William J. Collen

Patton, Boggs & Blow
1200 17th Street NW
Washington, DC   20036

UNITED ACTION FOR ANIMALS, INC.   (7)
205 E. 42d Street
New York, New York   10017

President: Eleanor E. Seiling (full-time, without salary)

Founded: 1967

United Action for Animals is a nonprofit foundation working for the "use of sophisticated modern methods which are presently available to replace live animals in research." It campaigns to inform the public "of the need to stop laboratory animal suffering by the use of available alternatives and the development of more."

Funding: Tax-deductible contributions [exempt from taxes under section 501(c)(3) of the Internal Revenue Code], interest and dividends, bequests, and grants; 1977 income was $124,904. Total assets were $828,326 as of December 31, 1977.

Washington Representative
and Registered Lobbyists: Dunnels, Duval, & Porter
1220 19th Street NW, Suite 400
Washington, DC   20036

Eleanor Peretsman
Great Neck, New York   11022

Publications: List available upon request.

UNITED AUTOMOBILE, AEROSPACE & AGRICULTURAL IMPLE-
MENT WORKERS OF AMERICA   (9)
8000 E. Jefferson Avenue
Detroit, Michigan   48214

Washington Office: 1125 15th Street NW
Washington, DC   20005   202/296-7484

The United Automobile, Aerospace, and Agricultural Implement Workers
of America is the international union of all members of the United Auto
Workers.

Registered Lobbyists: Eugene I. Casraiss, Jr., Howard G. Paster, Betty
S. Robinson, Stephen I. Scholossberg, Jerry R.
Tucker.

UNITED EGG PRODUCERS   (3)
3951 Snapfinger Parkway, Suite 580
Decatur, Georgia   30035   404/288-6700

Founded: 1968

Executive Vice-President and General Manager: Al Pope

Washington Representative: Betty Vorhies
499 S. Capital Street SE, Suite 411
Washington, DC   20003

United Egg Producers is a national federation of egg marketing
cooperatives with members in forty-eight states.

Membership: Six regional member cooperatives—Northeast Egg
Marketing Association, National Egg Company, Midwest Egg Producers,
Northwest Egg Producers, Western Egg Company, and Southern Califor-
nia Egg Cooperatives.

Registered Lobbyists: Thomas A. Davis, Michael R. McLeod, Betty
Vorhies.

Publication: *United Variations*

UNITED FARM BUREAU FAMILY LIFE INSURANCE CO.   (6)
130 East Washington Street
Indianapolis, Indiana   46204

Registered Lobbyist: Sutherland, Asbill, & Brennan
1666 K Street NW
Washington, DC   20006

UNITED FARM BUREAU MUTUAL INSURANCE CO.   (6)
130 East Washington Street
Indianapolis, Indiana   46204

Registered Lobbyist: Sutherland, Asbill, & Brennan
                        1666 K Street NW
                        Washington, DC   20006

UNITED FOOD & COMMERCIAL WORKERS INTERNATIONAL
UNION   (9)
AFL-CIO
1775 K Street NW
Washington, DC   20036

Registered Lobbyists: Douglas Couttee, Walter L. Davis, William J.
                        Olwell, Michael L. Tiner.

UNITED FRESH FRUIT & VEGETABLE ASSOCIATION   (6)
727 North Washington Street
Alexandria, Virginia   22314   703/836-3410

Founded: 1904

President: Bernard J. Imming

The United Fresh Fruit and Vegetable Association is a national trade
association whose member companies are engaged in growing, packing, and
distributing fresh fruits and vegetables and providing goods and services to
the industry. Members handle approximately 80 percent of the tonnage of
fresh fruits and vegetables sold in the country.

Membership: 2,700 firms

Registered Lobbyists: Bernard J. Imming, Robert C. Keeney, Roger
                        Stroh.

Publications: *Spud Light, Fresh Forum* (weekly)

UNITED STATES BREWERS ASSOCIATION, INC.   (6)
1750 K Street NW
Washington, DC   20006   202/466-2400

Executive Vice-President: Allan A. Rubin

UNITED STATES TUNA FOUNDATION   (6)
525 B Street, Suite 2290
San Diego, California   92101

Registered Lobbyist: David G. Burney

UNIVERSAL LEAF TOBACCO CO., INC.   (6)
Hamilton Street at Broad
Richmond, Virginia   23260

Registered Lobbyist: Will E. Leonard
                       900 17th Street NW, Suite 714
                       Washington, DC   20006

UNIVERSITY OF HAWAII AT MANOA   (10)
College of Tropical Agriculture
Honolulu, Hawaii   96822

Washington Representative
and Registered Lobbyist: Vorys, Sater, Seymour, & Pease
                              1800 M Street NW, Suite 800 S
                              Washington, DC   20036

U.S. BEET SUGAR ASSOCIATION   (6)
1156 15th Street NW, Suite 1019
Washington, DC   20005   202/296-4820

Founded: 1911

President: David Carter

The U.S. Beet Sugar Association is an organization including all beet sugar
processing companies, except one, that process beets from 15,000 farmers
at fifty-one plants supplying 30 percent of U.S. sugar needs.

Membership: The Amalgamated Sugar Co.; American Crystal Sugar Co.;
Buckeye Sugars, Inc.; Holly Sugar Corp.; Michigan Sugar Co.; Monitor
Sugar Co.; Spreckels Sugar Division, Amstar Corp.; U and I Inc. (plant
closed in 1978); Union Sugar Division, Consolidated Foods Corp.; and
Minn-Dak Farmers Cooperative.

Registered Lobbyists: David C. Carter, Van R. Olsen.

U.S. CANE SUGAR REFINERS ASSOCIATION   (6)
1001 Connecticut·Avenue
Washington, DC   20036   202/331-1458

Founded: 1936

President: Nicholas Kominus

The U.S. Cane Sugar Refiners Association is an organization of eleven of the fourteen companies that are engaged in refining cane sugar in the United States, accounting for over 90 percent of the cane sugar refined in the country. Members are the small, independent cane sugar refiners. The two largest cane sugar refiners are not members.

Membership: Amstar Corp.; Imperial Sugar Co.; The National Sugar Refining Co.; North American Sugar Industries, Inc.; Revere Sugar Corp.; Savannah Foods & Industries; The South Coast Corp.; Southdown Sugars, Inc.; Supreme Sugar Co., Inc.

Registered Lobbyists: Nicholas Kominus; Thomas G. Abernathy, Sr.;
                        Pepper, Hamilton, and Sheetz

U.S. CATHOLIC CONFERENCE, AND CATHOLIC RELIEF SER-VICES   (7)
1312 Massachusetts Avenue
Washington, DC   20005   202/659-6600

General Secretary: Thomas C. Kelly, U.S. Catholic Conference
                     Bishop Edwin B. Broaderick, Catholic Relief Services

Founded: 1943

Catholic Relief Services is the official overseas relief and development agency of the Catholic church. The U.S. Catholic Conference is a national-level action agency of Catholic bishops representing the concerns of the church on policy issues.

Funding: Donations

Publications: List available upon request.

WESTERN COTTON GROWERS ASSOCIATION OF CALIFORNIA   (2)
P.O. Box 512
Fresno, California   93709

Registered Lobbyist: Kenneth E. Frick

WESTLANDS WATER DISTRICT   (10)
P.O. Box 5222
Fresno, California   93755   209/244-1523

Washington Representative
and Registered Lobbyist: Timothy V.A. Dillon
                              1850 K Street NW
                              Washington, DC   20006

The Westlands Water District is a public body organized to administer the distribution of water under the federally financed Westlands Water District.

Membership: Landowners and water users in the district

WHEAT AND WHEAT FOODS FOUNDATION   (6)
14 East Jackson Boulevard, No. 1010
Chicago, Illinois   60604

Registered Lobbyist: John F. O'Neal
                        600 New Hampshire Avenue NW, Suite 952
                        Washington, DC   20037

WHEY PRODUCTS INSTITUTE   (6)
130 North Franklin Street
Chicago, Illinois   60606

Registered Lobbyist: Leighton & Conklin
                        2033 M Street, Suite 800
                        Washington, DC   20036

WILDLIFE MANAGEMENT INSTITUTE   (8)
1000 Vermont Avenue NW
Washington, DC   20005   202/347-1774

Founded: 1911; incorporated in New York in 1946.

President: Daniel A. Poole

The Wildlife Management Institute is a national, nonprofit, private membership organization supported by industries, groups, and individuals promoting better use of natural resources for the welfare of the nation.

Membership: 600 to 700

Publications: *Outdoor News Bulletin*, list of others available upon request.

WILDLIFE SOCIETY   (8)
7101 Wisconsin Avenue NW, Suite 611
Washington, DC   20014   301/986-8700

Executive Director: Fred Evenden

Founded: 1937

The Wildlife Society is an association of those professionally employed in the biological or related fields of wildlife conservation whose aim is to develop and

promote sound stewardship of wildlife resources and the environment upon
which wildlife and man depend.

Membership: 7,000

Publication: *Journal of Wildlife Management, Wildlife Society Bulletin*; list
of monographs available upon request.

WOMAN'S LOBBY, INC.   (7)
201 Massachusetts Avenue NW
Washington, DC   20002   202/547-0044

Director of Food Stamp Reform: Pam MacEwan

Founded: 1972

Woman's Lobby is a national organization with affiliates in forty states
working solely on legislation pertaining to women.

Funding: Membership dues, contributions.

Registered Lobbyists: Kristina Kiehl, Pam MacEwan, Maya Miller, Ann
                                    Regenstein, Anne Schnitt, Carson Miller, Carolyn
                                    Woolley.

WOMEN INVOLVED IN FARM ECONOMICS (WIFE)   (4)
Marian Lenzen
Box 484
Sydney, Nevada   68651

Founded: 1976

National President: Betty Majors

Women Involved in Farm Economics is a national organization with eighty-
six local chapters and ten state associations whose members are wives of
farm operators.

Membership: 1,000

WORLD HUNGER YEAR   (11)
P.O. Box 1975
Garden City, New York   11530

Founded: 1975

Cofounders: Harry Chapin, Bill Ayres

Director: Wray MacKay

World Hunger Year (WHY) is a nonprofit education and resource organization dedicated to developing people's awareness of the cause of hunger so they may take appropriate action to bring about changes. It provides resource and curriculum materials for the classroom and helps organize community groups around issues of food, land, and hunger.

Funding: Contributions and sale of publications.

Registered Lobbyist: *See* Food Policy Center

Publication: *Food Monitor*

WORLD WATCH INSTITUTE   (11)
1776 Massachusetts Avenue NW
Washington, DC   20036   202/452-1999

Founded: 1974

President: Lester Brown

The World Watch Institute is an independent, nonprofit research organization created to identify and focus attention on global problems.

Funding: Private foundations, United Nations, government agencies; Edna McConnell Clark Foundation, $50,000 in 1977; Rockefeller Brothers Fund, $200,000 in 1977.

Publications: List available upon request.

YAKIMA INDIAN NATION   (12)
P.O. Box 151
Toppenish, Washington   98948

Registered Lobbyist: Rebecca D. Shapiro & Associates
                       111 C Street SE
                       Washington, DC   20003

THE ZUNI INDIAN TRIBE   (12)
Zuni, New Mexico   87327

Registered Lobbyist: Boyden, Kennedy, Romney, & Howard
                       1000 Kennecott Building
                       Salt Lake City, Utah   84133

Appendix B
Agriculture
Committees and
Subcommittees in the
House and Senate,
1979-1980[a]

Senate Committee on Agriculture, Nutrition, and Forestry

Democrats
Herman Talmadge, Georgia, Chairman
George McGovern, South Dakota
Walter Huddleston, Kentucky
Richard Stone, Florida
Patrick Leahy, Vermont
Edward Zorinsky, Nebraska
John Melcher, Montana
Donald Stewart, Alabama
David Pryor, Arkansas
David L. Boren, Oklahoma

Republicans
Jesse Helms, North Carolina
Robert Dole, Kansas
Milton Young, North Dakota
S. I. Hayakawa, California
Richard Lugar, Indiana
Thad Cochran, Mississippi
Randolph E. Boschwitz,
  Minnesota
Rogert W. Jepsen, Iowa

Senate Subcommittees

Agricultural Credit and Rural Electrification
  Zorinsky, Chairman
  McGovern
  Huddleston
  Hayakawa
  Jepsen

Agriculture Production, Marketing, and Stabilization of Prices
  Huddleston, Chairman
  McGovern
  Stone
  Zorinsky
  Melcher
  Pryor
  Boren
  Young
  Helms
  Lugar
  Cochran

---

[a]Listed in order of seniority.

Agriculture Research and General Legislation
  Stewart, Chairman
  Leahy
  Stone
  Talmadge
  Lugar
  Dole
  Young
  Boschwitz

Environment, Soil Conservation, and Forestry
  Melcher, Chairman
  Huddleston
  Stewart
  Talmadge
  Jepsen
  Hayakawa
  Cochran
  Helms

Foreign Agricultural Policy
  Stone, Chairman
  Zorinsky
  Talmadge
  Boren
  Pryor
  Cochran
  Lugar
  Dole
  Boschwitz

Nutrition
  McGovern, Chairman
  Leahy
  Melcher
  Dole
  Helms
  Hayakawa

Rural Development
  Leahy, Chairman
  Stewart
  Pryor
  Boren

Boschwitz
Young
Jepsen

House Agriculture Committee

Democrats

Thomas S. Foley, Washington,
  Chairman
Eligio de la Garza, Texas
Walter B. Jones, North Carolina
Ed Jones, Tennessee
Dawson Mathis, Georgia
George E. Brown, Jr., California
David R. Bowen, Mississippi
Charles Rose, North Carolina
Frederick W. Richmond, New York
Richard Nolan, Minnesota
James Weaver, Oregon
Alvin Baldus, Wisconsin
Tom Harkin, Iowa
Berkley Bedell, Iowa
Glenn English, Oklahoma
Floyd J. Fithian, Indiana
Leon E. Panetta, California
Ike Skelton, Missouri
Jerry Huckaby, Louisiana
Dan Glickman, Kansas
Daniel K. Akaka, Hawaii
Charles Whitley, North Carolina
Tony Coelho, California
Thomas A. Daschle, South Dakota
Kent Hance, Texas
Beryl Anthony, Jr., Arkansas
Charles W. Stenholm, Texas

Republicans

William C. Wampler, Virginia
Keith G. Sebelius, Kansas
Paul Findley, Illinois
Steven D. Symms, Idaho
James P. Johnson, Colorado
Edward R. Madigan, Illinois
Margaret M. Heckler, Massachusetts
James M. Jeffords, Vermont
Richard Kelly, Florida
Charles E. Grassley, Iowa
Tom Hagedorn, Minnesota
E. Thomas Coleman, Missouri
Ron Marlenee, Montana
Larry Hopkins, Kentucky
Bill Thomas, California

House Subcommittees

Democrats

Conservation and Credit
  Jones, Tennessee, Chairman
  Harkin
  Huckaby

Republicans

Madigan
Jeffords
Kelly

Democrats	*Republicans*
Glickman	Coleman
Hance	Marlenee
Brown, California	Hopkins
Richmond	
Baldus	
Bedell	
English	
Panetta	
Daschle	

Cotton

Bowen, Chairman	Heckler
Coelho	Thomas
Jones, Tennessee	
Hance	
Stenholm	

Dairy and Poultry

Baldus, Chairman	Jeffords
Rose	Kelly
Akaka	Hagedorn
Coelho	Hopkins
Jones, North Carolina	
Whitley	
Anthony	
Stenholm	

Department Investigations, Oversight, and Research

de la Garza, Chairman	Wampler
Brown, California	Heckler
Fithian	Grassley
Skelton	
Glickman	
English	
Daschle	

Domestic Marketing, Consumer Relations, and Nutrition

Richmond, Chairman	Symms
Panetta	Heckler
Nolan	Grassley
Glickman	
Akaka	
Harkin	

Democrats   *Republicans*

Family Farms, Rural Development, and Special Studies
 Nolan, Chairman   Grassley
 Akaka   Sebelius
 Harkin   Coleman
 Daschle   Thomas
 Anthony
 Richmond
 Bedell
 Panetta

Forests
 Weaver, Chairman   Johnson, Colorado
 Anthony   Symms
 Huckaby
 Coelho
 Nolan

Livestock and Grains
 Rose, Chairman   Sebelius
 Bedell   Johnson, Colorado
 English   Hagedorn
 Daschle   Coleman
 Stenholm   Symms
 de la Garza   Marlenee
 Fithian
 Skelton
 Jones, Tennessee
 Nolan
 Baldus
 Hance

Oilseeds and Rice
 Mathis, Chairman   Findley
 Jones, North Carolina   Thomas
 Bowen
 Whitley
 Stenholm

Tobacco
 Jones, North Carolina, Chairman Kelly
 Whitley   Hopkins
 Mathis
 Rose
 Baldus

Appendix C
Network of Mutual Support and Assistance to National Citizens' and Rural-Oriented Groups with Food and Agricultural Interests

Many of the citizen and consumer groups have little or no membership. So through a "networking" process they give one another assistance and mutual support in a number of ways. The basis for network associations listed in this appendix is as follows: Joint authorship of articles by staff members, joint appearance before congressional committees to testify, membership on committees or boards of respective organizations by a single individual, reports or articles supporting or publicizing activities or publications in a newsletter or publication of that organization, source of information for articles appearing in that organization's publications, author of articles by staff member in that organization's publication or newsletter, sponsor or contributor to a conference or other activities of that organization.

Organization or Group	Groups Receiving Support or Providing Assistance
Action Center (Institute for World Hunger)	Center for Science in the Public Interest, Earthwork/Center for Rural Studies, Interfaith Center on Corporate Responsibility, Conference on Alternative State and Local Policies, National Land for People, World Hunger Year
Agribusiness Accountability Project	Center for Community Change, Migrant Legal Action Program
Bread for the World	Catholic Relief Services, Overseas Development Council
California Rural Legal Assistance	Children's Foundation, National Association of Farmworkers Organizations, National Land for People, Legal Services Corporation
Center for Rural Affairs	California Rural Legal Assistance, Conference on Alternative State and Local

Organization or Group	Groups Receiving Support or Providing Assistance
	Policies, Emergency Land Fund, Legal Services Corporation, Migrant Legal Action Program, National Family Farm Coalition, National Land for People, National Rural Center, Roger Blobaum & Associates, Rural America
Center for Rural Studies/Earthwork	Agribusiness Accountability Publications Project; American Friends Service Committee, San Francisco chapter; California Church Council Producer-Consumer Food Organizing Project; California Food Policy Coalition; Institute for Food and Development Policy; National Land for People
Center for Science in the Public Interest	Bread for the World, Community Nutrition Institute, Environmental Defense Fund, Institute for Food and Development Policy, Interreligious Task Force on Food Policy, Overseas Development Council
Children's Foundation	Community Nutrition Institute, Rural America
Coalition of Consumer Organizations (1977 testimony)	Center for Science in the Public Interest, Congress Watch (Public Citizen), Community Nutrition Institute, Consumer Federation of America, National Consumers Congress (merged with National Consumers League)
Community Nutrition Institute	Center for Science in the Public Interest, Food Marketing Institute, Consumer Federation of America
Conference on Alternative State and Local Policies	Agribusiness Accountability Project, American Agri-Women, Community Nutrition Institute, Center for Rural Affairs, Center for Science in the Public Interest, Emergency Land Fund & National Association of Landowners, Environmental Action, Environmental Policy Center, Food Research Action Center, Institute for Local Self-Reliance, Interfaith Center on Corporate Responsibility, National

Organization or Group	Groups Receiving Support or Providing Assistance
	Association of Conservation Districts, National Association of County Officials, National Association of Farmworker Organizations, National Catholic Rural Life Conference, National Center for Appropriate Technology, National Family Farm Coalition, National Farmers Union, National Farmers Organization, National Land for the People, National Rural Development and Finance Corporation, Natural Resources Defense Council, Rural America, Rural American Women, World Hunger Year
Consumer Federation of America	AFL-CIO Industrial Union Department, Amalgamated Meat Cutters & Butcher Workmen of America, Cooperative League of the U.S.A., International Association of Machinists, National Consumers League, National Council of Senior Citizens, National Farmers Union
Consumers Opposed to Inflation in the Necessities (COIN)	AFL-CIO Center for Science in the Public Interest, Community Nutrition Institute, Congress Watch, Consumer Action Now, Consumer Federation of America, Environmental Action, Exploratory Project for Economic Alternatives, Food & Beverage Department, Food Research & Action Center, Friends of the Earth, International Association of Machinists, National Consumers League, National Council of Senior Citizens, National Family Farm Coalition, Network Rural America, Public Citizen, U.S. Catholic Conference
Environmental Defense Fund	National Audubon Society
Food Research & Action Center	Center for Science in the Public Interest, Childrens' Foundation, Community Nutrition Institute, Interreligious Task Force on

Organization or Group	*Groups Receiving Support or Providing Assistance*
	U.S. Food Policy, National Association of Farmworker Organizations
Institute for Food and Development Policy	Agricultural Missions, Center for Rural Studies/Earthwork; Conference on Alternative State and Local Issues, National Council of Churches, World Hunger Year
Interreligious Task Force on U.S. Food Policy	Bread for the World, Church World Service, Friends Committee on National Legislation, Lutheran World Relief, Overseas Development Council, U.S. Catholic Conference, World Hunger Education Service
Legal Services Corporation	California Rural Legal Assistance, Migrant Legal Action Project
National Association of Farmworker Organizations	Children's Foundation, National Land for People, National Rural Housing Coalition, Rural America
National Catholic Rural Life Conference	Center for Rural Affairs, Conference on Alternative State and Local Policies, Institute for Food and Development Policy, National Center for Appropriate Technology, National Family Farm Coalition, National Land for People, Rural America, West Side Planning Group
National Child Nutrition Project	Children's Foundation, Community Nutrition Institute, Food Research and Action Center
National Council of Senior Citizens	National Consumers League
National Family Farm Coalition	Ad Hoc Coalition on the World Conference on Agrarian Reform and Rural Development, COIN, Rural America, The Rural Coalition
National Land for People	Agribusiness Accountability Project, California Rural Legal Assistance,

Organization or Group	Groups Receiving Support or Providing Assistance
	Center for Rural Studies/Earthwork, Institute for Policy Studies, National Association of Farmworkers Organizations, Rural America
Network	Center for Rural Studies/Earthwork, Center for Science in the Public Interest, Common Cause, Community Nutrition Institute, Cooperative League of the U.S.A., Food Research and Action Center, League of Women Voters, National Catholic Rural Life Conference, National Farmers Union, National Family Farm Coalition, National Land for People, Public Citizen, Rural America
Public Citizen	Citizen Action Group, Congress Watch, Health Research Group, Litigation Group, Tax Reform Group, Visitor's Center
Rural America	AFL-CIO, Agribusiness Accountability Project Publications, California Rural Legal Assistance, Children's Foundation, Food & Beverage Trades Department, Green Thumb, National Catholic Rural Life Conference, National Farmers Union, National Land for People, National Rural Center
	Consumer Federation of America, Community Nutrition Institute, Exploratory Project for Economic Opportunities, Family Farm Coalition, Food Research and Action Center, Institute for Policy Studies, Legal Services Corporation, National Center for Appropriate Technology, National Rural Center, National Rural Electric Cooperative Association, Roger Blobaum & Associates, Rural American Women, Rural Coalition
Rural American Women	Center for Community Change, Center for Rural Affairs, Children's Foundation,

Organization or Group	Groups Receiving Support or Providing Assistance
	Common Cause, Industrial Union Department, AFL-CIO, National Association of Counties, National Rural Center, National Rural Development & Finance Corporation, Women's Action Alliance
Rural Coalition	Center for Community Change, Conference on Alternative State and Local Policies, League of Women Voters, National Association of Farmworkers Organizations, National Catholic Rural Life Conference, National Family Farm Coalition, National Rural Center, National Rural Housing Coalition, Network, Rural America, Rural American Women, Children's Foundation, United Auto Workers
World Hunger Year	CARE, Children's Foundation, Cuba Resource Center, Food Policy Center, Institute for Food and Agricultural Development, Interfaith Center on Corporate Responsibility, National Land for People, President's Commission on World Hunger, Rural America

Appendix D
Contributions by Food and Agricultural Political-Action Committees, 1977-1978

Organizations and Connected Committees	Number of Congressional Candidates Supported		Total Contributions ($)
	Democrats	Republicans	
Producers and Cooperatives			
American Association of Nurserymen Nursery Industry Political Action Committee	3	4	850
American Horse Council, Inc. Horse Industry Committee on Legislation and Taxation	15	8	9,050
American Rice Growers Cooperative Association Rice Producers Political Education Committee	3	3	4,050
American Rice, Inc. Political Action Committee	16	3	13,350
Arizona Cotton Growers Association Farmers Committee for Political Action	4	3	5,100
Associated Milk Producers, Inc. Committee for Thorough Agricultural Political Education	145	77	456,151
CF Industries, Inc. Political Action Committee	6	7	2,775
California Almond Growers Exchange CAGE/PAC	27	13	18,750
California Canning Peach Association Cling Peach Growers for Effective Government	7	3	3,175
California-Arizona Citrus League Fund	22	11	9,100
California Rice Fund	3	2	8,400
California Westside Farmers, Inc. Federal Political Action Committee	8	3	7,500
Citrus Central, Inc. Florida Cooperative Citrus Growers Political Action Committee	3	2	8,000
Dairymen, Inc. Trust for Special Political Agricultural Community Education	86	20	181,600
Georgia Committee	6	2	15,950
Kentucky Committee	4	3	18,000
Louisiana Committee	6	3	18,750

Appendix D (*continued*)

Organizations and Connected Committees	Number of Congressional Candidates Supported		Total Contributions ($)
	Democrats	Republicans	
Producers and Cooperatives (continued)			
Mississippi Committee	3	2	11,500
North Carolina Committee	5	—	4,500
Tennessee Committee	4	2	10,000
Virginia Committee	1	2	6,000
Farm Bureau			
Alabama	2	—	2,000
West Central Missouri	1	—	540
North West Missouri	—	1	609
Michigan Farm Bureau Political Action Committee	—	5	1,600
Farmers and Ranchers Midwest Political Action Committee (Des Moines, Iowa)	1	3	2,500
Kansas Cooperative Council Political Action for Cooperative Effectiveness of Kansas	—	1	464
Michigan Milk Producers Michigan Milk Political Action Committee	5	6	1,620
Mid-America Dairymen, Inc. Agriculture and Dairy Educational Political Trust	144	53	228,900
National Cattlemen's Association Cattlemen's Legislative Action Fund	77	92	45,175
National Council of Farmer Cooperatives Political Action for Cooperatives Effectiveness (PACE)	46	23	42,216
National Rural Electric Cooperative Association Action Committee for Rural Electrification (ACRE)	155	55	192,450
Colorado Advocates for Rural Electrification	—	3	855
Iowa ACRE	3	4	4,500
Louisiana ACRE	6	3	5,900
Mississippi ACRE	6	5	5,700
Missouri ACRE	9	2	4,670
Ohio ACRE	1	4	950
National Wool Growers Association National Sheep Industry Committee for Good Government	4	2	1,100
Pacific Egg and Poultry Association Western Egg and Poultry Action Committee	7	4	1,900
Pear Growers for Responsible Government	5	5	925
Rice and Soybean Political Action Committee	8	3	14,500
Sunkist Growers, Inc. Sunkist Political Action Committee	13	6	11,250

Appendix D (*continued*)

Organizations and Connected Committees	Number of Congressional Candidates Supported		Total Contributions ($)
	Democrats	Republicans	
Producers and Cooperatives (continued)			
Texas Cattle Feeders Association BEEF - PAC (Beef Political Action Committee)	18	10	13,800
United Dairymen of Arizona Arizona Dairymen Political Action Committee	—	2	750
United Egg Producers EGG-PAC (Egg Industry Political Action Committee)	22	4	3,550
Business			
American Bakers Association Bread PAC	42	30	40,350
American Feed Manufacturers Association Feed Industry Political Action Committee	10	14	4,050
American Frozen Food Institute Freezers Political Action Committee (FREEPAC)	3	—	1,300
American Meat Institute Meat Industry Political Action Committee	12	53	8,300
American Sugar Cane League of U.S.A. Committee	112	67	72,495
American Textile Manufacturers Institute American Textile Industry Good Government Committee	73	45	55,750
California Canners and Growers Association Committee on Agricultural Policy	15	10	15,742
Chicago Board of Trade Auction Markets PAC	55	31	96,400
Chicago Mercantile Exchange Commodity Futures Political Fund	68	85	230,225
Cotton Warehouse Association of America Government Relations Committee	19	3	3,225
Independent Bakers Association Bake PAC	2	5	1,750
Independent Bankers Asssociation of America Independent Bankers PAC	72	33	36,762
National Agricultural Aviation Association Agricultural Aviation PAC, Inc.	6	1	1,350

Appendix D (continued)

Organizations and Connected Committees	Number of Congressional Candidates Supported		Total Contributions ($)
	Democrats	Republicans	
Business (continued)			
National Agricultural Chemicals Association NACAPAC	8	5	3,210
National Canners Association Canners Public Affairs Committee	6	14	2,475
National Confectioners Association Government Improvement Group	8	14	13,800
National Cotton Council of America Committee for Advancement of Cotton	46	30	15,550
National Fisheries Institute Fisheries Political Action Committee	11	8	3,175
National Independent Meat Packers Association Independent Meat Packers Political Action Committee	5	8	1,300
National Limestone Institute NLI Political Action Committee	46	31	10,360
National Nutritional Foods Association Political Action Committee	3	1	1,600
National Pest Control Association Political Action Committee	6	9	2,300
National Soft Drink Association, Inc. NSDA Bipartisan Political Action Committee	6	3	1,125
National Turkey Federation Turkey Industry Political Action Committee	16	11	5,645
Poultry and Egg Institute of America Poultry and Egg Industries Committee for Political Action	6	5	1,800
Tobacco Institute, Inc. Tobacco People's Public Affairs	127	101	75,975
The Board of Trade of Kansas City, Mo. Kansas City Grain and Futures Traders Voluntary Political Action Committee	9	5	2,200
United Fresh Fruit and Vegetable Association United Political Action Committee	18	13	7,600
U.S. Beet Sugar Association Beet Sugar Political Action Committee	74	48	13,965
U.S. Cane Sugar Refiners Association Cane Sugar Refiners Political Action Committee	4	—	600
Wine Institute Political Action Committee	18	7	14,323

Appendix D (*continued*)

Organizations and Connected Committees	Number of Congressional Candidates Supported		Total Contributions ($)
	Democrats	*Republicans*	
Consumers and Others			
Amalgamated Meat Cutters and Butcher Workmen AMPOCE	101	13	111,500
Committee for Humane Legislation Political Action Committee	6	1	2,350
Consumer Federation of America CFA Political Action Fund	13	1	62

Environmental Action
  Environmental Action's Dirty Dozen
    Campaign
	7	5	19,937

National Association of Federal Veterinarians Political Action Committee	7	5	1,800

Source: Federal Elections Commission

Index of Names

Index of Subjects

About the Author

Harold D. Guither is professor of agriculture economics and extension economist in public policy at the University of Illinois at Urbana-Champaign. He received the B.S. degree in agriculture and the M.S. and Ph.D. degrees in agricultural economics from the University of Illinois. He is coauthor of *Mission Overseas* (1969), author of *Heritage of Plenty* (1972), and coauthor and editor of *Who Will Control U.S. Agriculture?* (1972). He has written for the *American Journal of Agricultural Economics, Agricultural History*, national public-policy extension projects, and several farm magazines and trade publications. He has also worked overseas under a University-AID project, for a private agricultural consulting firm, and as a legislative assistant in the U.S. House of Representatives.